SOD THAT
FOR A
GAME OF SOLDIERS

SOD THAT
FOR A
GAME OF SOLDIERS

MARK EYLES-THOMAS

KENTON PUBLISHING

Published by KENTON PUBLISHING
The Granary
Hatham Green Lane
Stansted
SEVENOAKS
Kent TN15 7PL
+44 (0) 1474 853669

www.kentonpublishing.co.uk

First published in Great Britain in 2007 by
KENTON PUBLISHING
ISBN 0-9546223-2-4

2 4 6 8 10 9 7 5 3

Typeset by Decent Typesetting, www.decenttypesetting.co.uk
Printed in the UK by CPI Bookmarque, Croydon, CR0 4TD

Every effort has been made to contact copyright-holders but some were
untraceable. We would be grateful if relevant owners could contact us.

www.sodthatforagameofsoldiers.com

Acknowledgements

There are several people that I wish to thank for assisting in the creation and subsequent printing of this book. However, before I do, I feel that it is essential for me to explain the motivation behind the book, 25 years on.

For years I have evaded journalists and their persistent quests for the 'hidden truths' of the Falklands Campaign. Always believing that their quest would be at the expense of other people's feelings and would conclude in the compilation of an editorial full of 'exposes' and 'shock horrors', which were far from the real events. Never in a million years did I ever dream of writing a book on my own personal experiences. That was until one individual put it to me that if my experiences went unwritten they would follow me to the grave and by so doing would be lost to history forever. History... that made me ponder. As an ex-soldier I often read interviews and articles from service personnel that appeared in the newspapers from time to time, which through editorial revision seemed either to lack the emotion of the event or failed to encapsulate the true spirit of the Armed Forces. As a consequence the 'truth' is often misrepresented or opaque. Through writing and publishing this book ourselves, at our expense, we hope to have maintained that spirit and those 'truths'.

Special thanks to:

Mike, Su, Brigitte and Kenton Ridley, Carey Edwards, Nick Casson, Vince Bramley, my daughter Cher-Leigh, my son Dominic, and my wife Trish for reliving every word and understanding the pain. I love you (MBHTZG) x. To all the families affected by the Falklands and other conflicts – please know how proud we were to serve, and that not all the heroes can be awarded medals.

And finally to all serving members of Her Majesty's Forces – may your journey home be safe and unhindered.

CAUTION

This book is my own account of my personal experiences of the Falklands Campaign. It will not glamorise or glorify events or ennoble people. The soldiers' names as written are real, but I fully acknowledge the implicit obligation I have to the families who have been tragically affected by the loss of their loved ones. I would not wish in any way to further their pain. However, to maintain the truth I have recorded in some detail events that can only be described as graphic, and may be severely distressing. I would respectfully ask that should you have experienced such a tragedy as losing a loved one through the Falklands Campaign that you think carefully before reading this book. Alternatively, I hope perhaps that in some small way this may assist you in your search for compassionate closure. For those of you who may follow in our footsteps please consider the content of this book. Should the Forces still be for you – serve well and keep safe.

For those who may subsequently change their mind,

consider that you may well owe your decision and subsequent safety to the silent voices of my absent friends and to those who have fallen (unvoiced) before them. Please always remember their brave deeds and that they too were loved. Never forget them or apologise for their actions. And finally, as a last general recommendation, tell your children about them.

> *"Dulce et decorum est pro patria mori:*
> *mors et fugacem persequitur vuirum,*
> *nec parcit inbellis inventae*
> *poplitibus timidove tergo."*

Horace, *Odes* iii 2.13

God Save the Queen!

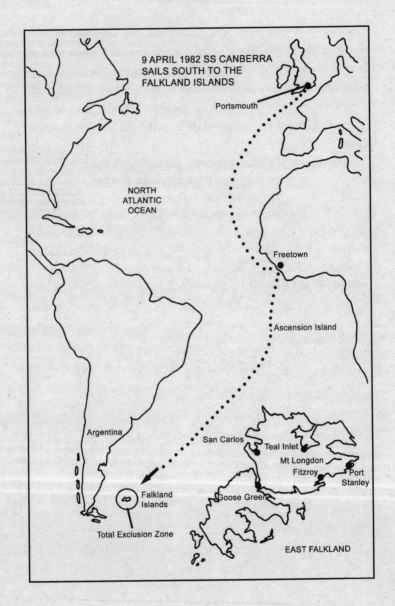

Prologue

2200Hrs (Local Time) – 11th June 1982 – Mount Longdon, Falkland Islands.

I can clearly see the moon on the horizon. The evening air is crisp, the night sky, unclouded. Away from artificial light and air pollution, the moon is sharp and bright, creating a brilliant aura around the mountain. A sudden explosion followed by screams of pain breaks the silence as Corporal Milne steps on an anti-personnel mine. Immediately machine gun tracer rounds rain down on us. Flares light up the sky. Spontaneously, I go to ground through instinct and training. Mount Longdon, previously cold, dark and still, has come alive.

The mountain and our initial objective 'Fly Half' are still some 100 yards away to my right. Our section, now compromised and out in the minefield, is vulnerable to the enemy gunfire, exposed like rabbits caught in a car's headlights.

Corporal Milne's screams are now muted. Instead, we hear the horrendous groans of a man in serious pain – shock is setting in. For a few brief seconds we lie there in the cold damp grass, doing nothing, taking stock of what is unfolding before us, knowing there to be land mines all around. The enemy continues to fire automatic weapons in our direction. It will only be a matter of time before they have us firmly fixed in their sights and we are annihilated. We must take action.

Still lying on the ground, Jas turns to me and says, "I'm going to Corporal Milne to inject his morphine."

Jas edges slowly towards to him. No one else moves, says or does anything, anticipating Jas to initiate a second explosion. Moments pass while the enemy continue to fire. Eventually I crawl forward to Jas; Corporal Milne is in severe shock.

"I've injected the morphine," says Jas, "but it doesn't seem to ease any of his pain. I'm going to give him mine". This may seem the correct and Christian thing to do but, as any infantry soldier knows, the single morphine syrette you wear around your neck, taped to the cord of your dog tags, is for personal use should you require it. The way things are unfolding it is a very brave action at this early stage of the battle. Jas doesn't see it that way and injects his morphine into Brian. Ron Duffy crawls over to us.

"I think he's lost the lower part of his leg," whispers Jas.

"Okay, don't tell anyone else what you have seen, lads," says Ron. "Bad for morale."

A decision is taken to leave Ron attending to Corporal Milne, while the rest of the section continue through the minefield towards the enemy gunfire. I survey the ground that I must cover, knowing there are land mines ahead. But as I slowly raise myself from the ground, I cannot move however hard I try. I tell myself time and time again to take a step forward but my legs ignore the order. I stay motionless contemplating the unthinkable. I pray to God to give me strength and take an initial stride but nothing happens. Then a thought enters my head. If I want to see Mum and my sister Jo again I've got to move forward. Suddenly I do. Fearing that each step I take could lead to the loss of a lower limb or even death, my weapon visibly shakes in my hand. The lads behind shout at me to slow down. They are placing their feet in the footprints I've left on the frost-covered ground. Resentfully, I comply and my momentum is stifled for a brief moment. The enemy's accuracy increases as they fire down at us from a number of bunkers higher up the mountainside. In minutes it's a free-for-all as our section disperses, seeking cover from the onslaught.

The enemy fire is more intensive now that we have gone to ground. I'm alone, lying flat on the slight up-slope trying to make myself invisible as the rounds from enemy guns zip through the air just above my head. There are no foxholes here. I look up and can make out the large dark boulders, pitch-black crags and light grey rock faces from where the enemy are firing. I can see other members of the section slightly ahead of me to my right, in what appears to be a disused peat pit, a far better place to seek safety than the open space I'm in. They are older, more experienced soldiers and I dare not presume I can join them. With the enemy fire continuing in my direction, they seem to appreciate my predicament and gesture towards me. Within seconds I am with them, unified, accepted, a comrade.

I fear, however, that this night may well be my last…

CHAPTER ONE
Genesis

The Creation and the Fall

I am informed I was born at 5.20 am on Tuesday, 30th June 1964, in a corridor of Rochford General Hospital, in Essex. Nice to know that in forty years the National Health Service hasn't changed much, although corridor usage is now maximised to its full potential and includes accident and emergency admissions, along with various other sectors of patient welfare and abandonment.

It appears I was quite impatient and couldn't wait for the delivery room. Mind you if I knew then what I know now, I think I would have waited a tad longer.

Dad and Mum proudly took their new-born son back to their council house at 157 Nether Priors, Basildon New Town, and quickly settled into their proven routine of making each other's life hell.

I, on the other hand, set about mastering the general day-to-day duties of a new born child – namely eating, drinking, screaming and filling my nappies, the last of which, I am told, I did very well. These activities continue to this day but not necessarily in that order, nor, I hasten to add, with the same conviction or sense of achievement. Somewhere along its path my life became, quite simply, more complicated.

I was baptised according to the Roman Catholic faith Mark

Robert Jason Eyles Thomas. Mark, Robert and Jason, following my father's initials M. R. J. for Michael Robert James. Eyles was my mother's maiden name and, of course, my father's surname was Thomas. Mum preferred the name Jason and from that moment on she and the rest of my family including Dad, always referred to me as Jason.

Dad, I am told, soon became 'restless' and 'wandered'. Mum on the other hand decided it was time to relocate, and in December 1967 crossed the then channel from Essex to Kent, obtaining a headship at an infant school along with a council house, on an estate in the small village of Hoo, near Rochester.

Life wasn't easy for Mum, with two kids – my sister Joanne was born a year earlier – her newly-gained headship and the countless other duties of a single parent. Consequently, Dad reappeared on the scene during the latter part of 1968.

This reunion, and the remarriage that followed, was an ambitious undertaking. One I would liken to the Northern Ireland peace process. Although both parties were often drawn to the table for negotiations and dinner, a suitable settlement could never be reached and an uncompromising separation throughout 1971 concluded in a second divorce in 1972. Mum stayed with us children in Hoo, and Dad left.

Stories of me masterminding a mass break out from the local nursery should have sounded early warning bells for my mum that life with her son was not going to be easy or peaceful. Mum sought solace through education and discipline, placing me in the charge of nuns at a Roman Catholic Convent School in nearby Frindsbury.

The nuns and I never really saw eye to eye. I believed they concentrated their efforts on making my life absolute hell.

They believed I was a lazy, illiterate, idiot who required education and discipline. Things came to a head when, at the end of one playtime, I refused point blank to re-enter the classroom. This resulted in me being tied to my chair. Now how would that fit in with today's teaching practices? You can see the School League Tables and Prospectus now:

PUPILS	A GRADES	B GRADES	C GRADES	TIED TO CHAIRS
FEMALE	50	30	10	0
MALE	0	10	30	50*

* Denotes number of male pupils tied to chair and does not include those pupils who were tied to their chair on more than one occasion.

Another dispute arose when I locked myself in the loo. This led to the Mother Superior, on her hands and knees in a most undignified pose, pleading with me from beneath the door to free myself and unlock the toilet.

Something had to give and as I was still unable to read even the most basic passages my education was considered to be suffering severely. Finally, I was removed from the caring attention of the nuns and the security of my classroom chair to attend another school nearer to home, at Chattenden.

The majority of those attending Chattenden Hill School were drawn from the children of H M Forces. Their parents were stationed at Chattenden Barracks and the school was conveniently located at the top of the road.

Unfortunately for the school, this often meant children only attended until their parents were posted on. This is not conducive to a learning environment and Chattenden School was no exception. Competition to be bottom of the class was fierce and often led to playground disruptions. Being of a competitive nature, I entered into this spirit, and wholeheart-edly subscribed to the non-learning culture.

The scars of attending Chattenden School are still with me today. I am not speaking metaphorically, but literally. On one occasion, whilst defending a female pupil's honour, I was picked up by two older boys and rammed, head first into the school railings. Six stitches later, a headache that would have killed a legion of the finest Roman soldiers, and an unsympa-thetic message from the girl stating that she could fight her own battles in the future, led me to believe that girls were stupid, unfathomable and best left to their own devices.

I am told that during an eventful parent's evening, where, in front of the other parents, Mum openly and successfully questioned the headmaster's teaching regime and the school's philosophy, it was decided I would be removed from the school. I was almost seven years old and still unable to read.

Responsibility for my education now passed to Hoo St. Werburgh Infants School, where Mum was the headmistress. The children who lived on the estate or came from the village attended the school and everyone knew everyone. My read-ing disability was a major concern to my parents and a serious embarrassment to me as I was due to attend the junior school the following term. I was quite pleased with my placement in Mrs Hughes' class. After all she was a slim, tall, striking look-ing lady, with long, shoulder length, dark brown hair, not your usual deputy headmistress type!

Mrs Hughes' teaching technique was different to anything I had experienced before. She allowed pupils to follow up areas of their own learning interests and did not stifle their imagination through stringent and often boring and unchallenging curriculum activities. Her teaching method seemed to remove the pressure from me and I soon became keen to learn and subsequently, and more importantly, happy to master reading.

I have fond memories of sitting on an outside step in the sunshine with Mrs Hughes after school reading the Happy Venture books. Whatever happened to Dick, Dora, Nick and Fluff?

I can honestly say that without her patience, compassion and obvious teaching ability, I never would have learned to read in such a short space of time, just one summer term. I am eternally grateful to Mrs Hughes, for all the untold unpaid hours she unconditionally gave up.

Oh, by the way, Nick the dog ate Fluff the cat and was, as a consequence, impounded and later put down. Dora became pregnant at the age of fifteen and got a cameo part in EastEnders. Dick hit the booze and is now a recluse somewhere in Wales.

Hoo Junior School was in the same grounds as the Infants' School, their boundaries separated by a large grass bank, though the school fields were shared.

My sister Joanne was already at the school and doing rather well, which I thought was bloody typical of her. I was in Mr Geater's class. A strict, loud teacher, he resembled the Detective Jack Frost, played on TV by David Jason, though much taller. Mr Geater's temperament was, however, more akin to a volcano, ready to erupt at the slightest provocation, than Jack's easy, if sarcastic, manner. Mr Geater had an amazing talent for being able to bring his ruler down, with lightning speed and accuracy across your knuckles before you'd even realised he had caught you talking. He practiced this ability with me, with painful efficiency and regularity.

The eleven-plus exam was still the driving force behind any future academic placement. Quite rightly Mr Geater championed this. I, on the other hand, was more concerned with my up-and-coming cycling proficiency test and playing for the school's football first team. This slight divergence of priorities was closely monitored and controlled by Mr Geater's ruler.

About this time the peace process with Dad and Mum finally broke down affecting us all badly. Joanne suffered at school and subsequently failed her eleven-plus. Immaturely and incorrectly, I blamed Mum for the break up of the marriage and became rebellious. Mr Geater's ruler technique improved dramatically throughout this period of my life.

With Dad gone, evenings and night times were the hardest. Mum would often spend the night crying in her bed. Jo and I could hear her through our thin bedroom walls and we would try to comfort her. Mum always put on a brave face and would lie in her bed with her arms around us, telling us story upon story of when we were younger and what we would get up to. Hours would pass with us two listening intently to her, laughing and giggling and finding comfort together. We would always ask for just one more story and Mum being the loving person that she was would always oblige. Eventually we would all drift off to sleep in the same bed ready to repeat the routine the following night.

Hoo St. Werburgh was a typical village where nothing exciting seemed to happen to anyone. You were born there, worked there for either BP or Berry Wiggins and married someone from the next street. The newlyweds would then have children, who then played on the estate and went to the same school and were taught by the same teachers. Eventually people died and depending on their denomination were usually buried at one of the two churches in the village.

Our housing estate had its own parade of shops for the essentials:- a newsagents, hairdresser, chemist and a greengrocers. It was also blessed with a large recreational park, covered with Tarmac where there were swings, a large slide, a witch's hat and a hobbyhorse. The village hall was at the top end of the 'rec'. Occasionally there would be a disco or a birthday party but mainly the hall was just something to look at whilst we whiled away the hours playing and smoking on the swings.

For the weekly shop, families would venture down to the village where they could peruse the aisles of the Co-op and later on, Liptons. The village also boasted a launderette, a bookies, an off-licence, a number of general hardware stores, three pubs – The Five Bells, The Bridges and The Chequers – a fish and chip shop, a bank and a police station.

Everyone knew everyone else's business. This removed any need for prying. The effective and efficient grapevine was supported by an infrastructure that would be the envy of any modern day military communications network. This set-up ensured those who needed to know were kept informed of the latest events, sometimes before they had even happened. This was an accepted practice that aided and controlled the resources of the village and the estate ensuring their distribution to the right quarters, as and when needed. It also made sure discipline was directed swiftly and where required.

Various people held rank within this framework and although they were accepted as a useful source of information and help to most parents, to us kids they were 'nosy parkers' and were given a wide berth. Generally respect was only given to the more influential and important members of the community: Mr Brice, the local landowner, Police Sergeant Herd who oversaw police operations throughout Hoo, Mum the Infants' School Headmistress, Mr Lawrence the Junior School Headmaster, both vicars and most of the strict, loud male teachers, especially Mr Geater and his ruler.

Our gang was formed around this time. Stuart McAllister, formerly Stuart Doctor, was a 'Just William' type of character who could argue with his fists and was unfortunately for him, always upsetting his Glaswegian father, Jim. Stu had three sisters, two older and one younger than him. Ian Pritchard, who we nicknamed Horace, was a slim, cheeky chancer who always saw the funnier side of life. Horace had an older sister and a brother, Horace Senior, who eventually went into the Army. Vincent Tipple was a tall, dark-haired comedian who lived with his older sister, younger brother and his mum and dad in a caravan at Hoo marina. Vince never had any money or fags, although he smoked profusely. Aaron Wilson was a rotund lad who was raised by his Nan and Grandad and, as a consequence, was spoilt. Aaron always seemed to have more money that anyone else; he also had a Bay City Rollers suit, not that I think he would admit to this now. Aaron would spend far too much time combing and messing around with his hair. Adam 'Woody' Woodhouse was a footballer who also played for the school's first team. Woody was an only child and lived at the top end of the estate. Martin Wood, who we called Pecker, was quite an intelligent lad if slightly naïive and was the subject of everyone else's jokes and, when he got tedious, Stu's fists. He lived with his mum and her truck driver boyfriend, his three sisters and his brothers. With the exception of Pecker and me, none of the others were in the top stream in the Junior School:- another testament to Mrs Hughes's teaching ability.

After school the gang would meet in my shed and embark on a number of 'social' and 'unsociable' activities. We would, play football on the 'rec' or in a road, go swimming at the Hoo pool, make camps at the Marina, swim in the River Medway, play British Bulldog, knock down ginger or over-hedges-through-gardens. Mum rarely knew where I was or what time I would appear. Not that she didn't care for my welfare or my safety it was just the way things were and that's the way I liked it.

I can't recall when or how 'Operation Guz' first happened but I think it was Stu who came back to the shed one night and said he had seen the local shopkeeper placing empty Corona fizzy drink bottles in the back yard of Welhams shop. The shopkeeper paid a deposit for these 'returns'. Operation Guz required three people and would be undertaken during the darker hours. One person would go over the back gate and would pass the bottles over the fence. The second person had two functions, as lookout observing the entrance into the back yard area and to handle the bottles passed over the gate by the first person. The third person acted as another lookout, situated at the top of the stairs leading to the front doors of the flats that overlooked the back of the shops.

The bottles were taken back to my shed and stored for a

short while. They would then be returned to the shop and the deposit claimed. Initially we all took turns in all aspects of the operation but it was soon obvious that when Stu and I went over the fence we always got more bottles. The others would often cry wolf and say that they'd heard a noise or that there weren't enough bottles in the yard. So Stu and I took over the main duties of the 'op' sometimes doing it without the other gang members' presence or knowledge.

It was on one such occasion, while Stu was exploring the yard that he found where the shopkeeper kept the full bottles. JACKPOT! We were now pinching full bottles, drinking the contents, then taking the empties back and being paid by the very person we were stealing from:- an early form of recycling.

It was not long before we considered other premises for our newly-found talents. Letts was a tool shop located next to the village police station. With its black and white Tudor-style frontage and pegged-tile roof, the detached shop could be described as quaint. It was also situated some five hundred metres away from the main row of shops. During the day it was a hive of activity but after normal trading hours Letts was isolated and vulnerable, like a calf away from his mother and the safety of the herd.

Stu and I recognised this vulnerability and removed a small pane of glass from one of the Georgian windows at the rear of the shop so we could climb inside. Before long we had stripped the place of any tools we could carry in our duffel bags. This included an all singing, all-dancing modern iron that Stu presented to his mum, telling her he had saved up his pocket money and bought it for her. How proud she was!

Stu's dad, our Fagan, knew all about the break-in and took the tools to work where he sold them on to his colleagues. He gave us a few quid for our endeavours and kept the rest to spend on whatever horse took his fancy in the 3.30 pm at Epsom, or his other favourite pastimes, playing cards for money and drinking. In all, we thought, another successful and profitable operation without any repercussions. Our downfall came when we became over-ambitious and broke into the Co-op.

The back of the two-storey Co-op in the middle of the village was masked from view and its architecture provided us with an easy and concealed climb to the top of the building. And so on one cold, dark night, dressed in a combination of black civilian clothing and Army kit, we gained access through an old skylight in the roof. Stu, who was inside the store, passed cigarettes and sweets up to Woody and I on the roof, to place in the duffel bags. A passer-by out walking her dog noticed a flashlight in the store and came to investigate. Woody and me ran off and sought refuge at an earlier agreed rendezvous point, a garage behind the Co-op. Many anxious moments passed while we waited for Stu to come – but he never did.

Woody and I agreed to go home as it was now getting very late. Making our way along Bells Lane, laden down with the duffel bags, a woman and a very large German shepherd dog approached us. She had seen us behind the Co-op at the scene of a crime. She tried to grab hold of me and I threw my duffel bag at her and managed to escape. We ran to my house, terrified at how the evening was unfolding.

Shortly after, there was a knock on the door. Half expecting the police, I answered it and to my surprise and initial relief found Stu, out of breath, on the doorstep. He had encountered the same woman who was now armed with my duffel bag, which had my name and address emblazoned across the front of it. He had also escaped her clutches but knew it was only a matter of time before the police would be involved and we'd be nicked.

I still recall the feeling of panic as I yelled to Mum that I was going back out and did what is technically referred to in the trade as 'a runner'. The three of us wandered the streets contemplating our options. Woody soon became worried about the time and decided to go home. Stu and I stayed out and sat down at the parade of shops by the phone box.

Eventually we agreed I would ring my dad, who was now living in Dartford and tell him of our situation. As I said to Stu, we could rely on him to hide us 'villains' until the heat died down, after which we could re-enter life as 'normal people'. Dad turned up and we sat in the car, waiting a clean getaway. Dad had another viewpoint. He would happily take us to the police station were we could do the right thing and hand ourselves in.

Stu did a runner but Dad caught up with him halfway across the rec, dragged him back to the car, put him inside and applied the child safety lock.

The policemen were surprisingly pleased to see us. Nothing anywhere near as exciting as this had happened in the village for as long as they could remember. As the story unravelled they were amazed at what we had achieved at such an early age. They had even put the Letts burglary down to a professional job. Woody's parents were awoken and informed that they were missing a party down at the local cop shop and that the evening would be incomplete without their attendance. Woody got the hiding of his life.

Dad did his best to convince the policeman that charges should be brought against us to teach us a lesson. Mum did her best to ensure that the matter would not get out of hand and destroy her reputation in the village. Stu's mum did her best to keep the iron!

The evening ended with the police emptying the contents of the shed, a long lecture on the consequences of a life of crime and, thankfully, no official charges being brought against us. Sergeant Herd said we were free to go home and we were elated.

In contrast, Stu's mum, Mary, lost her iron and her pride.

My parents agreed it was probably best if I went to live with Dad. Mum only meant this as a temporary measure, Dad interpreted it as permanent – and that's how things stayed. The year was 1974, I was ten years old and on my way to Dartford, to a new home, a new family, a new school and a new beginning.

CHAPTER TWO
Exodus

The Liberation from Egypt

The first night I spent with Dad and Mavis, his new common-law wife, was at her mother's house, somewhere in East Ham. I had to sleep on a camp bed in the same room as my new stepsisters, Cathy and Christine. Both wore glasses and I can remember feeling odd about this as no one in the gang did, or anyone else that I knew for that matter. It was like they had a disease or something or were really, really intelligent boffins. At first, I never thought they were going to be my kind of kids.

Both were very nice to me and told me wonderful stories about their childhood, where they had lived, about their Mum and her family. They both went out of their way to help me, as much as they could, to feel comfortable and part of the 'newly established family'. Unfortunately all I could do was tell them tales of how Dad had left Mum a number of times before, and that this was probably just another episode in his transient life. Not the best start, as the girls and Mavis became very upset.

In the morning Dad and Mavis packed up the car with us kids and we embarked on the journey to Dartford and my new home, 76 Mill Road, Hawley. The house was white-painted, slim, elongated, detached, and two-storey with three bedrooms. The front garden was non-existent and Dad was

17

required to park his car outside. The small garden to the rear of the house was bordered by a farmer's field, which extended as far as the eye could see and gave the house a rural feel. This made a pleasant change to the constraints of the council estate I had come from.

The bedrooms had already been allocated and I was required to share Christine's bedroom, as we were approximately the same age. This was contrary to what Dad had said to the solicitor and most probably what Mavis had told her ex-husband. I was not to tell Mum of this breach, as it would cause an untold number of problems for everyone. My parents were already embroiled in a new row. This one was regarding my departure from Hoo and whether it was meant to be permanent or temporary. Their emotions were volatile to say the least and, as I also didn't want to upset Mavis or the girls again, I decided I wouldn't tell Mum or the gang members for that matter, and resigned myself to sharing a room with a girl...

To be honest Christine and I hit it off immediately. I don't know whether this was because we felt like we were both pawns in our parents' marital disputes and got comfort from each other's company, or that it was reassuring to have someone else's constant and caring attention. It may have been that I was badly missing my mum and Joanne and that Christine was an immediate and available substitute mother and sister; but, for whatever reason, we always seemed to get along fine, being around the same age and disposition, and we quite simply, just clicked.

The school holidays had already started. This meant that the anticipation of starting a new school was postponed for the immediate future and playtime ruled. We were allowed to explore the local area and fields at our leisure and without supervision. Cathy who was older and very artistic would go off on her own sometimes and draw things, including painting a figurehead of our dog, a black cocker spaniel called 'Grocer' on the back gate, but generally the three of us would venture off together, into the big unknown.

We would return to the house for mealtimes, although these always consisted of stew or bread and jam, money being extremely tight. The main aim at these mealtimes was to eat quickly and get out of the house before jobs were found for us to do. We would then continue to roam the streets or the fields to the back of the house for hours on end. These excursions were where Christine and I found that we had much in common. We would explore new locations and talk for hours about nothing and yet, everything. She would tell me about her Dad and her friends at her old school, and I would tell her about Mum and Jo, living in Hoo and all the gang members. We had the same humour and zest for life that helped us escape from the harsh reality of each other's parents' divorce proceedings. These brought friction and tension, as both sides frequently tried to apportion total blame for their marriage break-up to the other person and by so doing, eliminate or assassinate that other person from the chambers of fondness, lying deep within the minds of their children. The basic truth was that Christine and I both loved each of our parents. She didn't blame me for the break up of her parents or for having to share her room and I, in turn, didn't blame her. We just wanted to be left alone and outside of the grown up world full of hate, blame and self-pity.

One day Dad came back with an old automatic Honda 50cc

motorbike. He took the bike and us three out onto the farmer's field and taught us all how to ride it. Being the boy of the group and his son, I expected to go first, but being the youngest, had to wait until last. This was my first experience of being treated unfairly in my opinion, although in Dad's opinion a fair, logical and impartial way of ensuring that all were involved. It was an experience that I did not warm to as I felt Mavis never applied the same ruling.

Riding the bike soon became our main entertainment. We were not kids who sat in front of the telly. As there was only one telly in the house in the front room this would have meant sitting with Dad and Mavis. Watching telly would have quickly been transformed into an afternoon of explaining our lives away or getting involved in conversations about our other parent or being made to do meaningless and often arduous jobs about the house. It was always better to be out of the house and not interrupt or interfere with their routines.

It was not long before the holidays ended. My new school was Oakfield Lane Junior at the bottom of the Tree Estate in Dartford. Cathy and Christine had both passed the eleven-plus and went to Dartford Technical School For Girls, a sure testament for the wearing of NHS specs. So I started my new school alone. I knew no one and hated it. My first few months there were murder. I would often run away from school not caring for the consequences, to a phone box on the main road. There I would reverse the charges to the school where Dad worked to ask him to pick me up and take me home. After a stern lecture from Mavis that Dad could not be interrupted at work, I decided to skip this part of the proceedings and simply walk home without anyone knowing.

This caused havoc and before things got 'out of hand' I was sat down where it was explained to me, in no uncertain terms, that everyone was feeling the same anxiety that I was feeling and that it wasn't easy for anyone else either. My actions were deemed to be selfish and uncaring for the other members of the family and this 'chastisement' made me feel isolated – a total outcast. I badly missed the warm compassion and understanding of my Mum, which the girls had available to them with Mavis. Although Dad was there he was not an individual who would express his feelings openly. I was very unhappy and couldn't get my message across. In the end and in the interests of peace, I succumbed to the emotional blackmail and begrudgingly completed the term at Oakfield Lane School while Dad and Mavis found me a senior school.

Before my next birthday Dad took me to his cricket club. He loved the game with an intense passion and had played for his public school Mill Hill, the Royal Navy in the Far East, and various clubs throughout his life. As a lad from the council estate, I had never played before or appreciated its subtleties, preferring to kick a football around the streets with my mates. One evening, I was introduced to Len Morris, a Saturday first eleven player and the coach for the Horton Kirby Colts team.

Len was probably in his late thirties and lived for sport – all sports; as long as you could compete fiercely and drink sociably afterwards. His enthusiasm was addictive and his ability with colts unrivalled. Assessing my potential, I was asked to pick up a cricket stump and take a batsman's stance. To his absolute delight and mine, he proclaimed me "a natural".

Len was also a wicket-keeper and before long was teaching me the basics of standing behind the stumps. My introduction to cricket was complete and very soon I was in the Colts team and competing fiercely, as Len had taught me to, against the neighbouring villages.

The year was 1975, I would be eleven in June and finally I felt I had a purpose in life:, to play cricket well. During the summer holidays the Kent under-eleven cricket team was touring Wales and I was invited. For two weeks I lived with a family whose son was playing for the Welsh team. Phillip North was fanatical about his cricket and his Welsh sweater and cap were both in a display cabinet in his bedroom. To his credit, Phillip later went on to play professional cricket for Glamorgan.

Being eleven already, I was technically exempted from being selected for the under- elevens team but the manager, Colin Oliver, was having none of this. With permission from the Welsh manager, he selected me for a game against Newport Cricket Club in Gwent. Everything that could possibly go well for me happened on that day. I took seven stumpings in the game, a statistic that I am yet to find matched, and Kent stuffed Newport out of sight. I was on cloud nine but was banned by the Welsh manager from playing against Wales in the 'test match'.

Colin Oliver presented me with my under-elevens cap in the changing rooms before the game against Barry Island, where I learned I could not be selected for that or any other match on the tour. I was upset to say the least but comforted when he informed me I was the only individual ever to be awarded a Kent under-eleven cap for performance and not attendance.

In the September I joined The Downs School, a comprehensive renowned for its sporting facilities. Once again I knew no one. For the first few weeks I wandered around the school aimlessly and anonymously until an incident happened that was to change my school life dramatically.

As we filed into the assembly hall the kid in the row in front of me, from another class, sat down and his school bag that was strung around his back, fell across my legs. I noticed that he had spelled Kawasaki incorrectly on his bag and pointed this out to him. He thought that I said that he 'smelt' funny and promptly smacked me in the face. Because the assembly hall was packed with teachers I couldn't retaliate but the red mist had arisen in me and I told him I would see him at one of the schoolbreaks.

After assembly we went off to our lessons and, with the red mist now dispersed, I never gave it another thought until, during a break, I went into the boys' toilets. There to my utter disbelief was this kid and about ten of his mates smoking and playing a game of penny-up-against-the-wall. All of a sudden I no longer wanted to go to the loo but simply get the hell out of there. Unfortunately, I had been seen and he made a beeline straight for me. I was trapped. While he was ranting on at me and trying to involve his other mates, the red mist reappeared and I belted him, and continued to do so. He never managed to land one punch on me. He was, however, much taller than me and I couldn't hit him in his face. Suddenly someone picked me up and I was level with him, face to face, so I belted him all over the place and he gave up. The person who had picked me up let me go and I turned around to see Mark Vincent with a big grin on his face. Mark had been taught football by my dad at his old junior school.

I thanked him and walked out of the toilets, back towards my form room. En route I was stopped by a tall, thin, blond lad who was in my class. His name was Darran McGill and he informed me that, "I could hang around with him if I wanted to". Not having any other offers at the time, I decided I would and our friendship began there and then. Dal and I had the same mischievous manner and sense of humour and were the first two pupils in our year to be selected to play rugby for the school. I was picked first, although he would never admit to it and still doesn't.

Dal and I got into all kinds of trouble and it wasn't long before we were in front of our head of year Mr Jarvis for messing about during the Christmas school choir concert. The Head of Year, who was afflicted with a terrible shedding skin complaint, believed I was potentially a sound pupil who had been led astray by Dal, whose surname he had encountered several times before in his teaching career.

Our punishment was to count the dinner tickets after each school meal. Strangely we were trusted and unsupervised. Each pupil was required to write their name, class and the date on the reverse of their green dinner ticket and it wasn't long before we realised that some of the tickets had the details of the pupil who had bought them written on the back in pencil. This could easily be erased without trace and the dinner ticket reused. We were in business. We no longer needed to buy our own dinner tickets, which in turn meant we could pocket the dinner money being given to us by our parents. It also meant that any pupil who had forgotten or had lost their ticket for that day could come to us and buy one. They could also swap one for anything we fancied, like sweets, fags – although Dal didn't smoke – or homework being completed for us. Absolutely anything we wanted. We viewed it as a kind of charitable gesture to those in need. Another form of recycling. The Head of Year, who had no idea what we were doing, soon informed us that our punishment was over. We respectfully told him that we didn't mind carrying on. He agreed and that's how things stayed, right up until we left school.

Cricket was going extremely well. I was now established in the Kent under twelves' side and had also played regularly for the under thirteens. Dad enjoyed my success but Mavis resented more and more the time he was spending with me at cricket nets and matches. Cricket focused his time and attention on me and took it away from her. She would frequently pass comments about the money that was spent on my cricket clothes, equipment, travelling costs and net fees. Money she felt could have been spent elsewhere, on the new home or other family members. I couldn't understand this at the time, as the clothing and equipment was a requirement and not a luxury, and Dad's attendance at nets and matches was his wish and to his enjoyment.

Cathy and Christine were always fully supportive of my achievements and never said anything untoward or let it be known that they in anyway felt they were missing out. They would often ask me where the game had been played, how the game had gone and if I had played well. They seemed genuinely interested in what I was doing and their words and actions always made me feel that the internal wrangling was unique to Dad and Mavis and that it was in my best interest to keep out of the way.

Cricket continued to go extremely well and I even captained the Kent under-thirteen side for a whole season, unbeaten. By now Dad had decided cricket would be my chosen career when the time came to leave school and his attitude changed from "as long as you enjoyed the game, that's the main thing" to a more serious, "you really need to improve that part of your game if you are going to play at the top level".

He would often say, "When you're good, son, you're exceptional but when you're bad you're terrible"; so most weeknights were spent practising my game. Dad would throw endless cricket balls at me and I would practice over and over again a specific batting stroke he considered to be weak. He would then talk me through my mind-set and the need for me to remain totally focused throughout my innings, "Concentration is the key", he would say. I would then have to don a pair of wicket-keeping gloves and stand in the middle of the cricket square while he threw balls in from the boundary. This was another area of my game that he disliked and I would be severely reprimanded if I caught a ball untidily or, God forbid, I dropped a ball he had thrown.

I suppose this was when my attitude towards the game started to change. It is easy to maintain a youngster's motivation when the people around them enjoy and praise them for what they have or are achieving. At that time most people around me found cricket boring. The game wasn't televised in the same way that is today and so only the 'purist' followed the sport or people from private schools. Those attending comprehensives mainly focused on football, rugby, netball and athletics. My school was unaware that I was even playing for the county, let alone had captained it. Many assemblies were spent watching and applauding other members of the school receiving congratulations and accolades from the headmaster for attending a district or North Kent trial for football, netball or athletics. I never got a mention, which led me to the conclusion that I had chosen the wrong sport. At one point I had been the only pupil playing for the county who wasn't attending a private school! My school didn't seem to want any recognition for this and the Kent cricketing authorities, being snobby at the time, didn't advertise the fact.

Throughout the fourth and fifth years at school, Dad became more intensive with his criticism and after each match for the county I would receive a full debriefing on everything that in his eyes had gone horribly wrong. I had been playing for the county two years above my own age group and by now had cemented my position within the under-fifteens side. Dad, however, left nothing to chance and would tear into me if he felt I could have played better. He would then drop me off at home feeling pathetic and useless and go off to the pub with Mavis, only to repeat the process and the entire debriefing conversation with me once the pub had kicked him out and he had returned home. He would come into my room worse for wear, wake me from my sleep and go on at me for hours. Sometimes he would become aggressive saying I was taking my talent for granted and becoming complacent and that without cricket I was nothing; as academically I was a clown. I would eventually be saved by Mavis when she would call him to bed, but this was not before I had acknowledged his criticism and promised to do better next time.

These conversations were too much for me and I started to

resent each game I played, knowing that it would bring me criticism later. I swore to myself that at the first opportunity I would pack the game in. And that's what I did. During one heated conversation I told Dad that I hated the game and was only playing it for him. The constant practice and his eternal criticism was driving me mad and that I would be happy if I never held a cricket bat or put on a pair of wicket-keeping gloves again. I told him I intended to join the Forces and would be leaving home at the first possible chance. He said I wouldn't last six months in the Forces. There the conversation ended, as did my cricket, and for that moment my relationship with Dad.

In May, 1980, Dad and Mavis both gave up teaching and took over a pub. The Wheatsheaf in Southfleet, near Gravesend in Kent was a 500-year-old Courage house with a thatched roof, wooden beams and littered with history. We moved in lock, stock and barrel and lived there from that date on. On the down side it had no central heating or upstairs toilet and was freezing 365 days a year. People would travel for miles around to visit the Wheatsheaf and from Thursday to Sunday you were lucky to get in the door. The pub had a reputation for daytime food and during those hours enjoyed a professional clientele. During the evening until about 7pm the locals would come in and Dad would put a pot of pheasant stew or something similar over the large inglenook fire and there'd be crisps and cheeses on the bar. After seven o'clock, when the locals had gone, couples would fill the pub and a romantic ambience would ensue. As the relationship with Dad was quite strained I would spend any holiday time I had back in Hoo with Mum, Jo and my old friends.

The final weeks at school were a drag. Dal had been expelled for refusing to wear uniform. Dad and Mavis attended a parents' evening where the school tried to talk them into convincing me to stay on. I wasn't interested and refused to give it any serious consideration. My future I had decided was in the Marines as I had already sat the entrance exam and had passed the medical. Furthermore, I was being considered as a potential officer cadet, along with another pupil from school, based on the exams that I was taking and the grades I expected. The school could therefore go and whistle.

Like most things in life, unexpected events can crop up and impact on the outcome of ready-made plans. Peter, the other pupil, decided he didn't want to join the Marines after all. Then my friend from Hoo, Stu McAllister contacted me and said he was no longer joining the Marines but was now joining the Parachute Regiment. When I asked him what they did he simply said, "Everything the Marines do, but they also jump out of planes".

Well, that was a good enough sales pitch for me. So I contacted the Marine office in Chatham and told them, "Thanks but no thanks" and went down to the Army recruiting centre, also in Chatham, and sat the entrance exam for the Army. I passed and the recruiting chap couldn't believe me when I told him I wanted to be a Para. He told me I had a very high pass mark and as such could choose any of the top bands of jobs within the Army. I think at the time the highest paid trade was Aircraft Technician. He was adamant I was throwing away a golden opportunity but I wouldn't be swayed and off I went to Didcot, in Oxfordshire, for a couple of days to the

Army's selection centre. My joining date for the Parachute Regiment was 9th September, 1980.

Stu joined the regiment a couple of weeks before me. His birthday was earlier than mine and as he would be seventeen in the same year he could join Recruit Company immediately. I had to join Junior Parachute Company and complete a year of service there prior to transferring to Recruit Company. When Stu left to join, the whole of the street and almost the entire village turned out to wave him off, which made him feel very special. When he turned up at The Parachute Regiment depot and was told he was a week early, he had to go all the way home again. He then spent the next week hiding from everyone, feeling a bit stupid.

CHAPTER THREE

Leviticus

The Ritual of Sacrifice

The bus stop, where Mum and Joanne waved me goodbye when I left to join the Army, still stands on the Hoo main road. The three of us had walked, suitcases in hand, through the alleyway opposite Mum's house, past the parade of shops, turning left at the end by the phone box, where I had phoned Dad all those years ago. Crossing the road and the 'rec' brought us out onto the main road near the bus stop at the entrance to the Masonic Hall.

I was wearing a pair of faded Levi jeans, white trainers, a blue velvet jacket with a T-shirt underneath. My hair, which came well below the jacket collar, sported a centre parting, which I believed to be extremely trendy. The bus was late which left me feeling awkward, waiting for the inevitable tears and soppy farewells. When the bus came in sight I didn't think Mum and Joanne were ever going to release me from the incapacitating bear hug they now had me in.

Once released, I boarded the bus and immediately went upstairs and sat on the back seat. I looked back to see Mum and Joanne still practising their wrestling techniques, this time with each other. I felt a sudden surge of emotion for them both and wished I could have behaved better at the bus stop and said the things one should say at such a time but I hadn't and it was now too late. I turned to look ahead and never saw Mum and Joanne leave the bus stop.

Eventually, I boarded the Aldershot train, which was communal and, as is always the way when you want to sit down, soon packed. The suitcases played their part in ensuring I was not as sharp as I would have liked in finding a seat. After an uncomfortable period standing with two suitcases between my legs, I decided to abandon them so that I could repair to the corridor outside the first class compartments in the next carriage. There, I met another lad who, after I'd scrounged a fag off him, informed me he was joining the Army. Not wishing to get into a conversation about him and his life, I offered a rather tart, "Really" and left him. The suitcases required a chaperone, I decided. I did not.

The train pulled into Aldershot where, for the first time, I saw a soldier in uniform. He was a menacing-looking Corporal who would undoubtedly have been snapped up by the Kray Brothers. He was bawling at the top of his voice for any lads awaiting transport for Depot Para. I, not wishing to appear intimidated, casually walked up to him and informed him that my name was Mark Thomas and that I was waiting to go to Depot Para. He stopped for a brief moment, observing my hair, then my dress. I honestly thought he was going to have me for breakfast or worse still, just have me. He recovered to look at his list and thumbed down to the T's.

"Thomas, yup – you're on my list," he said. "Get yourself on the wagon outside".

Getting on the wagon was much harder than I had envisaged. Like the train, it was cram-packed with lads. The tailgate to the rear of the lorry had been dropped but as there was no space for my suitcases I couldn't throw them aboard. In a decisive attempt to save face, I once more abandoned them and, as there was a foot hole at either end of the tailgate to assist with your climb, decided to simply step aboard. I soon discovered there was a definite technique to this. After several failed attempts and absolutely no assistance from those on board, I was ready to turn around and get the next train home. The Corporal soon appeared and deciding it was time to depart, hoisted my suitcases and me into the abyss of the wagon and slammed shut the tailgate.

Falling off the wagon outside Browning Barracks: Depot – The Parachute Regiment, was, I discovered, much easier than getting on. Another Corporal had his own list of platoons in Junior Parachute Company, to which each arrival was assigned. When he asked me my full name and I told him, "Mark Robert Jason Eyles-Thomas", he burst out laughing and said in a sadistic tone, "With names like that you should have been an officer. Do you think you're better than every-one else?"

I did not answer him and vowed never to mention my full name again, and when required, would introduce myself as just "Thomas".

I was in 3 Platoon, situated on the top floor of Queripel VC block. Each three-storey building was named after a renowned Parachute Regiment soldier or a recipient of the Victoria Cross. Captain Lionel Queripel won his VC posthu-mously at Arnhem in 1944. Each floor contained six rooms that could comfortably house 12 men. Each room was parti-tioned so six men would share each side of the dividing wall. There were four other rooms, the Platoon Office, a Non

Commissioned Officer bunk, a storeroom and the washroom. My room was at the end of the corridor nearest the stairs. No one else was in the room when I got there. Each of the six bed spaces had been allocated by surname in alphabetical order. I located mine and nosily looked at the other names. In one corner by the window I read the name Scrivens, written in chinagraph. I rubbed out the letters E, N and S and lay on my bed to await the others. Ian Scrivens was the first to turn up. He was six-feet tall with a skinhead haircut and drainpipe jeans, cut to the top of his black ten-hole Dr Marten boots, one of which was laced up with a bright yellow lace, the other with a red one. He was wearing a bomber jacket. He went over to the locker with his name on and declared that his name was not Scriv but Scrivens. "Really," I said, hoping he wouldn't notice the black mark on my right index finger. "Thomas," I continued, and left the introductions there.

When everyone had arrived, the Corporals took us into the corridor that ran the length of the top floor and introduced themselves. There were four Corporals, all Non Commissioned Officers, one Sergeant, the Senior Non Commissioned Officer, and one Lieutenant, the Officer. The platoon was broken down into four sections, each commanded by a Corporal. The Sergeant would oversee the Corporals and the Lieutenant was in overall command. I was in 1 Section commanded by Corporal Tom Camp.

Our Sergeant, Aussie Howells, had a reputation as one of the hardest men, if not the hardest man, in the 3rd Battalion, Parachute Regiment. He looked older than his years, with the weathered face of a sailor, as if he had spent too much time outside in the wind and the rain. Apparently, Sgt Howells held the record in 3 Para for having the most fights while the regiment were serving in Germany, and never losing one. He had reportedly been stabbed in his right arm during one of these encounters and this restricted his ability to salute officers in the manner according to the drill movement. He would, however, carry out his own version of a salute to any officer he encountered but no one ever said anything to him about this! His demeanour, though, was nothing like the stories of brutality told about him. He radiated a sense of calmness that made you want to get to know him or be respected by him. It was obvious that he was held in high regard by all of the other SNCOs and NCOs serving at Depot Para.

The Platoon Commander, Lieutenant Neil Young, was a striking-looking man. He spoke with an educated voice that in no way diluted his action man appearance and charisma. He had an air of sophistication about him and was always dressed immaculately. His blond hair accentuated his tanned complexion and brown eyes, making him an ideal son-in-law prospect. Although he obviously knew this, his vanity never appeared to be more than just an inner confidence or self-belief.

Lieutenant Young had been a young PC in charge of a platoon in 2 Para when the IRA blew up their vehicle full of Paras at Warrenpoint, Northern Ireland, in 1979. When medics and ambulances arrived to deal with the casualties, the IRA detonated a second bomb to devastating effect – killing eighteen soldiers, sixteen of them from 2 Para. This experience seemed to provide a hidden motivation deep within him and gave him a determined and vengeful manner.

The barracks had its own barber, although I think by trade, he was a butcher or mechanic. When it came to my turn, he smiled at me and asked whether I wanted a wash and blow dry. Very funny, I thought, and ignored him as I sat in the chair. He promptly removed the attachment from the shaver and with one single stroke gave me a strip of the shortest cropped hair, from the centre of my forehead to the nape of my neck. He then turned off the shaver and announced that he was going to lunch. He'd be back in an hour. I, meanwhile, had to sit there, looking like the opposite of a Mohican, and await his return. This amused everyone in the barber's shop, with one exception. Very funny man the barber, very funny.

We were taught how to wash, iron and wear all of our kit issue correctly. Morning and afternoon parades were carried out each day and any individual who failed to present himself in a manner acceptable to the inspecting NCO or Officer was severely punished.

Our immediate objective was for the Corporals to teach the platoon drill to make sure we passed off the square in line with the training programme. Passing off the square was a big thing. Not only were we in competition with the other Platoons in Junior Company, but the Corporals also had their own competition regarding which individuals and which section would let the platoon down. Woe betide anyone who was responsible for losing their bet!

Passing off required the whole platoon to complete various drill movements, in unison to the complete satisfaction of the Company Sergeant Major (CSM), a Warrant Officer, and the Officer Commanding (OC) Junior Company, who held the rank of Major.

This was not easily achieved and led to many a 'beasting' being handed out to those uncoordinated, bet losing offenders. After hours of 'square bashing' everyone got the hang of it and our platoon passed off. We were then allowed to wear the maroon beret of the Regiment but with a small blue plastic backing behind our cap badge. This told everyone we were junior soldiers and not the real thing.

Within a short space of time people started to leave, deciding the Army or the Regiment wasn't for them. This whittled the numbers down dramatically and very shortly we were down to four in a room.

At NAAFI break the Corporals distributed our mail. I was one of the fortunate ones, receiving a number of letters, mainly from Mum, Joanne, Cathy, Christine and Claire, my girlfriend at the time. Claire would cover the envelope with the acronyms S.W.A.L.K. and H.O.L.L.A.N.D. plus lots of hearts and kisses and small drawings of men hanging from parachutes. The corporals loved all this and I'd get the piss taken out of me in the corridor in front of the whole platoon. On more than one occasion, I would have to read the whole letter out to everyone. The contents of her letters, in keeping with the envelopes, were always extremely embarrassing and I would cringe every time they called my name, hoping she hadn't written to me. I wrote to her, at Nottingham University where she was studying, imploring her to stop drawing on the envelopes, as I was getting grief. She, on the other hand, thought it was great fun and continued to do so. The relationship ended shortly afterwards, as did the piss taking.

The OC decided every junior Para was to watch the Six O'Clock news to keep abreast of world events. So each night the duty NCO would appear at the block and escort the whole of Junior Company over to the NAAFI to watch the TV news. This was a complete pain in the neck, other than on Monday nights when the whole of Junior Company was required to report to the gymnasium for 'milling' – the term used by the Parachute Regiment for two individuals knocking hell out of each other for two minutes. Participants would have to demonstrate their ability to fight with maximum aggression and a determination to win. Individuals who failed to satisfy the Physical Training (PT) staff would have to re-fight, be branded 'wimps' or not suitable for the Regiment. Milling has been described as boxing without Queensbury Rules and most certainly without any 'queens'. Due to the vast numbers of juniors, two-minute bouts were often cut to a minute or until someone was hurt or knocked out. Monday was the only night no one got up to leave immediately after the news ended. The duty corporal was the only exception. He couldn't wait to see the fighting.

The curriculum for Junior Parachute Company included vast amounts of Adventure Training, viz. canoeing, rock climbing, abseiling, pot-holing, navigation, sailing and hiking. Apart from the rock climbing, these activities were great fun. Rock climbing was horrendous. How anyone can get enjoyment from hanging by a thin thread over a three hundred foot high sheer cliff face will always beat me. Cpl Stuart Windon would take us for these 'external leadership' courses. He was a mountain goat who could have climbed a four hundred foot sheet of polished glass naked if required to do so. Fear, apprehension and anxiety were not in his vocabulary. He'd look at us with a puzzled expression as we quaked uncontrollably at the foot of the mountain. During one group climb we had to scale an overhang – a rock that juts out from the main face and impedes your ascent. During the initial stages of the overhang, the climber finds himself clinging to the rock for dear life, his body parallel to the ground with nothing but air between himself and impending death, or at the very least, life as a cripple. Our group of four climbers was made up of Scrivs, Neil Grose, Baz Barrett and myself. Scrivs and Grose set off first, Baz and I were to follow. The climb was in two phases. Phase One was to climb one hundred and fifty feet to a ledge. I use the term 'ledge' loosely. Phase Two was to tackle the overhang and then on to the summit two hundred feet further up. When Scrivs and Grose completed Phase One and were starting the second phase, Baz and I set off. We reached the ledge and were told by Cpl Windon to secure ourselves until Scrivs and Grose had completed Phase Two. Baz and I sat on a lump of rock no wider than a gnat's cock, secured to a 'twig' that was trying hard to impersonate a bush, with our feet dangling into the oblivion. "You owe me a fag," said Baz.

"What are you talking about?" I replied.

"The day we joined the Army, when we boarded the train for Aldershot. I was the bloke in the corridor. You bummed a fag off me," he joked.

"Really?" I said, concentrating on not falling to my death.

"That's what you said back then," he laughed.

"Baz, if we get out of this alive I'll buy you twenty bloody fags – now shut up will you!" I snapped back.

Cpl Windon shouted down that the other two had success-fully completed Phase Two but there was now only time for one more climber. Baz looked round to see me already half way down the mountain with a huge smile on my face. "I'll have the fags waiting for you when you get down!" I shouted up to him.

"Okay, mate," he said, although to be honest I don't think he actually used those precise words but I believe that's what he meant to say. I didn't care anyway. I was gone.

Adventure training exercises always took us to remote villages. Places in Devon, Scotland and Wales you had never heard of but always welcomed the British Army as newcomers and a source of entertainment. We loved these outings and couldn't wait to be allowed out to explore the village. We would always head for the local disco or noisiest pub, knowing that it would be packed with the three essentials – booze, girls and local milling opponents.

Scrivs, myself and another member of the platoon, Jason Burt, were absolute nightmares. Walthamstow boy Jason was the cockiest cockney you'd ever met. Handsome, with a Mediterranean complexion, the girls just loved him. The three of us would stroll into the local pub as if we owned the place. After a quick 'recce' of the talent we would agree on who were to be the lucky ladies for the night. We would then set about our 'mission'. Jas and I would go over to the girls and ask whether they wanted a drink or a dance. Jas would do the initial talking and the smiling, as his charm and looks were impossible to resist, and I would take his lead. Should the boyfriend get out of hand or take umbrage, I would also initiate the milling. Should it get totally out of hand, as quite often happened, Scrivs would step in. From that moment on the whole thing would resemble a brawl in a cowboy saloon.

Quite often everyone from the platoon got involved and on one memorable occasion in Ashburton, Devon, nigh on the whole of Junior Para was fighting.

Whenever the police became involved or the matter was reported to the OC, Junior Para would get a right rollicking, not for the evening's events as fighting was an important part of being a paratrooper, but for getting caught.

We were now getting to know our own strengths and weaknesses and those of the other members of the platoon. Whenever an individual needed assistance it was given, unconditionally. In the main, individual idiosyncrasies were accepted, as long as it didn't disrupt the achievements of the platoon. Anyone lacking in fitness was taken out by the more capable lads for extra training. If a person lacked confidence, he would be urged on at milling by everyone in the platoon and then taken down the pub and accepted as someone willing to tackle and conquer his fears. Those who could not present themselves in a manner befitting a Parachute Regiment soldier were given additional instruction and help with their kit. For anyone committed to the platoon and the regiment, help was always at hand. The atmosphere in the block was fantastic, radios and cassette players blasting out music at every available opportunity. No one was criticised for their preference. Scrivs was a Motown fanatic and would play Smokey Robinson's 'Tears Of A Clown' over and over again. It would make us laugh to see this six-foot skinhead, who was as hard as iron, prancing about like Bambi, and whenever or wherever the song came on we would all look for him and imitate his dance.

Baz, or 'hideous gargoyle', as he was affectionately known,

worshipped The Stranglers. Their music would reverberate around his room giving anyone within a two-mile radius a splitting headache. No one could imitate his dance or the faces he would pull when doing it. Nevertheless, we would watch him for hours and fall about in fits of laughter when he introduced a new movement or facial expression.

Grose had no personal musical preference and loved listening to whatever was being played at the time. There was no nickname for Grose. The Army liked to shorten things for ease and the lads adopted this practice and subsequently most surnames were shortened. My nickname was Tom, gleaned by simply shortening Thomas. Grose's surname was short, as was his first name Neil, so the work had already been done. No one saw any need for change. Referring to him as Grose was in no way derogatory and he received the same affection as everyone else. Grose was a homely lad and was proud of the fact that he had an older brother serving in the Army. He disliked being away from his mum, dad, brother and younger sister. He would often remark that I reminded him of his brother. I believe he found some comfort in the similarities he saw in us. I liked Grose and would take him out with me down town when I was drinking. He enjoyed the crowd and the cheekiness of the banter. On one occasion when I had left him to his own devices for too long due to the attentions and affections of a female, he got blind drunk. I couldn't believe my eyes when I returned to him. He was out of it, laughing and giggling like a schoolboy.

"Jesus," I said. "If only Mum and Dad, could see you now." He didn't care. He was having the time of his life and didn't want to leave. Finally, I dragged him away from the bar and started to walk back to camp. It was obvious Grose's legs weren't working as well as they should have been and before long I was giving him a fireman's carry, with the occasional piggyback. I think he proposed to me several times on the journey but all I just kept telling him was not to be sick all over me. Now and then, to my utter revulsion and his total amusement, he would pretend to be sick. When I eventually got him back to camp he was unconscious. I had to put him to bed and stay up all night to make sure that he wasn't sick in his sleep. The following morning when I recounted the evening's events to him, ending with me as Florence Nightingale, he was even more amused despite his colour, which was, in the words of the song, a 'lighter shade of pale'.

On another occasion, waiting in the queue to use the phone to ring home, I overheard Grose talking to his mum. It was obvious from his body language and the pitch of his voice that the conversation was difficult for him. I opened the phone booth door and could see that he had got himself into a bit of a state. I nodded to him and took the phone from him. His mum told me that he was feeling homesick and was thinking of calling it a day. As any mother would be, she was very concerned for her son's welfare. I assured her that he was fine and doing well. We had all, at one time or another, experienced moments like this when you missed home and thought of packing it in. I promised her that I would look out for him and personally take care of him. Mrs Grose thanked me for my reassurances and looked forward to meeting with me one day. I took Grose back to the block and showed him a letter I had received from my mum on a similar occasion. I'd had a tremendous time on leave back at home with all my friends and hadn't wanted to return to camp. Mum listened to me sympathetically concluded that if I no longer wanted to be in the Army then I should return to camp and inform them in the correct manner, and not go absent without leave, AWOL. On returning to camp, I received a letter from Mum, saying how nice it had been to see me on leave and how I had grown. The discipline and training from such a prestigious regiment would stand me in good stead for the years ahead of me and how proud she was of my achievements. I kept this letter close to hand as her words were heartfelt and, I told Grose, had inspired me through that difficult time. I was convinced they would continue to do so whenever the occasion presented itself again. Grose was amazed that I had felt the same way and, putting the matter down to experience, decided to stay.

Fitness and soldiering soon became the main topics of the training programme. By design, paratroopers are required to jump out of aircraft with all the kit necessary to complete their mission, most probably behind enemy lines where re-supply would prove difficult if not impossible. Each paratrooper was required to be physically able to carry the equipment to complete the mission and if the situation called for it, be fit enough to get himself home, under his own steam and initiative. My experience of fitness, prior to joining Junior Para, was a game of football or cricket, with the occasional sprint for safety when a game of knock down ginger went terribly wrong.

This was a different kettle of fish altogether. We were initially introduced to fitness by a gentle 'road walk and run' but within weeks we were running in webbing belt order.

Webbing is the personal equipment worn by a soldier into battle around his waist; its function was the storage of ammunition, food and water. To simulate the weight, sandbags were used. Belt order had to weigh thirty-five pounds and the Physical Training Instructor (PTI) would weigh each man's webbing. There were no exceptions or excuses. Runs would increase in distance from two or three-mile jaunts to the ultimate ten miler, to be completed within two hours. Dress was always boots, denims, puttees, red PT vest, combat jacket and helmet with each man required to carry his personal weapon, a 7.62mm SLR, self-loading rifle. Without a fully loaded magazine, the rifle added a further nine pounds to the weight being carried. The combat helmet controlled body temperature, by acting as a pressure cooker!

The Paras' method of advancing on foot is known as 'tabbing', short for Tactical Advance to Battle (TAB). This is a combination of running and, when dictated by the terrain, walking at an extremely fast pace. Tabs were undertaken daily and soon included, in addition to belt order, bergens – back packs for carrying all the essentials for surviving out in the open; sleeping bags, clothing and additional rations. The bergen also leaves the aeroplane attached to the paratrooper when he is parachuting.

In addition to tabbing, fitness periods would include the assault course, steeplechase, telegraph pole races, stretcher races – where the stretchers weigh around one hundred and eighty pounds – as well as swimming and gymnasium workouts. Gym workouts were gruelling. The PT staff would 'beast' us until we could no longer go on. When everyone was too exhausted to continue and the PT staff became bored, they would play their own sadistic version of space invaders to amuse themselves. This required the platoon to line up against one of the gym walls in three ranks. We would then have to move in a crab-like fashion from one wall to the next, making a noise similar to an electronic amusement game found in pubs. The three or four PTIs competing against each other would then throw or kick medicine balls at us. When you were hit by a ball, you were dead. The PTIs earned ten points for each one of us they hit and were very competitive. We just got bruised. Every now and then they would send one of us running across the back of those who were left, as a 'space ship' with a noise to match. The value if hit was one hundred points.

The image of sixteen-year-old boys playing soldiers doesn't do justice to the professionalism and high standard of soldiering achieved in Junior Para. The instruction was always of the highest order and although the availability of kit and ammunition was not always what one would have expected, the instructors would improvise in their own inno-vative ways and the battle lessons always appeared cutting edge and real.

Range days and live firing happened regularly and each soldier would have to demonstrate his ability to be able to use all the Platoon weapons. This included his personal weapon the SLR, a semi-automatic rifle with a range capability of between 100 and 600 metres; the General Purpose Machine Gun, or GPMG with range capability up to 1,800 metres in Sustained Fire Role; the Light Machine Gun or LMG, the Browning 9mm semi-automatic, hand held pistol; (mainly used by officers), the 9mm Sterling sub-machine gun or SMG;

the 84mm Carl Gustav anti-tank weapon, the 66mm disposable anti-tank rocket launcher and hand grenades.

In addition, Regimental history was taught and we would learn all about where the Parachute Regiment had fought, the battle honours won, the individuals who had shown exceptional courage, the medals that had been awarded and the lessons to be gleaned from these previous encounters. Regimental pride and honour was paramount and was enforced at every available opportunity, as was the Regimental motto, Utrinque Paratus (Ready For Anything). We were different from the other regiments and corps within the British Army. Other regiments and corps, we were told, were issued their berets during basic training. This was because it was worthless, a 'crap hat'. This was how our regiment referred to all other soldiers in the British Army who were not Parachute Regiment. They were 'crap hats' or simply 'hats'. Field Marshal the Viscount Montgomery of Alamein, Monty as everyone knew him, had once said of the Parachute Regiment:

What manner of men are these that wear the maroon beret?
They are, firstly, all volunteers and are then toughened
by hard physical training.
As a result they have that infectious optimism and that offensive
eagerness which comes from physical well being.

They have jumped from the air
and by doing so have conquered fear.
Their duty lies in the van of battle;
they are proud of this honour and have never failed in any task.

They have the highest standards in all things whether it be skills
in battle or smartness in execution of all peacetime duties.
They have shown themselves to be as tenacious and determined
in defence as they are courageous in attack.

They are, in fact, men apart.

'Every man an Emperor'

It was a hard act to follow. Our regiment's coveted red
beret, parachute smock and parachute wings, had each to be
earned at different stages of our training in Recruit Company
and were never just issued. The Parachute Regiment was an
elite fighting force and only those who could maintain its
reputation for fitness and courage would succeed. This was
never regarded as brain washing or an indoctrination process
but as plain and simple fact. The drop out rate in the Junior
Parachute Company was high and Recruit Company, they'd
tell us, would be higher still. The Paras would happily release
to the 'hats' those individuals deemed unworthy. We felt
special, a cut above the rest.

Stu McAllister had been at the depot all the time I had been
there and we'd occasionally meet up. This was not easy as the
juniors would often be away and being in Recruit Company,
Stu was up to his neck with day training and night exercises.
Recruit Company had only twenty-six weeks to change a man
off the street into a fully-fledged paratrooper. The timetable
for recruits incorporated both day and night time activities
and every hour was utilised to maximum affect. Stu always
looked knackered and would tell me he would 'pass come

hell or high water, as there is nothing to go home for'. I agreed with him and we shook hands on it – our pact was made. However, Stu did have a problem with his Sergeant because on one parade, when called to attention, he had slid his foot in as the Royal Marines did. This was opposed to the Army way of bending the knee waist high and ramming the foot home. The Sergeant was on him like a flash. When Stu told him he had been used to Marine drill from the cadets at school, the Sergeant punched hell out of him on the parade ground, in front of everyone. The Marines were disliked by the Regiment and were not rated, as was anyone associated with them.

I made a mental note never to mention to anyone that I had once wanted to be a Royal Marine and worse still, a Marine Officer.

Soon we were ready to move up to Recruit Company. From the initial intake of some two hundred boys, and the original three platoons in the September of 1980, there were now only two platoons and approximately sixty of us left. The transfer to Recruit Company would be undertaken platoon by platoon. The first thirty would go across to Recruit Company and join 476 Platoon in September, 1981, at training week four (passing off the square). The second batch would join 477 Platoon later but in week one of training.

I remember being in camp and pressing my kit, ready for the transfer to Recruit Company while watching the wedding of Prince Charles and Princess Diana. The Prince of Wales was our Regimental Colonel-in-Chief. I wasn't sure at the time which one of us was making the bigger mistake.

CHAPTER FOUR
Numbers

The Census

Recruit Company started for me in September 1981. Stu had successfully completed his training and had left the Depot to join 3 Para in Tidworth, Wiltshire.

Our Platoon 476 was comprised of about thirty newly enlisted lads straight off the streets and the 30 of us junior soldiers who were transferring across. Our officer was to be the same Lt. Young who had taken us through Junior Company and our Sergeant was Sgt Bradshaw, a terrifying figure from 2 Para. He wore the SAS smock of the Special Air Service and looked as if he'd just spent four years in the woods living off the land. He gave the impression his preferred choice of weapon in combat would be a blunt spoon and he would enjoy every minute of removing your heart with it, via your nose. He would scream and bawl at anyone who so much as looked at him. No one messed him about and when he said jump you screamed back at the top of your voice, "How high and for how long, Sergeant!"

Lieutenant Young gathered the juniors together and said we all looked too cocky, as if we didn't need to undergo Recruit Company training. Perhaps our time would be better served if we were allowed to go straight to our battalions.

"How would you fancy that, Thomas?" he asked.

"Sounds all right to me, sir," I said, standing to attention.

"Not quite, there's a small matter of 'P' Company to be settled first," he replied. I knew I'd said the wrong thing. He then made us all remove the blue plastic backing from our cap badges and he exchanged them for the green ones of Recruit Company.

P Company, or Pre-parachute selection, is reputed to be one of the hardest physical and mental tests in the British Army, designed to take an individual beyond his limit by testing both his mental and physical endurance. Successfully completing P Company meant you would be allowed to remove the green backing from your beret and would then go on to three weeks of Advanced Tactical Training in the Brecon Beacons. Those who failed had the option of joining Retraining Platoon to have another attempt or to transfer to a 'hat' regiment.

We were then introduced to our Corporals. Cpl Lewis was to be my section commander and, like Cpl Camp who had taken me through juniors, was from 2 Para. Cpl Lewis had also been Stu's section commander in Recruit Company. He seemed okay.

Passing off the square went smoothly and we were soon into the hard fitness regimes the Parachute Regiment is renowned for. Backs covered with bergen burns and webbing sores were everyday occurrences, as were blistered feet. Burns and sores would be smothered with talcum powder to remove the moisture and then covered with a dressing. Blisters would be popped to release the fluid and the same procedure for burns and sores would be followed. No one would miss a run through these injuries, for fear of being 'back-squadded' or 'binned'.

Each Friday evening we would form a single line, in alphabetical order, to receive our pay from Lt Young. Sgt Bradshaw would accompany him and maintain discipline. On receipt of his pay, the recruit would declare, "Pay checked and found to be correct – Sir!" He would then sign his name against the entry on the pay register, stand to attention, salute and disappear as quickly as possible to get changed and head off down town. On one particular Friday, spirits were high. Sgt. Bradshaw stood up and bellowed, "Be quiet!" After a short while the chatter started again and Sgt. Bradshaw lost it completely. "Right!" he shouted, "Everyone outside now!" Within seconds we had formed up outside the block in three ranks.

"Who was talking?" he demanded. No one moved or said anything. "Who was f-ing talking?" he shouted, his face bright red with frustration. Again no one moved. "Right!" he bellowed. "If no one owns up to talking I will have you all over the assault course all night and until the last one of you drops. Now for the last time, who was f-ing talking?"

The Assault Course and I had never got on – in fact I was allergic to it. To me it was nothing but pain from the moment you set off until the moment you finished. The majority of 'hat' courses are known by a more familiar name – 'an obstacle course'. A thinking man's bit of fun, if you will. Ours was not fun. It was an assault course and by definition required you to attack each obstacle with passion and commitment if you were to succeed. Most obstacles had ice-cold, knee-to-waist high water features that removed all air from your lungs, leaving you gasping frantically for breath.

The course had always been my weakest discipline and I hated it with a passion. There were times where I had thrown up trying to meet the time, only to be told by the PTI that I'd failed and was required to do it all over again. I even hated the journey from the barracks up to the course, knowing that within a few minutes I would be freezing cold, soaking wet and struggling for air. If ever there was a reason for leaving the Parachute Regiment it was the Assault Course. Very quickly I weighed up the pros and cons of doing the Assault Course all night or taking a hiding from Sgt Bradshaw. Although a beating would be painful it would be over far quicker than the Assault Course, so I stepped forward.

Sgt. Bradshaw glared at me and I realised I had made the wrong decision. "Well you weren't talking to yourself, Thomas!" he snarled, turning to the other recruits "So where is the other culprit?" A moment passed and another lad stepped forward. Sgt Bradshaw viewed the proceedings for a moment, "Right, the rest of you get away!" he snapped. In seconds the two of us were left alone with Sgt Bradshaw.

The Sergeant strode up to me and, with his face millimetres from mine, bellowed, "You must think I'm f-ing stupid Thomas!" I tensed but said nothing, expecting his first punch at any time.

"Your name begins with a 'T' and this idiot's," he said, pointing at the other lad, "begins with 'M'. What were you shouting to each other down the line?" Again I said nothing. He turned his back to me and faced the block. This is it I thought. When he turns around he's going to punch the living daylights out of me. Sgt. Bradshaw didn't move. My eyes looked up at the block and I could see most of the platoon watching us from the windows. So could Sgt Bradshaw. "Get away from the windows!" he roared. The platoon disappeared.

Sgt Bradshaw turned back around to face me. "I admire what you have just done," he said calmly. "I know it wasn't you talking in the line and you know what punishment I had in mind, yet you still sacrificed yourself to save the others," he continued. Jesus Christ I thought, I'm going over the Assault Course. Turning to the other lad he snapped, "You're nothing but a copy cat!" By now I was totally confused and wished he would just get on with it and put us out of our misery. "Follow me, you two," he said turning on his heels and heading off towards the block. Sgt Bradshaw took us to the Platoon Office and gave us both a toothbrush. He then marched us to the toilet area and told the other lad that he was responsible for cleaning the urinals while I had to clean the toilet bowls. He announced that he would be back to inspect them later. At around two o'clock in the morning Sgt Bradshaw returned to the block to find us both working as directed. The punishment was over, he said, we should get our heads down ready for tomorrow's training programme.

From that day on Sgt Bradshaw viewed me in a different light and would occasionally look in my direction and give me an approving nod. Subsequently, my fear of him disappeared.

P Company was all too suddenly upon us and on the Monday morning of the twelfth week Lt Young formed the platoon outside the block. We stood in three ranks, hearts pounding and adrenaline rushing. Dressed in gym kit, names emblazoned across the chests of our red PT vests and our P

Company number painted on our shorts, we were ready for our first test – milling. This was the moment to prove ourselves worthy of the Regiment, he said. To follow in the footsteps of others, people like Queripel VC, Pearson VC, John Ridgway and Chay Blyth, paratroopers who had rowed the Atlantic, and our next King – Prince Charles.

He then read out Rudyard Kipling's poem 'If'.

If

If you can keep your head when all about you
  are losing theirs and blaming it on you;
If you can trust yourself when all men doubt you,
  but make allowance for their doubting too;
If you can wait and not be tired by waiting,
  or, being lied about, don't deal in lies,
  or, being hated, don't give way to hating,
  and yet don't look too good, nor talk too wise;

If you can dream – and not make dreams your master;
If you can think – and not make thoughts your aim;
  If you can meet with triumph and disaster
  and treat those two impostors just the same;
If you can bear to hear the truth you've spoken
  twisted by knaves to make a trap for fools,
  or watch the things you gave your life to broken,
  and stoop and build 'em up with worn out tools;

If you can make one heap of all your winnings
  and risk it on one turn of pitch-and-toss,
  and lose, and start again at your beginnings
  and never breath a word about your loss;

If you can force your heart and nerve and sinew
to serve your turn long after they are gone,
and so hold on when there is nothing in you
except the Will which says to them: "Hold on";

If you can talk with crowds and keep your virtue,
or walk with kings – nor lose the common touch;
If neither foes nor loving friends can hurt you;
If all men count with you, but none too much;
If you can fill the unforgiving minute
with sixty seconds' worth of distance run –
Yours is the Earth and everything that's in it,
And – which is more – you'll be a Man my son!

By the time we were told to turn to our left and 'double' to the gym I was on cloud nine ready to murder my milling opponent. The PT staff formed us up in a single line with the tallest on the right and in descending height the shortest on the left. This meant that those either side of you were about your same height and should therefore be about your same weight. They then proceeded to call out two P Company numbers these numbers would be milling opponents. When my number was called, I stepped forward. Hearing the second number called I expected to feel the presence of someone close by me in the line stepping forward. This didn't happen. Curiosity got the better of me. Optimistically I looked to my left to the shorter people. No one there. To my right stood a lone figure, the tallest lad in the platoon. Chaz Paxton was one of the new recruits and a boxer. He had boxed all his life and lived for the sport. He was the spitting image of the British, European and World flyweight champion Charlie Magri, complete with the eyebrows, nose, boxer's chin and deliberate speech. Chaz Paxton's advantage over Magri was his height and his reach – a reach that would keep any opponent at a safe distance, while his jabs would be rearranging his challenger's face. Surely there'd been some mistake. Surely they would notice this lad towered above me and change him for a more suitable opponent. Not wishing to emit an ounce of concern I maintained my facial expression, though my eyes scanned the gym looking for any kind of activity that might have allayed my fear. I saw none, though I do believe Lt Young had a wry smile on his face. I thought back to his comments, all those weeks ago, about juniors being too cocky and my subsequent reply. Shit, I thought, He who laughs last – laughs loudest.

Chaz and I were called to the ring. Cpl Lewis, who was in my corner, gave me the following words of encouragement, "F-ing hell Thomas, all you can do is your best." I thought, I'm going to be killed. The bell sounded and the initial seconds of the contest were a blur, arms flailing everywhere. I caught Chaz a number of times with some very good hits but his jaw, as for the rest of his body, seemed to absorb the blows. I didn't feel Chaz hitting me, although he obviously was. Overall, I felt the contest was going my way. Then he hit me on the forehead with such force I swear I could see stars, white dazzling dots in front of my eyes spattered on a canvas of blackness. Fortunately, my legs did not give way. I gritted my teeth and persevered, but my strength had been sapped and I considered it was only a matter of time before my legs followed suit. The bell was now sounding frantically and the PTI, who was acting as referee, stepped in and tore us apart. Captain Gandell, the Officer Commanding P Company, was responsible for awarding the match by holding up a red or blue table tennis bat. We looked to him, bloodied and exhausted, to see both bats raised in the air, denoting a draw. I went back to my corner and received much praise from Cpl Lewis, although to be honest I didn't give a hoot for what he was saying. To me a draw meant the maximum ten points. I had successfully passed my first test in P Company.

Monday afternoon was the ten miles 'Battle March'. Boots, denims, putties, red PT vest, combat jacket, SLR and bergen weighing 35lbs. All bergens were weighed prior to the start. At 1400 hrs we set off. The start of the battle march is always in three ranks, although as the march progresses and individuals drop back, the platoon formation becomes less disciplined. I was near to the front of the Platoon, a position that I wished to maintain as an individual who drops back from the front is required to run or walk twice as fast if he is going to catch up again. The course for the ten-miler is the training area around Aldershot – woodlands, sandy banks, heath lands and hills with 'Long Valley' as its masterpiece, where the Army tests tanks and other large tracked vehicles. These vehicles sink deep into the soil leaving huge ravines that, when the weather is wet, fill with water that soon stagnates. The ground is then impossible to walk on and the recruit sinks deeper into the mud with each step he takes. Energy levels are sapped trying to remove each foot from the stronghold of the mud. When the weather is dry the ravines play havoc with the ankles and prove difficult to overcome. Either way, Long Valley is extremely demanding, and with the added pressure that the march has to be completed in 1 hour 45 minutes for the maximum ten points, stress levels are soon raised.

Before long we were at the top of 'Flagstaff Hill'. This was approximately the halfway point and the Platoon was now straddled over quite a distance. There were around twenty of us in the front group, roughly a third of the platoon and I felt confident that I was doing well and only a twisted ankle or other injury would prevent me from finishing with the front runners.

We were soon heading back to where the battle march had started and I was sure that I was going to finish in the top group. Instead of turning into camp, the lead PTI turned out towards the training area once more and my heart sank. The problem is that you are never told the exact route for the ten miles to be completed and there is no way of knowing how many miles have passed and how many are still to come. As the main road came into view my bergen felt as if it had doubled in weight. The front group was down to five. The other four recruits were much taller than me and looked comfortable, taking each step in their stride. I on the other hand was struggling to keep up with the pace that was being set and my legs felt as if they had lead weights attached to them. The PTI instructed the group to 'double' and I searched for every ounce of strength that I could muster to stay with them, my heart was pounding and my lungs were ready to burst at any moment. As we turned into the wood on to a small track off the main road the PTI told us to sprint to the finish line. I watched as the others left me for dead. I couldn't compete with their huge strides and as the finish line came into view, I could see the other four lads sitting on their bergens. I was so demoralised. I had managed to stay with them for 99.99% of the way and on the final sprint had nothing in my reserve tank to offer. I sat with Scrivs, who had finished in the front group and swore. The PTI came over and congratulated us on finishing in the front group, and told us to get a drink and wait for the others to arrive. "Staff" I said, "I didn't finish in the front group". "Yes you did", he replied. "You lot are all here in under 1 hour 45 minutes, the maximum – well done". I was jubilant, although Scrivs kept telling me that technically I hadn't finished in the front group. "How many points did you get more than me?" I would ask him. "Then piss off!"

The evening was spent digging the trenches we were to sleep in that night to sap any strength that the body had left. After a meal of 'Airborne Stew' we were sent out on a night navigation course. Once more we were required to cover the terrain that had been the route of the ten-miler. From checkpoint to checkpoint we would go gathering a stamp from each one that indicated to the staff that we had completed the course in its entirety. No team could return to their trench until they had collected all the stamps and it wasn't until the early hours of the morning that our team, soaking wet from the constant rain, finished the course and got back to the trenches.

We got up the following morning at around 0500 hrs and were required to fill in the trenches that we had dug, ready for the next test – the 'Stretcher Race'. This test was to represent the withdrawal of an injured comrade from the battlefield across rigorous terrain. The stretchers were constructed of scaffold poles and steel sand tracks that had a combined weight of approximately 180lbs to simulate the casualty and the actual stretcher weight. The race was conducted over a seven and a half mile course. We were broken down into only six teams of eight due to the dropout numbers. Six recruits were required to carry the stretcher and the other two members of the team would act as stretcher 'reliefs', giving every member a break when instructed by a PTI. They were also to assist with the carriage of all weapons. A thunder flash initiated the race and within 200 metres recruits were dropping out. The PTIs and our NCOs were screaming at us to get going and overtake the stretcher in front of us. The stretcher was horrendous to carry. If the individual carrying the stretcher on your opposite side was taller than you the whole weight of the stretcher fell onto your shoulders. Whenever you ran with the stretcher it would pound up and down against your shoulder, and with little or no muscle to protect the shoulder bones the pain was excruciating; this was the main contributor to so many lads dropping out. Long Valley was a bog due to the previous night's downpour and once again proved impossible to tackle. We lost two members of our team to Long Valley, which meant that relief from carrying the stretcher was few and far between. I detested the individuals who had packed it in as it meant more work and more pain for those of us that were left. During the final stages of the race our stretcher team was down to five, four carrying the stretcher and me carrying the five weapons, equivalent to 45lbs. Cpl Lewis was fuming that we were the penultimate stretcher and was shouting obscenities at us. He told me to run ahead of our stretcher and sprint home, with the weapons. I did as I was told and overtook two of the four stretchers that were ahead of us. This gave him some satisfaction although it was, to be truthful, a hollow victory. When all the stretchers had been loaded onto the wagons we were allowed breakfast and Cpl Lewis came over and sat with us. We thought by being second to last that the points awarded to us would be minimal. "Not at all" he said, explaining that the test was not about coming first, second or last – although it would have been nice to win! – but was about how an individual performed towards the overall team objective of completing the course. Those who had dropped out had not considered the ramifications of their actions to the other team members or to the team's objective; but the remaining lads had persevered when the odds were stacked against them. We had in his eyes and in the spirit of the test completed our mission, which was the 'airborne way'. Happier with his version of events than my own, I crammed the 'scoff' down my neck.

With breakfast cleared away we were ready to undertake the next event of the day – the 'trainasium'. By now the heavens had reopened and the largest hailstones I had ever seen were falling from the sky. The words, "cancelled due to bad weather" are not associated with the Regiment and in true airborne fashion we were soon running the catwalks, jumping the gaps and shuffling the bars. The confidence course went well with the one exception of a recruit falling from the fireman's pole, some thirty feet up, to the concrete base below. He didn't actually break anything but was totally winded and couldn't carry on so the medic rushed him off to hospital to be on the safe side, although to be honest I think the medic just wanted to get out of the rain. Psychologically this was a disaster to us, but each man needed to complete the course to pass and no one on that day failed to do this.

Lunch was taken back at camp with enough time for a change of clothing ready for the final event of the day – the 'Assault Course'.

The 'Assault Course' was another timed event that required you to go around it three times in less than 7 minutes 30 seconds to pass. The journey out to the Course was in the main uneventful, although I still hadn't quite come to terms with the fear and trepidation that I held for it. We were broken down into teams and the event was begun. I can't remember how many teams there were or when I was called forward to start, all I know is that I completed the Course that day in less than six minutes 45 seconds, a personal best. It may have been the additional pressure associated with P Company or that my technique for mounting the obstacles was at an all time high, but whatever it was I was thankful in the knowledge of a definite pass.

Tuesday night was spent back in camp washing kit ready for the following day's tests.

Wednesday morning brought the first of the two tests – the 'Steeplechase'. The Steeplechase is another timed event requiring the recruit to complete two miles of cross-country terrain in less than 18 minutes. Various obstacles and quite hazardous five-foot jumps into ice-cold water scatter the course just to add to the fun. Once again the start of the course is initiated by a thunder flash and the whole platoon sets off together. There is always an awful lot of niggling, elbowing and general hounding for a better position at the start and this continues at each obstacle and water jump. Apart from making the time, the main concern for each recruit was not slipping at an obstacle or twisting an ankle when landing. Like most cross-country courses, after about halfway round the pack spreads out with the leaders like foxes being chased by a pack of hounds. It is always better to be at the front of the pack removing the possibility of injury by others and allowing yourself more concentration at each obstacle. My strategy was always to set off like a hare and get away from the others as soon as I could. To ensure success I would then have to maintain my distance from the pack and make every effort not to slip or fall at the jumps. The Steeplechase always went well for me and although I wasn't in the top six 'sprinters'. I was in front of the next main group to cross the finish line – another pass.

All that was now left was the 'Log Race'. The Log Race symbolises a gun barrel being carried by a seven-man team over a distance of one and a half miles. The gun barrel was a telegraph pole weighing about 200lbs with seven ropes attached to it. Three men were positioned either side of the 'log' with one man situated at its head. It was a short straight course with a hill in the middle, and the race lasted about 15 minutes. Each team was required to carry the log to the hill, climb to the top of the hill by one route, then come down another route and sprint to the finish line. Sounds very easy in theory and as such I considered the phases of the course to be as follows. The initial phase – pick up the log and run to the hill – should be okay and due to the adrenaline pumping not too much pain. The second phase, climbing the hill – tiring bit of pain going up the hill but should be manageable. Final phase, down the hill and back to the finish line – very painful and tiring but on the home stretch so therefore bearable.

In practice, however, it was horrendous. The race was started when each team was lined up behind their respective logs. When the thunder flash went off we all sprinted to our logs and were off. From the very moment I put my left hand in the loop of the rope and took the weight of the log the pain was intense. It is impossible to describe the physical pain and the mental challenge one experiences during this race. Our team hadn't even made the hill when a lad from my side of the log dropped out. I thought the pain and the race was never going to end. Every step was murder and my shoulder felt as if it was being wrenched from its socket. As I was unable to change hands or positions on the log there was nothing I could do to reduce the pain. It was quite simply a matter of grinning and bearing it. On the way down the hill and whilst jostling for the front position, our lead man lost his footing and fell over. There was nothing we could do to stop our momentum and within seconds we had trampled him into the sand and the stones. Expletives rang out everywhere, from the NCOs, members of our log team and the lad on the floor. The finish line seemed an eternity away and our team, with only five members left, was losing ground on the front log. Suddenly the lad who had fallen was back on the log, not in his lead position but on my side where there was a vacant position. I immediately felt some relief when he took his share of the log weight and my spirits were lifted. We crossed the finish line just behind the first log and were congratulated on beating the logs with more members in their teams than ours. Those who had fallen off the logs were tasked in putting themselves and the logs on the wagons. The rest of us were marched back to camp to await the results of 'P' Company.

The atmosphere was tense within the block as no one had any idea of whether they had passed or failed. Those who had failed the ten-miler or had dropped out of the other events had already been shipped out of the block leaving only those who had completed all of the tests. The sections had been sent to their rooms to await the arrival of the section commanders and the impending results. We sat on our beds not saying or doing anything. Scrivs soon got up and starting packing, "What are you doing?" I asked. "Confident are we?"

He looked at me in his usual all knowing way and said in a very matter of fact fashion, "If I've passed I'm going to Brecon. If I've failed I'm going to Retraining Platoon. Either way I need to pack." I couldn't believe what I was hearing. The word 'failed' had not even entered my head, although I didn't wish to start packing for Brecon for fear of appearing too complacent. I hadn't given any thought to what I would do if I failed. Would I go to Retraining Platoon? No, I wasn't going through all that again but what about my pact with Stu? With no readily available answer I decided to postpone my anguish until Cpl Lewis announced the results. The way ahead would hopefully be defined for me.

The minutes passed like hours but eventually Cpl Lewis came into our room and closed the door behind him. He appeared relaxed and confident, understanding our apprehension as he looked around the room. "Anyone here thinks he could have done better?" he asked.

One lad stood up and said, "Yes, Corporal, I think I could have done better."

Cpl Lewis looked at him for a moment and then said, "You'd better wait outside then."

The recruit left the room and silence prevailed. Eventually Cpl Lewis broke his expression and smiled, "Congratulations, you're all going to Brecon," he said. "Get your kit packed now as we leave in the morning."

For a brief moment no one said anything then the room erupted. Within minutes the whole block was alive and we were running around the other rooms to find out who had passed. The majority who'd transferred from Juniors had passed. Unfortunately, a few who joined straight from Civvy Street had failed, including the lad still standing outside our door.

Within ten minutes my locker was empty, my suitcase, sausage bag and bergen packed ready for the trip to Wales – but not before I'd removed the green backing from my cap badge.

Advance Tactical Training in Wales is all about soldiering. Here field craft, weapon skills and tactical knowledge are integrated into effective personal and platoon fighting skills. Recruits are assessed individually regarding their own combat ability and live firing is an everyday occurrence. Early mornings and late nights are the order of the day and sleep deprivation assists in providing a tense and stressful environment. Wales is a 'battle camp' where recruits are required to 'double' wherever they go; to the loo, to and from scoff, when retrieving weapons from the armoury – absolutely everywhere. Add the unique Brecon weather, freezing temperatures, snow when you least expect it and torrential downpours that would be the envy of any tropical rainforest and you have the perfect climate to ensure soldiers soon become demoralised. We were in Brecon for three weeks during

November and not one day passed where it did not piss down!

The Parachute Regiment relishes such conditions and with the added spice of 'airborne initiative' happily provided by the NCOs, we were soon providing covering fire while chest-deep in freezing streams.

The grand finale in Wales is a three-day defensive exercise with the Platoon situated at the imaginary forward edge of a battalion position. On the last day the Gurkhas attack the defensive position and the platoon has to 'bug out'. This tactical withdrawal is conducted over four miles and is exhausting. The Gurkhas push forward at every opportunity but eventually the platoon breaks free and the order to 'tab' is given. After about a mile of 'tabbing' the transport came and parked at the side of the road halfway up a steep hill. This was a wonderful sight and informally signalled to the recruit the end of the exercise.

When we approached the wagons, they sped off and morale fell through the floor. Lt. Young gave the order to continue 'tabbing' the ten miles back to camp. One lad packed up there and then. This was the final straw for him. Dejected and exhausted, the rest of us soldiered on. As we broke the top of the hill the wagons could be seen pulled over at the side of the road about a hundred metres further on. Not raising my hopes again, I ignored them and programmed myself for a long hard slog back to camp. As we drew level with the vehicles, Lt. Young stopped the platoon and ordered us to unload our weapons and make them safe. The exercise was over. I do not remember the journey back to camp, as I was fast asleep.

Later, I was given a lecture on how a lot more had been

expected of me. The trainers were disappointed with my C grade. I nearly burst out laughing with relief. C grade was enough to secure a pass. It meant I was on my way to RAF Brize Norton, in Oxfordshire, for four weeks of parachute training and the infamous Spotlight Club.

Brize Norton was completely different to anything we had been used to. Our corporals' attitudes towards us changed immediately. We were no longer just recruits but their colleagues and members of the Regiment. At first we were very sceptical about this and when we were told a coach would collect us from the block at 0900 hrs to take us to the hangers, we thought they we having us on. Morning parades were usually held at 0800 hrs, so 0900 hrs was most probably a trap. So at 0800 hrs we all stood outside the block waiting for the NCOs just in case. No one came. We couldn't believe it when at 0900 hrs a green coach pulled up and took us to a hanger less than half a mile from our block, certainly a pleasant change from the 'doubling' everywhere at Brecon camp.

The hanger was typical of the sort you would see in any World War II film. The badge of No.1 Parachute Training School, a parachute with crossed torches below it, hung above the large double doors. The motto 'Knowledge Dispels Fear' was good to read even if it was a little optimistic.

An RAF Sergeant approached and 'invited us' into the hanger. Here things would be different, Sgt Bailey explained. There would be no shouting or bawling of commands; each recruit would be shown how to use each piece of equipment and the procedure for parachuting would be explained thoroughly. No one would be expected to jump out of an aircraft until they had complete understanding of both. Once we had attained this knowledge our fear would be dispelled, in keeping with the motto.

None of us was totally convinced by this philosophy. Jumping out of a plane eight hundred feet in the air, however you wish to dress it up, is an unnatural activity and should it go horribly wrong will ultimately lead to your death. A hideous death at that, presenting members of the Pioneer Corp with the decision whether to dig you out of the ground or just throw earth over you and cover you up!

After meeting the girls who packed the parachutes the potential pitfalls of parachuting were reinforced even more. The large sign above their heads in the packing room stating: REMEMBER A MAN'S LIFE DEPENDS ON EVERY PARA-CHUTE YOU PACK, didn't help at all.

Inside the hangar, parachute harnesses hung from the ceiling like huge chandeliers. We would spend hours dangling from these, practising drills ready for our first jump in week two.

Brize Norton to paratroopers is what Disneyland is to kids. The camp atmosphere is relaxed and peaceful. The dining halls resemble restaurants with tablecloths, condiments and cutlery laid on them. Soft elevator music played in the background. You could even order a steak cooked to your individual preference or a tossed salad with Italian or French dressing. We were all too busy pinching the knives, forks, spoons and ketchup bottles to really appreciate the aesthetics of the place. When the chef asked me how I would like my steak I told him, "On my f-ing plate, mate".

By the second week the RAF had removed the cutlery from the tables and we were required to provide our own. The ketchup, however, stayed and provided my now 'medium to rare' steak with a suitable garnish. There was even an area for you to cook your own eggs, a luxury never before afforded to us – and in the true spirit of things the blokes had a go. This was soon stopped when one of the lads set fire to the decorative curtain by the side of the frying area. The rest of us didn't mind, as every good experience with the regiment was always short lived due to someone's failings. Besides, this particular practice was difficult to master, very messy and best left to the 'hats'.

The Spotlight Club provided the evening's entertainment. Music was played each night with discos on Fridays and Saturdays. The ladies from the surrounding area would all be there dressed up in their finery looking for a suitable paratrooper to attend to their needs. Being young, fit and naïve, we would oblige. On a couple of occasions I met a girl called Joanne and eventually she took me back to her place for coffee and a chat. She asked me where I came from and I told her a small village in Kent called Hoo. "Oh" she said, "I had a boyfriend from there once, his name was – Stuart McAllister."

I couldn't believe it but as there was only rule in the Paras – that being 'there were no rules' – I thought no more of it…

During my stay at Brize, Stu wrote to me from 3 Para, welcoming me to the 'airborne brotherhood'. He congratulated me on succeeding where many others had failed and looked forward to seeing me when I joined 3 Para. I wrote back telling him all about my antics in Brize and the company I had been keeping. He loved it and replied that once I was in the battalion we would re-visit Brize together, but in the meantime I was to have as much fun as I could and enjoy every moment. Wise words I thought and set about the task with zeal.

Our first parachute jump was to be from a balloon and so on Tuesday, 1st December, 1981, we were taken by coach to the Dropping Zone at Hullavington. We drew our parachutes from the RAF vehicle. Each 'chute had a unique number which, along with the parachutist's name is recorded in a log, providing the RAF with an audit trail in the event of a malfunction. This procedure did nothing to boost our confidence!

Four of us stepped into a 'cage', an unnervingly flimsy construction hanging below the balloon. We were each secured to the cage by a strop, the long canvas static line that trails outside the parachute and pulls the main canopy out. The Parachute Jump Instructor (PJI) closed the cage door. I say closed, he actually placed a thin metal bar across the entrance. "Up eight hundred. Four men jumping," he shouted. Slowly the winch motor started and, with a slight jerk, the 'cage' and the huge grey helium-filled balloon, lifted from the ground.

The journey to eight hundred feet was slow and quiet, except for the noise of the winch motor. The PJI asked us all to recite a joke to take our minds off of the proceedings. No one could think of one. He then offered a ten pound reward to anyone who could get an erection. Once again we failed.

"You lot are no good," he said. "Don't worry about not jumping – I'm going to throw you all out," he scoffed.

The winch motor stopped and the ground crew shouted, "Up 800!" The absence of noise was unsettling, interrupted only by the occasional 'whoosh' of the wind. I was third to leave the cage. As I held the uprights on either side of the exit, the PJI told me not to look down but to concentrate on a small red lanyard hanging from the main body of the balloon, some ten yards in front of me.

"This is it" I thought, "No chance of bottling out now."

"GO!"

I stepped forward and Isaac Newton, true to his word, introduced me to the laws of gravity. The Standard Operational Procedure on exiting is to shout out, "One thousand, two thousand, three thousand, check canopy!" I managed "One thousand", got halfway through "Two thou…" when my testicles stopped my voice box from working. Not only could I not speak but I also found that I couldn't breathe, as my stomach had decided to relocate to my mouth blocking all intake of air to my lungs. To top it all my eyes were streaming and struggling to focus on the balloon that was now, and all too rapidly, disappearing from my hazed view. Within a flash my brain re-engaged and my testicles released their grip on my larynx.

"Check canopy!" I bellowed.

I looked up and to my relief saw the parachute canopy deploying – a magnificent, beige mushroom that opened fully and then closed.

Closed? What the hell? But before I could register the catastrophe the canopy had fully deployed again. Assured that the canopy had only 'breathed in' like a lung deflating before its next inhalation, I set about my air drills. Check your air space I recalled. Assess your drift. Pulling down hard on my rear lift webs to slow down my drift, I settled down to take in the experience. The view was incredible. Looking down my boots seemed small and insignificant against the backdrop of the fields and houses. The lads who had completed their jump looked even smaller and were gathered in a group obviously sharing their experiences and enjoying mine.

"Pull down on your lift webs harder, Thomas!" the PJI on the ground yelled through a loud hailer. "Feet and knees together! Prepare for your landing, chin on chest, elbows in!" As I came level with the horizon the ground came rushing up, too suddenly for my liking, and within seconds I was on the floor – rolling. The whole experience had lasted no more than thirty seconds from start to finish. Very similar to my first sexual encounter, I thought.

"What about your feet and knees? – They were all over the place!" the PJI yelled at me "Your air drills were crap." I was too busy with my Harness Release and Drag procedure to take any notice. HR&D can potentially be as dangerous as parachuting. Once the parachutist has landed he immediately unclips one side of his reserve and rolls over onto his stomach. To prevent the parachute re-inflating and dragging him all over the Drop Zone (DZ), he must deflate the chute as quickly as possible. "Sorry, Staff. I was trying," I said, too excited to enter into a full-blown conversation.

"I know, I know. I've heard it all before," he replied.

The other lads slapped me on the back and remarked how great it was to get some air under their boots. Sporting a huge smile I looked back at the cage and allowed myself a moment of self-praise. That's the nuts, I thought, and so am I.

I felt alive, independent and very capable.

I woke as the coach pulled up to the main gate of the camp. It is said, that one parachute jump is equivalent to eight hours of physical work due to the mental strains one experiences and I certainly felt shattered and was looking forward to lying on my 'pit'. The lads were having none of it. Within seconds of being back in the block their radios and cassette players were blaring the latest songs of the time (mainly the Human League's "Dare" album) and electric shavers were buzzing. Energy levels had been revitalised and everyone prepared for a night to remember at the Spotlight Club.

Our first plane jump was scheduled for Thursday 3rd December, 1981, at Weston-on-the-Green. Brize was covered in snow and everywhere we went snowballs were sure to follow. Walking back from synthetic training to scoff, we passed the Officers Mess and were ambushed. In the main, officers don't mix with other ranks. Although within the Parachute Regiment a mutual respect exists that, where appropriate, allows discussion prior to decisions being made, whilst still maintaining discipline. The ambush was anything but disciplined. Believing they had the advantage through the element of surprise, the officers were complacent and after the initial volley of snowballs and much guffawing, soon found themselves stranded and wanting. We, on the other hand, immediately rallied together and within seconds had suppressed their attack by providing superior volleys, enabling us to counter attack. Some of the 'hat' officers scrambled for the safety of the foyer leaving the Para Reg. officers to certain doom. Scrivs, Jas, Grose and I followed up into the foyer to complete the mission, only to be removed by the RAF orderly in charge of maintaining decorum in the Mess.

The encounter lasted about 15 minutes and had been great for everyone's morale, underlining the overall atmosphere at

Brize Norton and the Parachute Course Administration Unit (PCAU) in particular.

The next day we drew our parachutes ready to board the plane. There, up close and personal, stood the C130 Hercules aircraft or 'hercy bird', with its tail ramp down ready for boarding. The plane was cramped and the red, strapped, canvas seating was somewhat less than one would expect from an economy class flight. Both sides of the plane were utilised for seating and we sat with our backs to the windows facing each other. To add to our discomfort two additional rows of seating ran through the centre of the plane's fuselage. In all, sixty paratroopers with full equipment can be seated within the basic Hercules while 'Stretch Hercs' can carry up to ninety paratroopers. The engines were soon roaring as the plane accelerated down the runway.

The noise inside the aircraft was so intense the only way to communicate was to shout. Foregoing this, I just looked around and took in the activity. The PJI's were up and down the plane preparing for the drop. Some of the lads were trying to sleep, while others like me looked around, left to their own thoughts. Before long, one side door of the plane was slid open and a refreshing gush of air passed through the fuselage. The noise inside the aircraft increased ten-fold. The 'drifter' was beckoned forward to the door by the PJI dispatcher. The 'drifter' on this occasion was an instructor whose job was to exit the plane without steering his parachute to indicate to the pilot the strength and direction of the wind. The pilot could then on the next run take remedial action to ensure the main drop landed where it was supposed to.

The red light came on. The drifter took his arms from the

side of the exit door and folded them across his reserve. "Green On – Go!" Instantly he stepped out of the door and was gone from view. The dispatcher leaned out of the door checking the drifter was free of the aircraft and within seconds the strop was retrieved from the slipstream. The first stick of six was given the order, "Stand Up! – Hook up!" The plane banked preparing for its second approach to the dropping zone. When the PJI was happy all the lads had hooked up correctly he gave the order, "Check equipment!" Everyone checked their own equipment first and then inspected the person in front of them.

"Action Stations!" yelled the PJI.

All six men shuffled forward in unison by taking a short stride with their leading foot and dragging the trailing foot to it until number one had reached the door when all motion stopped. The aircraft steadied as it made its final approach.

"Green On – Go!" the PJI ordered.

"One, two, three, four, five, six!" he yelled in one-second intervals, slapping each man on the back as they came level with him and exited the plane.

I was number six in the final stick to be called forward, the very last person to exit the plane. My personal parachute logbook records the time was 1400 hrs. I remember feeling excited and apprehensive but not necessarily scared. The green light came on and as I approached the door all I was concentrating on was making a clean exit. This required a determined and aggressive 'push off' from the exit step to make sure I didn't 'inspect the rivets' as the slipstream sucked me all the way down the plane's tail. I didn't really achieve this. The moment I stood in the door thinking about stepping out, I was immediately sucked out into oblivion. God only knows what really happened in the next few seconds because, to be frank, my eyes were firmly shut tight and nothing was going to open them. The only thing I am certain of was being hurtled through the air at break neck speed. "One thousand, two thousand, three thousand. Check canopy!" I opened my eyes to find myself parallel to the ground looking down at the DZ a thousand feet below while my parachute, flopping spuriously in the wind and yet to deploy, was laid out ahead of me. Eventually, mainly due to the fact I was falling faster through the air than my parachute, the canopy took its right-ful place above me and deployed, breathed in and deployed again. I assessed my drift and pulled down on my lift webs ready for my landing.

Once on the ground with my parachute safely gathered in, I looked up at the sky to see the aircraft disappearing from view in the distance on its way back to Brize Norton. I felt a strange affection for the plane, an affinity even. The feeling of accomplishment and pride was overwhelming and I wondered if all those before me who had gone on to jump at Arnhem or on D-Day had felt the same emotions during their training. Back at camp we received congratulations and a long weekend pass.

I spent the weekend back in Hoo, where, I have to confess, the weekend was spent bragging about my exploits and how amazing and exciting it was to jump from a plane. I probably bored the lads silly with all the parachuting talk but it had been an incredible experience and I couldn't wait to tell them, over and over and over again!

Monday morning's air briefing revealed the 'sims' would

be increased from six to eight jumping at a time and that two sticks would exit the plane simultaneously, from the port and starboard doors. Again the jump would be made 'clean fatigue', which meant that we would not be carrying any equipment. In parachuting terms this is a 'fun jump'. After spending the weekend bragging about how cool it was to jump from an aircraft the harsh reality of having to do it all over again suddenly hit me. The Gods certainly know when and how to remind you that you are but a mere mortal. My weekend of constant boasting had obviously not gone unnoticed. Walking to the plane I felt very unsettled. The excitement had gone to be replaced by a feeling of "What could go wrong?" I was no longer the airborne warrior who couldn't wait to get some air under his boots. Now I was confused and in two minds whether I wanted to jump. Murphy's Law, which states 'what can go wrong, will go wrong' bounced around my head. I boarded the plane with the 'Port Stick' and took my seat.

Shuffling towards the door I wasn't my normal self. Thoughts came flooding back of my previous experience of being thrown around in the slipstream, being yanked as my parachute strop ripped the parachute from its housing and the vision of the DZ as I tensed in my exiting position, helpless, vulnerable and parallel to the ground. Nearing the door my legs didn't want to play. Instead of the manly and aggressive push off the exit step, I was dragged out of the plane by the slipstream, like an unwilling child being dragged to school by his mother. The side and tail of the plane were too close to me for my liking and although I did not collide with either of them it wasn't a pleasant experience. Back on the ground I felt much better and swore to myself that I wouldn't wimp out at the door next time.

Our first night jump brought much excitement as it was something new and we were all down at the hangar early, ready to get on and complete the jump. Inside the aircraft was lit with red lights to aid our night vision, giving the plane a warm welcoming feeling. I was the second stick to exit the plane, again from the starboard side and my position was No.6. When the doors of the plane were opened by the PJI the night air rushed through the fuselage and my adrenaline started to pump. On exiting the plane and completing the mandatory count down, I looked up to see the parachute wasn't as it should be. There was something peculiar in its appearance. Without hesitation my right arm shot across my chest to the red 'D' handle on my reserve and pulled it. Immediately the reserve parachute sprang out of its housing. As it deployed the rigging lines whipped across my face, adding to my confusion and desperation. The main 'chute then collapsed on top of my head as the reserve 'stole' its air, extinguishing all light. Panic reigned. Everything went black. I frantically pulled at the main chute to release my head from under it, trying to secure it between my legs as instructed in training. Precious moments were passing and very soon the ground would be upon me and I would not be ready for the impact. It seemed like an eternity before my head was freed from beneath the chute and I gasped for air. I looked down to see the ground rushing up at me and within seconds I had landed, clumsily. I lay still on the ground reliving the jump and wondering whether, by pulling my reserve chute, I had done the right thing.

The ground PJI raced over. "Why did you pull your reserve?" he asked.

"I didn't think my main chute had deployed properly, Staff" I replied anxiously, expecting a rollicking or a formal inquiry into the subject.

"You hit the ground before anyone else in the stick," he said. "This suggests you were falling faster than everyone else; there may well have been a problem so well done!" He took the number of my parachute once more and made a few notes before leaving me to pack both chutes away.

Our final jump, on Tuesday 15th December would be simultaneous 'sims' of eight with equipment, including weapons, and for the very first time from eight hundred feet. My equipment weighed in at sixty-two pounds. This was the all-important eighth jump. Completion would entitle us to wear our parachute wings. The jump went well and we were soon standing proudly on 'wings parade' inside the hangar awaiting the OC No. 1 Parachute Training School.

One would think the parade was simply a formality, a gesture of "well done, son, here are your wings. You've bloody well earned them". But in true HM Forces fashion the romance of the occasion was soon removed. The OC read out an official document with all the tact and diplomacy of a headmaster addressing his pupils:

"Once formally awarded your wings, you are deemed to have ACCEPTED, as long as you are medically fit to do so, the OBLIGATION to SERVE with a parachute unit on OPERATIONS, and to carry out PARACHUTE DECENTS when ORDERED or required to do so. For this, parachute PAY is AWARDED. Future failure or REFUSAL to carry out a parachute DESCENT will result in DISCIPLINARY ACTION being taken against you. This will almost certainly RESULT in a trial by COURT MARTIAL and the WITHDRAWAL of the right to wear the qualified parachutist badge with WINGS. If you are NOT PREPARED to accept this obligation, then you should SAY SO NOW".

Why didn't the bloke just say, "If you take the money, make sure you do the job"? It would have been a lot quicker. I would've loved for everyone on parade to have stepped forward in unison and, at the top of their voices, shouted, "Sod that, sir – we're off!" but no one moved or said anything, which spoilt things a bit. After a dramatic pause for effect, the OC was soon among us shaking us individually by the right hand and placing a gleaming set of wings in our left. How proud we all were.

Parade over, the last night was spent in the Spotlight Club, which included final farewells and promises of "We'll meet again – honest". We packed our kit and were on our way back to Aldershot for Rear Guard duties while the rest of the camp went on Christmas leave. In the New Year, when the main body of the camp returned, we were allowed our leave before returning for Exercise Last Fence and our Passing Out parade.

Exercise Last Fence was invented so the platoon could parachute into Hankley Common as an operational unit with all the equipment necessary to carry out a mission. It was our first taste of an operational exercise that started with a parachute descent. On the plane Grose looked over at me and said, "I'm only here because of you. I f-ing hate parachuting!" Grose now had a superstition of wearing the same thick red socks for every jump. I smiled at him and took up my position ready to exit the plane. Unfortunately, one of our platoon landed badly and sustained a very serious back injury, leaving him in hospital for weeks.

A film crew was at the depot at this time. The BBC had decided to make a fly-on-the-wall documentary and 480 Platoon were to be the chosen subjects. Unfortunately for them, every moment of their training, from their initial joining date on 11th January, 1982, was to be filmed and subsequently scrutinised by millions of viewers.

We, on the other hand, gave the cameras a very wide berth.

The week leading up to the Passing Out parade was spent practising drill and 'bulling' boots. Our platoon final piss-up was booked for a couple of days prior to the parade, to make sure we had sobered up. The piss-up went with a bang, if you get my drift. The NCOs had arranged for three strippers to liven up the event and even provided the girls with a bowl of fruit, which I thought was a nice welcoming gesture. The girls warmed to the fruit and I have never eaten a banana or peeled an apple in the same way since.

During the evening, these naked, well-equipped girls handed out awards for 'Outstanding Effort', 'Champion GPMG shot', 'Champion SLR shot' and 'Champion Recruit'. I received the Champion SLR shot award and a few suggestions from the girls on how I could improve my shooting technique. All of which I found useful and will happily impart to my son when he is of age.

Dad couldn't make our Passing Out parade on Friday, 22nd January, 1982, as he was on a cruise ship somewhere around the Mediterranean. To be honest I hadn't really expected him to. In all the time I was training he had only written to me once, and although I knew deep down he was proud of what I was doing, it just wasn't his kind of thing. Mum and Jo came along to the day I will remember forever. Along with the Chaz Paxton, Champion GMPG and Champion Recruit, Andy Townend, I had to march out in front of the whole platoon to receive my award, Champion SLR from the Inspecting Officer, Major Tom Duffy MBE. He didn't have the same kind of advice as the girls had offered me but he did shake my hand, something that the girls forgot to do. Mind you, I'm not sure Mum or the rest of the watching parents would have appreciated it if the Major had tried to mimic the girls. Dad probably would have, though. Anyway the parents all met each other, put faces to names and everything went swimmingly. After Lt Young's final address to the parents we were free to go on leave.

During this leave I bumped into Laura, the younger sister of a girl I had seen on one or two occasions. She immediately recognised me and stopped to chat. Laura, like her sister, was an attractive girl. Unlike her sister she was blonde. Her blue eyes had a sparkle that hinted she enjoyed living and having fun. After laughing and joking about and catching up on what we had both been doing, I asked her to come out with me that evening and she agreed. Unfortunately, I'd already arranged to go out with the lads that night, and as it was Friday, Stu would be home for the weekend.

When I told Stu and the lads that I was going on a date that night they went mad and complained that I had let them all down. I understood their moans and groans. At that time a girl was simply an accessory you took along on prearranged foursomes or for a smooch at the cinema. They certainly never interfered with a lads' night out, especially a party in Rainham we had known we were going to for weeks. I told them Laura was worth upsetting the plans for but to be on the safe side, I would take her to the Command House, a pub in Chatham, where the lads were starting the evening. If they approved of Laura, I would be forgiven and allowed to continue with the date unhindered. If they didn't, I would be quietly informed and would have to make my excuses, drop Laura back at her mum's and meet up with the lads at the party. All this would happen without Laura knowing. When I walked up to Laura's mum's house I must admit I was thinking, I hope she looks nice – otherwise I'm in for a right piss-taking session all night. She did and shortly after arriving at the Command House the lads got up to leave. When Stu passed me, I stopped him, pretending not to have noticed him before, and introduced Laura. Stu and the lads joined us at the table and the evening ended with us all going off to the party. Everyone was happy. The lads were all together and Laura was none the wiser. I spent the rest of my leave with her.

Reporting back to camp we were given our Battalions. The older members went off to 1 Para ready for their impending tour to Northern Ireland. The rest, most of us still only 17 and too young to serve in Ulster, went to 2 and 3 Para.

Lieutenant Young gave a final speech to the platoon regarding life in the various battalions and asked three of us to stay behind, "Cody, Crooks and Thomas". Unsure what we had done wrong the three of us hung around at the back of the briefing room. He came over and asked us to sit down. He believed we had the potential to become officers and once we'd entered battalion life and preferably completed a tour of

Northern Ireland, we should approach our OC and ask to be considered. We were amazed and elated and congratulated each other on a job well done.

The lads going to 2 Para were taken just up the road to Montgomery Lines while 1 Para were heading for Edinburgh on Castle duties. 3 Para were stationed at Tidworth, in Wiltshire, and our wagon soon turned up. I must admit it was quite hard saying goodbye to some of the lads heading off to 1 Para, Graham Collins in particular. We had been through Juniors together, spent many a leave in and around his home in Edmonton, North London, especially with Jas Burt and had enjoyed hours of fun. It was a shame we were going our separate ways – but that was life.

CHAPTER FIVE

Deuteronomy

Introductory Discourses

The 3 Para wagon roared off and from the back of it we gave the remaining lads various farewell signs that were appropriate for the moment. Some time later we arrived at our destination – Kandahar Barracks, Tidworth, home of 3 Para.

After 'debussing' we were told to change into PT kit and report to the gym. We were not shown any accommodation or allowed to unpack. 3 Para's philosophy was that if we failed the induction physical tests we would be back on the wagon and returned to the depot as rejects. After a severe beasting session in the gym and a run around the local training area at a pace Linford Christie would have been pleased with, we showered and changed back into working dress before forming up outside the gym to await the results of the physical tests. Physical Training Instructor Sgt Butters reported that we had all passed the induction tests and could now report to our CSMs.

Along with Jas, Scrivs, Grose, and Steve Jelf, I was sent to B Company where we were to report to a CSM Weeks. We had been warned he was a tough nut and not to cross him. We waited outside his office, not sure of what to expect and trying to pluck up the courage to knock on his door. Scrivs eventually took the risk. "Come in!" a voice shouted from the other side of the door. We all froze for a second.

"Come F-ING in!"

Scrivs went through the door and, like sheep, we all followed. The office was small and narrow with minimal furniture, a desk with a phone, a chair and a filing cabinet. A large-set man sat in the chair behind the desk with his back to us. We took up positions in front of his desk and stood there in silence. For a while nothing happened and then suddenly he swivelled around in his chair to face us and growled, "If anyone wants to know, I got these playing rugby!" He pointed to his eyes-both swollen, black, purple and very bloodshot.

"Jesus Christ!" I thought. "What have I let myself in for?"

No one said anything. The seconds passed into minutes as he looked us all up and down, weighing us up.

"Right," he smiled, "Burt, Grose, Jelf and Scrivens: 4 Platoon – Thomas: 5 Platoon." Still no one moved or said anything.

"The Company Clerk will show you to your rooms – Lewis!" he bellowed.

The door shot open and there stood the Company Clerk, "Sir?"

"Show these lads to their rooms."

We followed the Company Clerk to our rooms and he told us to unpack. None of the other lads were about at this time and, as I entered my room, I wondered what they would be like. Stories of life in the Battalion are full of tales of individuals getting 'filled in' when they first arrive. New intakes are always seen as being cocky having been the senior lads at depot, leaving full of high spirits and a little too much 'bravado' from nights at Brize Norton. New lads are referred to as 'crows', a derogatory term used to imply that they are still to prove themselves to the others and as such are not accepted by them. To add insult to injury, B Company had just returned from a trip to Oman and everyone had been live firing Kalashnikov AK47s and the like, and had all completed a tab up the Jebal Akdah. We, of course, hadn't.

The room was enormous compared to what I had been used to at the depot and looked more like a 'squat' than a barrack room. There were five beds, various pieces of furniture, lockers, bedside cabinets, a table with chairs, armchairs with clothes strewn across them and a large metal dustbin complete with lid. The walls were covered with pictures of naked women in various poses and the floor was littered with rubbish. I was shown my bed space and told to unpack, after which I sat on my bed admiring the wallpaper and waited for the others to arrive. Hours passed and eventually the door swung open and in came three lads. They looked at me and grunted. I didn't introduce myself. They all went to their respective bed spaces, removed their belts and berets and crashed out.

That went well, I thought.

The Company Clerk, who also shared the room, came in threw his belt and beret on his bed and announced that it was time for scoff. Like a flash the lads were awake, up and out. I was left alone again.

I knew that Stu was also in 5 Platoon and couldn't wait to meet up with him. Unfortunately, I didn't know what room he was in and couldn't just walk into any of the rooms looking for him. I was also very conscious that fraternising with the 'crows' could bring him grief from the other lads, so scoff time was probably the best opportunity to meet up with him. I eventually met Stu in the scoff house. He didn't give a damn about etiquette and came straight over and slapped me on the shoulder. "Good to see you, mate," he said, re-introducing himself to all the other lads. It was good to see a welcoming face. He soon filled us in with what had really happened to the CSM's eye. It had nothing to do with playing rugby and more to do with being jumped by a few blokes, while zipped up in his 'doss bag', one night in Oman.

"Nice to know 3 Para lads respect rank," I said to Stu. "Nothing to do with rank", he said. "If you go overboard or get a little out of hand the blokes don't forget it. Doesn't matter who you are. These things always have a habit of coming back and biting you when you least expect it." He continued, "Johnny Weeks is a right handful and can look after himself, so don't cross him!" We looked at each other and all replied at the same time, "We've been told that all ready!"

So here I was, finally in battalion, labelled as a 'crow', totally ignored by day and a social outcast of a night. For my sins I had been put under the charge of a 'psychopathic' CSM who obviously had one, two or possibly three outstanding issues to tackle in the coming months. To top it all, Stu told me the lads in my room – Dominic Gray, Tony Kempster, Pete Hindmarsh and the Company Clerk Lewis – were a nightmare "Just watch yourself tonight", he warned, "and until you're invited don't go drinking down The Ram pub. You'll get killed!"

I must admit I wasn't looking forward to going to bed that first night but things must take their course. Eventually I turned in for the evening. None of the lads were back from the pub when I entered the room, so I turned the lights off and decided to lay on top of my bed with all my clothes on – expecting the worse.

I was asleep when the first one, Tony Kempster, came in – but not for long. He kicked the door open sending the dustbin and all its contents flying. He did not attempt to switch the light on and the room echoed with expletives. Startled, I braced myself. Tony ignored me and made his way to his bed space, in the dark – colliding with every piece of furniture in the room on the way. He then dispersed his clothes to the four-corners of the room and lay naked on his bed. Moments later he was snoring – extremely loudly. Dominic Gray was next back, some ten or fifteen minutes after Tony. He also kicked the door open, fell over the dustbin now lying in his path and sent his bag of chips flying.

"F- it!" he mumbled and made his way to his bed, again without the aid of the light. He, like Tony, also flung his clothes all over the room and crashed out on his bed. "Two down", I thought. I can't remember the other two coming in as I had already fallen asleep.

At the weekend I decided not to go home but to stay and wander around the camp, which appeared to be massive and mainly constructed of red bricks with concrete lintels and floors. The story goes that it had originally been designed for somewhere out in India but the plans got mixed up and the English designs for Tidworth had been sent out to India and the Indian plans were sent to Wiltshire. Each double-storey block had a large veranda that ran the length of the building. Columns adorned with ironwork supported the veranda roofs and the large barrack rooms all had high ceilings and impressive fans.

On Sunday morning I decided to tidy up the room. On Sunday afternoon, while I was sitting on my bed, Tony Kempster came into the room looked somewhat confused and left. Shortly after, he came back and declared, "This is my f-ing room." I noted he had obviously had quite a bit to drink. He looked at me and asked, "Have you tidied up?" "Yes, I have," I replied, to which he promptly picked up the dustbin and emptied its contents all over the floor. He then walked over to the pile of clothes I had folded and placed neatly on the table and flung them all over the room.

"There you go," he said. "That's better!"

Feeling a bit of a pillock, I decided not to tidy the room again. Tony sat on his bed, turned his television on to watch football, opened a bottle of brandy and started taking large swigs from it. "Want a drink?" he asked. Knowing this to be an opportunity to get talking I accepted, and we sat on his bed watching football and chatting. Tony told me about the personalities in the room, the platoon, the company and then the battalion. He told me he had a brother, Dave, in 4 Platoon and that life in the battalion was fine as, and when, you were accepted. He finished the chat by reminding me that I was still a 'crow' and would remain one for some time and until proven.

Life in battalion was quite relaxed. Morning parades were really just a get together outside the platoon rooms. There were no formal inspections of the men as there had been every day in Juniors or Recruit Company, just the CSM calling the roll out to check everyone was present and that no one had absconded. He would then hand the platoons back to their respective officers who would then decide what the day's events would be. To be honest, nothing really happened in those first few weeks. B Company spent most of their time cleaning the kit and weapons that had been used in the recent excursion to Oman. The occasional run would be undertaken and that was about it. It was generally accepted that 3 Para spent most of its time out of camp in the 'cuds' – a word used to describe a wood, mainly associated with an exercise. The battalion prided itself on its ability to live off the land and saw barrack duties as bullshit and best performed by 'hats'. 3 Para was often referred to as 'gungey 3' due to the lads always being in the cuds and wearing camouflage cream 24/7. Their state of dress would, more often than not, reflect this. The practice of lazing around waiting for the next exercise or deployment wasn't therefore frowned upon by the superiors but accepted as the 'calm before the storm' as 3 Para did more than their fair share of exercises and soldiering duties.

At NAAFI break each day the five 'crows' would walk through the Royal Irish Rangers' camp, stationed in the adjacent barracks, to the NAAFI hut at the end of their camp. We'd each buy a pork pie, a pint of milk and a Mars bar and sit around for half an hour, chatting away or reading The Sun, while Scrivs played music on the juke-box, "Tears Of A Clown" and Soft Cell's "Tainted Love". We'd return to camp and do whatever was on the agenda – if anything.

For reasons I am unsure of I was moved from 5 Platoon to 4 Platoon. I think 4 Platoon were slightly under strength. The move meant I ended up sharing a room with Grose and a Scotsman called Ron Duffy, who was rumoured to be the battalion 'nutter' – and I mean that in the nicest possible way. Ron was a loner, an older man who was still a 'Private' soldier by rank. He was known for keeping a black book that he would enter the names of anyone who crossed him or pissed him off. Eventually, when the individual was least expecting it – usually while sleeping – Ron would take his revenge and attack them with whatever was to hand. He would use anything he could lay his hands on, like the heavy bumpers that were used to buff up the floors. He was even said to have attacked one lad with a wire coat hanger! Ron was fine to Grose and me and would offer us a nip of his whisky to put in our tea. He detested all music other than Scottish folk songs, labelling it 'punk rock'. He hated chocolate and all those who ate it, branding them 'sweetie bandits'. I never told Ron about the Mars bars we ate at NAAFI break. Ron's exploits were legendary throughout the battalion. In Oman, the Platoon Officer had awoken in his tent to find a 7.62 round placed on his chest on top of his 'doss' bag. No questions were asked but everyone knew who had done it and what the significance was. He had also previously unhooked the officer in the plane, prior to a jump and after the Parachute Jump Instructor had completed his final equipment checks. It was only when the PJI was called to the front of the plane by the pilots – a most unusual occurrence – that he noticed the strop hanging down and hooked the officer back up. When the PJI looked at Ron for an explanation Ron just looked back and smiled – a smile that told the PJI everything. Ron had the most amazing brilliant-blue eyes that were the windows to a much darker side – not that anyone dared stare at Ron. The PJI accepted the explanation by facial expression, emphasised by Ron's eyes, and the matter was dropped.

All the other platoon rooms would be filled with the latest sounds of the charts and by the blokes' banter. With Ron there our room was like a library – silent and rarely visited. Nobody dared play any music in earshot of Ron.

Grose and I both bought earphone attachments for our stereos. Ron appreciated our sacrifice and never entered our names in his black book.

My new Platoon Officer was a Lieutenant, Andy Bickerdike, my Sergeant was Ian McKay and my Section Commander was Cpl Brian Milne.

After a couple of weeks in 3 Para, the Regimental Sergeant Major (RSM) called the battalion together and requested, "Whoever has nicked the Royal Irish Rangers' mascot, a goat with a large beard, would they kindly return it!" Shortly after the parade was dismissed the goat appeared, minus its beard, on one of the lawns between the blocks. The animal had been housed in one of the drying rooms and had been sprayed bright green (the Irish Rangers' colour) and a luminous orange (for road safety). To be truthful it looked very good although I don't think the Irish Rangers appreciated the hair-styling, artwork or the effort and thought that had gone into to it. The battalion was confined to camp for a short period.

Shortly after, Baz Barrett and some of the other lads who had originally gone to 477 Platoon joined the battalion. Baz was assigned to B Company, 6 Platoon.

In March, 3 Para was placed on 'Spearhead', where a battalion could be given twenty-four hours notice to be deployed anywhere in the world. Each soldier and his company was required to have their full kit issue packed and ready to go at a moment's notice. 'Spearhead' usually meant being sent over to Northern Ireland for a tour of duty and accordingly the battalion packed itself off to Hythe and Lydd in Kent to complete Northern Ireland training. This was fantastic and for us 'crows', our first taste of urban warfare training. Days were spent in the mock-up village undertaking foot patrols and practising the 'actions on' for when the patrol came under fire. Each soldier wore a bib, with his unique number on the front and back, allowing his movements to be tracked by the aid of cameras strategically positioned throughout the village.

The village represented a fictitious community in Northern Ireland, complete with streets full of houses, shops, a discotheque, a small green and various anti-British slogans painted on the brick walls. The patrol was given specific tasks to carry out like: "Visit the butcher's shop and glean information about the whereabouts of Paddy O'Murphy".

Dummies with voice capabilities were situated throughout the village and in the shops and would shout out to the patrol passing by, "F-off Paras – Go home!" and a number of other mind blowing phrases to try and provoke a reaction. Others would inform you they had just seen a man dressed in black carrying a weapon into the back of No. 12. You were required to pass this message verbatim to the Patrol Commander, who would make a decision whether or not to follow up the information. A notebook and pencil in your top left-hand pocket were essential pieces of kit.

The whole experience taught us how to improve personal

patrolling skills and, more importantly, not to take anything at face value or trust anyone. After each patrol the section would sit in the debriefing room and analyse its performance, with the assistance of the street cameras, which would show where the patrol or an individual had made mistakes. Perhaps taking cover next to a bin that could subsequently explode or an individual being silhouetted against the background. The training was intensive but extremely rewarding and I enjoyed every moment of it.

We practiced sangar duties time and time again. This included the routine for relieving other members of your section from their posts; taking over their duty and being responsible for the sangar. You would be positioned in the sangar for an unspecified period while various weapons would be fired in and around the vicinity. You had to record these incidents including the date, time, type of weapon used, number of shots fired, location of weapon, direction of shot and any other relevant information. The walls of the anteroom, leading to the sangar positions were covered with black and white photographs of victims of car bombs, shootings, explosions, complete with mortuary tray and slab.

Just the right atmosphere to ensure everyone took the matter seriously and understood the ultimate price that could be paid.

Observation was also a key area for training. We would sit for hours on end in an Observation Post (OP) in a mock attic overlooking a number of streets. Each member of the OP would be responsible for observing a specific street and duly recording any incidents of interest. The OP's brief would be to look out for a number of people known to be living in the area and record their movements. If at anytime the OP saw 'Paddy O'Murphy' dressed in blue jeans and a yellow jumper, we were to radio this fact in immediately, otherwise radio silence was to be maintained at all times. The people (dummies) would then move about the streets, controlled like bumper cars at a fairground, dressed in various forms of attire. Blue jeans – green jumpers, yellow jeans – blue jumpers and all kinds of combinations to confuse the observer. We would record in a log those individuals of importance and their movements. Eventually 'Paddy O'Murphy' would show his face and we would radio the incident in. At the debriefing we would be shown that 'Paddy' had actually shown himself on a number of occasions, one being only minutes after we had initiated the OP, but had gone unnoticed by us. It was quite an eye-opening and thought-provoking experience.

Hythe and Lydd was where I first rubbed someone up the wrong way with near disastrous consequences. Late one night Scrivs, Jas and I had gone over to the NAAFI to get something to eat. Scrivs and Jas went off to the loo and I walked in the NAAFI and saw the blokes were queuing up at the bar to get drinks and food. Seeing that there were two queues, one for food and one for drinks, I went over to the food queue and asked for a steak and kidney pie with brown sauce. I went back to the platoon room to sit on my bed and eat it, knowing Scrivs and Jas would get theirs and do the same. I wasn't halfway through my pie when Taff Hedges, a Lance Corporal (L/Cpl) in the platoon and an older and much respected member came charging into the room and warned me to get out – and quickly.

"Why? What have I done?" I asked. "You pushed in the

queue in the NAAFI and the next bloke to be served was Stevie Hope. He's coming for you."

Everybody in 3 Para knew that name. Stevie Hope was the hardest man in the battalion, reputed to be an absolute nightmare when riled.

"I didn't push in," I said hoping for a reprieve.

"Just F-off now and hide yourself, he'll forget about it in a couple of days." I spent the rest of the night hiding around the barracks and, when it got too cold, I sought refuge in one of the toilets.

In the early hours of the morning Taff came into the loos and told me that Steve had given up searching for me and that it was safe to go back to my bed. The next few days were spent keeping a very low profile, I didn't go back to the NAAFI again and the battalion soon left Hythe and Lydd to return to Tidworth.

Towards the end of March the Falklands first came to my attention. The nightly news was full of how a group of Argentine scrap metal merchants had landed on South Georgia and had subsequently hoisted the Argentine flag. Days later we were informed, again by the news, that the Argentines had invaded the Falkland Islands. None of us knew exactly where the Falklands Islands were – only that they were somewhere off the northern tip of Scotland...

Very soon the battalion was holding intelligence briefings to keep us informed of the latest events regarding the Falklands. Notice boards lined the scoff hall adorned with information, press cuttings and pictures of the Islands. We soon realised just how far away the Falkland Islands were. Rumours were rife throughout camp and as the battalion was on Spearhead everybody hoped we would be sent to deal with the invaders.

I informed Mum that it looked like we would soon be deployed. As the Falklands appeared to be a cold and wet place not dissimilar to the Brecon Beacons I asked her to send me, as a matter of some urgency, the high-legged Canadian Para boots that I had left in my room during my last leave. Being Mum, she sent me a parcel containing a cake that she had baked, some other items of food and loads of sweets but forgot all about the boots I had asked for.

On Saturday 3rd April, the Commanding Officer, Lieutenant Colonel Hew Pike, informed the battalion that we would be going to Southampton the following Wednesday or Thursday. The blokes were ecstatic. Stu, Jas and I went to a Women's Royal Army Corps' disco, where Stu had been dating one of the girls, and that night over the telephone in the bar I asked Laura to marry me. She agreed and I spent the rest of the night wishing I was back home with her.

By Monday 5th April, the battalion learned it would be travelling to Ascension Island on the P & O cruise liner SS Canberra with various commando units from the Royal Marines. As all of our kit was already packed, our days were spent sitting around speculating on the immediate future. The following Thursday we arrived at the gates of Southampton dock where five girls were standing outside with banners, which read: "Go on the Paras!" and "We love you!" This 'enormous' send off was embarrassing to say the least. Everyone on the coach laughed out loud and told them to go home. I was only thankful that Mum, Jo and Laura were not among them!

As the coaches stopped at the dockside, there before us, in its full splendour, was the SS Canberra, looking magnificent. With the kit unloaded, we were instructed to climb the gang-plank and board the ship. The battalion band played on. We were guided to the Alice Springs Bar and sat around waiting to be told our cabin numbers. Officers of the Parachute Regiment and the Marines were to be assigned to A and B decks, Senior NCOs were on C and D decks. We, the nobodies of the campaign, were allocated a cabin on F deck – one deck above the water line and the perfect striking height for an Exocet missile.

After finding our cabin and dropping our kit off we reported back to the Alice Springs Bar where we passed the hours while other members of the battalion and the Royal Marines boarded ship. By now the dockside was a mass of people. Families had come to say goodbye to their loved ones. Eventually, we were told to line the side of the Canberra facing the dockside and wave farewell to all those present. The decks soon became too crowded and the single blokes were asked to step aside and retire to the bars and let the married men say their goodbyes.

The 17-year-olds, Scrivs, Jas, Grose, Jelf and myself, sat back in the bar and tried to get a drink.

"Sorry I can only serve you non-alcoholic drinks until we set sail", the barman said. "F-ing good this is!" said Jas.

The ship slowly pulled away from its berth and we watched from the bar windows as Southampton and her lights slipped away into the night.

CHAPTER SIX
Joshua

The Conquest of the Promised Land

Days on the Canberra were filled with PT and weapons train-ing. The PT sessions mainly involved running, for what seemed an eternity, around the green promenade deck dressed in boots, denims, puttees and red PT vest. These sessions were more mind-blowingly boring than physically enduring, and the body exercises held on the upper decks were a welcoming change. Very soon we were tabbing around the promenade deck with full kit and platoon weapons. When the sea was rough we would be all over the place, falling from one side to another. On the very rare occasions that the sea was considered too rough and the deck was awash with the spray, PT would be stopped or cancelled. I was shocked to see that the Marines undertook their training in shorts, trainers and casual sportswear. We very rarely saw them in full kit or with weapons pounding the decks like us. I often wondered how they would hold up when it came to tabbing the islands in full kit with 70lbs strapped to their backs. I can't say I relished the thought of doing PT daily or even twice a daily, as was often the case, but I understood the mind-set behind it and the need to maintain and increase fitness levels.

Our cabin was probably one of the smallest on the

Canberra. It housed four of us – Jas, Taff Parry, Andy Stone and myself. Being 'crows', Jas and I had the bottom bunks and the other two senior lads had the top. There wasn't room to swing a cat and when we had to change for PT or weapons training, two of us would get changed out in the corridor.

Nights would be spent in the Alice Springs bar, talking, playing cards or Yahtzee and drinking. We were all restricted to two cans per man per night but no one took any notice of this and the bar was soon drunk dry. An extra shipload of booze had to be sent for.

Late at night we'd lay on our bunks listening to the ship's disc jockey or playing tapes on our cassette players. I enjoyed these moments and often wondered what the lads in Ron Duffy's cabin were doing minus the music. Jon and Vangelis "The Friends Of Mr Cairo" was the album of the moment and everywhere you went the lads or the ship's radio would be playing songs from it, like "I'll Find My Way Home" and "State of Independence". The Mamas and Papas' "Monday, Monday" was another well-played song and even to this day whenever I hear it I think of the four of us in our cabin all happily singing along.

Those initial days on the Canberra passed slowly and it seemed to take forever to arrive in Sierra Leone, West Africa, where Canberra was due to refuel and take on supplies. It was now 17th April and the general feeling onboard was that we would probably only get to Ascension Island. By then the Argies would realise that Britain was serious about the sovereignty of the Falklands and pack up and go home. We would then turn the ship around and go home ourselves. We didn't consider there was much possibility of a conflict with the

Argies and saw the trip as a cruise with the chance to get a sun tan at the taxpayers' expense.

In Freetown, Sierra Leone, local traders paddled their small hollowed trunks out to the ship and encouraged the lads, who were now crammed along the sides of the ship and leaning out of their port holes, to buy their wares. Spears, shields and even a live monkey were handed up to the lads to view and purchase. The spears were thrown back with little or no thought for the safety of the traders, who would then have to dive off their home-made canoes and retrieve the spears from the bottom of the ocean. This amused the lads endlessly and the process continued until the traders realised they were being taken for a ride. The monkey was passed from lad to lad until it arrived at the top of the ship where it was returned unceremoniously to its owner with the same terminal velocity. The traders soon gave up and were replaced by other locals who asked for plastic containers, which they could use for fetching and carrying water. The lads unsympathetically filled large plastic containers with water and dropped them from the highest parts of the ship on to the locals below. Their flimsy craft couldn't sustain the impact of these large water bombs and were soon capsizing and sinking. We roared with laughter and the locals gave up all hope of assistance and retired to the safety of the shore.

That night Jas and I took our drinks out on to one of the ship's verandas and sat in chairs with our feet up on the rails and watched the sun go down. It was beautiful. The warm West African air and the smell of the sea made us feel like we were civvies on holiday. As darkness came we watched the flickering lights of the settlements in the distance and wondered what activity was happening in their camps at that very moment. We talked for hours through the night about life in the battalion, the excitement of the voyage and being part of history in the making. We were so proud to be part of the campaign and, better still, part of the Parachute Regiment. Life was great and when we returned home victorious after the campaign life was going to be even better, one great big party after another. The girls would swarm around us in the hope of exotic tales, daring deeds and exciting times and we, flush with our well-earned pay, new clothes and fast cars, would happily entertain them. Those same girls would all be invited to our eighteenth birthday parties, the parties that would be the social events of the year and the talk of the town for years to come. We remembered Graham Collins stuck in Edinburgh on Castle duties with 1 Para missing out on the whole experience, and swore to write to him the very next day and tell him just exactly what he was missing. As the night came and went and the new day dawned, Jas and I returned to our cabin happy, excited and full of great plans for the future.

Two days later on 19th April, the ship anchored at Ascension where we would be based for about two weeks. This would give the battalion a chance to practice landing craft drills and beach landings in preparation for the assault on the Falkland Islands. Being paratroopers these drills were totally new to us and we all wished we were parachuting into the Falklands instead – in keeping with our operational role. To be perfectly honest, none of us thought that we would continue on from Ascension. We believed the sea drills and beach landing practice were either a propaganda exercise for the Government back home or to create the right image for any satellite photos the enemy might be taking.

Beach landings were basic, boring and practiced with irritating regularity. The Landing Craft Utility (LCU) or LCVPs, smaller landing craft, would come alongside the Canberra and we would have to jump from the ship into its hold. This was a horrendous and dangerous task, as the Canberra was not designed for troop movements. Before you could attempt such a 'leap of faith' you would have to wait for the Canberra and the LCU to be rising at the same time with the sea swell.

The LCU and LCVPs were somewhat smaller than the Canberra and looked like makeshift rafts bobbing up and down on the waves some 10ft – 15ft below. This made the jump appear similar to those 'illusion jumps' of the 'trainasium'. In other words, bloody frightening. Once the vessels were rising and falling in time, the 'leap' had to be of such a distance to ensure that you didn't fall between the two vessels to be crushed when they, all too frequently, collided together. It was all or nothing. You had to pray that if you did make it the lads in the LCU would steady your fall and not leave you to 'pile in' to the vessel's metal deck. To add to the problem, some bright spark then decided we should all have our platoon weapons and carry the weight we would be carrying when landing in the Falklands. It was absolute mayhem; how someone didn't break an ankle I will never know. Return journeys were even worse and I nearly burst out laughing when we arrived back, soaking wet from one session, complete with full kit and platoon weapons to find a scramble net over the side of the Canberra and the Navy lads beckoning us to climb up it. The lad with the 84mm Carl Gustav, weighing 36lbs by itself, also had his personal weapon, a Sterling sub-machine gun (SMG) plus webbing, fully laden in excess of 45lbs. All in all he would be climbing the net with an additional weight of around 100lbs. Still, if he had fallen he probably would have reached the bottom of the ocean before the vessels collided together and crushed him, proving the saying that every cloud has a silver lining!

The Navy guys realised the net was a complete waste of time and opened one of Canberra's external doors on a lower deck, and we scrambled aboard with their much-needed assistance.

Ascension Island was a typical exotic Forces location. Stuck in the middle of nowhere, barren and covered in useless volcanic ash that got everywhere it wasn't meant to. On the plus side the sea was crystal clear and the beaches golden.

Occasionally, on completion of the beach landings, we would be allowed to strip off and swim in the sea. This was what the Army refers to as Rest and Recuperation (R & R) and civvies call 'quality time'. Either way we loved every minute of it and couldn't wait to discard our equipment and clothes and dive uncaringly into the sea. Every now and then some-one would shout out that he was being bitten by Trigger fish and we would all scramble to the shore and wait for the shoals of fish to disperse.

Trigger fish are extremely ugly and have small but sharp teeth. One of them would take a nip at your leg or any other exposed part of your body and this would initiate a mass attack from the rest of the shoal. After a while, the shoal would lose interest due to the absence of bodies in the sea and move off. We could all return to repeat the process.

Jas and I did write to Graham telling him all about our experiences and life on the Canberra. By now 2 Para had also been called up and were sailing south on the MV Norland. We goaded Graham about 1 Para being absent from the excursion and sent him photos of Jas and I holding up signs we had made stating, "FIGHTING 2 + 3 PARA", "FIGHTING 3 – FRIGHTENED 1". We both had huge smiles in the photos and most of them included the mandatory hand signals that men make to each other when suggesting that the other is lacking in something! We sent him a box of matches with a picture of the Canberra on it, telling him that eventually he would get off sentry duty and go on exercise with 1 Para to practice his soldiering-skills. When this happened, and it could be some time yet, he would have to make a fire to cook himself scoff. He was to use the matches so he could think of us doing it all for real. We added a footnote to say matches were extremely dangerous and it would probably be best if he was supervised when using them, or better still gave them to someone older to look after until the moment came to use them.

Graham wrote back with the comments that one would have expected and included in his letter a small 'action man' Union Jack flag for us to fly in Port Stanley when victorious. Jas and I took photos of the Union Jack located in a place where the sun doesn't shine accompanied with messages written on either cheek and promptly returned it to him. Graham appreciated the sentiment!

On 3rd May we heard how the enemy battleship 'The General Belgrano' had been sunk by a British submarine from outside the 200-mile Total Exclusion Zone, or TEZ, the UK had declared around the Falkland Islands. The mood on the ship changed. Britain really was serious and had informed the enemy just how serious she was!

The following night we learned that one of our ships, HMS Sheffield, had been sunk. The reality of being at war hit home. From that moment we knew we would be landing on the Falklands, whether diplomatic negotiations were still going on or not. Both countries had struck their blows.

Our Prime Minister, Margaret Thatcher, was world renowned for being bloody minded and determined. There was no way she would stand by while the UK sustained casualties and losses. This was for real and there was more than just pride and honour at stake – there was now loss of lives. For the very first time I considered the ultimate consequence of being a soldier.

On the afternoon of 6th May, SS Canberra set sail from Ascension Island. The sea was constantly rough and the weather far colder than we had previously experienced. PT became vicious, weapons training more intensive. Daily first aid lectures were well attended and without the usual quips and jibes from the blokes. Each man gave blood as a matter of routine and stock levels were monitored. Surprisingly, no one complained if their blood group stock level was low and they were asked to give blood again and again. Interestingly, blood can only be maintained for a certain period of time and we were informed to keep the blood donations confidential and not write home about them in case the enemy found out and would conclude that landings would be inevitable within the blood's life span.

One afternoon the battalion was told to report to the cinema for a 'Scale A' parade, which meant everybody. The whole of

3 Para sat in attendance, the CO and RSM included, waiting for a lecture on Arctic Warfare from two Marine instructors. The two Marines stood behind their podiums situated at either end of the stage looking extremely serious. Our blokes were not impressed. The lights dimmed and the lecture started with one of the Marines lit up by a spotlight. He talked for several minutes about survival in extreme conditions and then the spotlight faded on him and immediately swung over to the other guy who went on about another area of Arctic Warfare. This continued for some time with all of 3 Para switching their vision from one side of the stage to the other – in sequence with the spotlight. We must have looked like spectators at Wimbledon watching a tennis match. After about an hour and a half of neck-breaking waffle the two Marines finished their briefing. The spotlight went out and the main lights came back on. No one in 3 Para moved, clapped or did anything. The two Marines stood there for a moment and an awkward silence fell around the cinema; then one of them asked, "Has anyone any questions?" Immediately one of the blokes stood up and said, "Yeah – how much are the whores in Port Stanley?" The whole of 3 Para fell about laughing, the CO put his head in his hands and the RSM shot up and shouted, "Right everyone file out!" That was the first and last lecture we received from the Marines.

Since leaving Ascension Island, Canberra had been escorted by two battleships, HMS Ardent and HMS Argonaut. Not that this changed anything to us soldiers. Our time was concentrated on ensuring that our kit was fully serviceable and functioning in the correct manner.

Lessons and briefings were now focusing on the equipment

we would be carrying when landing, operational strategic planning – where 3 Para fitted into the overall master plan – platoon and section drills and 'garrotte squads'. Garrotte squad was the affectionate name given to an individual or group of people whose task was to silence a sentry or an enemy position with minimum noise or fuss. Equipment included the obvious 'cheese wire' and bayonet, to the more imaginary collapsible spade trenching-tool. We practiced techniques for stalking the position and silencing the sentries. Jas and I found this extremely amusing, although the corporal taking the lesson didn't and threatened to fill us both in if we didn't take it seriously. So we did!

One afternoon during the daily briefing from Sgt Ian McKay, which took place outside our cabins by one of the F Deck stairwells, the platoon was informed that any individual who had not yet taken out insurance with the Pay Clerk should do so. To be honest, I hadn't given insurance a thought and as I hadn't a wife or family who were dependent on my income, I thought no more of it. A day or so later, when Jas and I were laying on our beds Sgt McKay came into our cabin and informed us that according to his list neither of us had taken out insurance.

"Get your arses up there now!" he said.

So Jas and I trotted off to the pay counter and joined a queue of people to do exactly that. Jas was immediately behind me in the queue and I was soon called forward to the counter to complete the necessary forms. With my forms completed, that was the last I thought about insurance. I did write home and tell Mum I had taken it out, although I knew this would worry her. To be honest it scared the hell out of me, as insurance cover is not the sort of thing a normal 17-year-old concerns himself with. If I had not been told by Sgt McKay to take out insurance I wouldn't have – it was as simple as that.

On 18th May, SS Canberra moved into the TEZ. A news broadcast informed the world that the Canberra with 2,000 men on board had joined the main fleet, and that for security reasons we would be moving to HMS Intrepid. The blokes cursed the media and its blasé attitude towards understanding the fine line between giving information to the British public and supplying the enemy with intelligence.

The following day B Company left SS Canberra in the giant LCUs and the smaller LCVPs and we made our way to HMS Intrepid. Our webbing was fully laden with our personal ammunition supply and 24 hour rations, ready for the landings. In addition, we wore around our necks a bandolier of 200 rounds for the GPMG, which weighed 12lbs. Our bergens already bulged at the sides with an additional 48 hours' rations, a sleeping bag, spare clothing and other essential items, like the trench tool.

Our entrance to HMS Intrepid was impressive. As we neared, the ship took on water and lowered itself deeper into the sea. This allowed our LCU to sail directly into its hull. Intrepid's rear doors were then shut and as the water pumped back out, the ship rose along with the LCU snug in a berth inside her. We had to simply walk up the landing ramp of the LCU and on to the ship's side. From there, though, things went downhill.

HMS Intrepid was full to the brim with soldiers and their kit, plus the ship's usual crew. The grey metal corridors and passageways were tiny and certainly not designed for a soldier and his overweight kit. Everywhere you went you hit your head, knocked your knee or got your kit stuck. To top it all, there was nowhere for us to stay or sleep, as the majority of spare spaces had already been taken. In the end, Scrivs and I climbed down several manholes and ladders, with all of our kit, and ended up sleeping in a cramped store room with two battalion medics. Within minutes I hated the ship and couldn't wait to get off. The ship's crew walked around the passageways with their anti-burn 'flash protector' kit, looking like extras from an episode of Dr. Who. Their heads, necks and chests were covered with flameproof white canvas type material, leaving only a small gap for their eyes. They wore huge white gloves or mittens to protect their hands. We were left wondering what would happen to us, who weren't issued with these essential pieces of clothing, if the ship were struck.

That evening, as Scrivs and I made our way back to the storeroom, a naval officer grabbed us and asked if we were first aid trained. He told us to follow him to the ship's galley. En route, he told us a Sea King helicopter carrying thirty SAS men had plummeted into the sea while cross decking from HMS Hermes to Intrepid. The survivors were being brought aboard and we were to assist him in any way possible. The scene that greeted us in the galley was not one I was prepared for.

The achievements of the Special Air Service are legendary and the Regiment is rightly considered by the British public to be unrivalled throughout the world – the elite, the best of the best, an organisation to be truly proud of. Within the Army the SAS is held in the utmost respect – a formidable fighting force that can adapt to any situation and provide unforeseen solutions to seemingly insurmountable problems.

As I surveyed the galley I could not believe what I was seeing. Men who had survived the crash lay on tables and on the galley floor with helpers desperately trying to remove their freezing wet clothing and cover them in warm, dry blankets. On other tables lay those men who had not survived. Medics still worked frantically with these men, never giving up hope. Orders and requests for assistance were being barked out everywhere and within seconds the naval officer, a rating, Scrivs, and I were carrying one of the survivors down a passageway towards the captain's cabin. Once inside, the SAS trooper was placed in a warm bath with his extremities, fingers and toes, placed outside of the bath. He slipped in and out of consciousness, shook uncontrollably and his teeth pounded together. Each time he lost consciousness he would be woken up and asked what his name was and what day it was. Each time he woke he would ask after his mates and whether they had managed to get out of the helicopter. Slowly, but surely, he warmed through enough to increase his blood circulation. He kept saying he had gone back to the wreckage and managed to free two of his mates from their seat belts but the water had been too cold. He must have blacked out as he could remember nothing from that moment on. We had been told the South Atlantic was so cold a man would have suffered from the effects of hypothermia within thirty seconds of entering the water. Within ninety seconds he would have lost consciousness. Some of the SAS men had been in the water for more than fifteen minutes.

After a while, the naval officer was satisfied the trooper was going to be all right and returned to the galley, leaving Scrivs and me to attend to the trooper who was now coming round.

The blue colouring throughout his body that had been evident when we first placed him in the bath was slowly disappearing, as was his involuntary shivering. One of his legs was severely strapped up. He told us how he had been traversing, climbing sideways, on Pebble Island, when he had slipped and had torn the ligaments in his leg. He was the patrol medic and in true SAS spirit he had strapped his leg up and soldiered on.

"The blokes always need a good medic – and I'm the best," he joked grimly. He complained for a few minutes about losing his medical equipment, which had taken years to acquire. He then returned to asking about his friends.

"Go back and find out will you?" he asked.

Scrivs and I didn't want to move or be the bearers of bad news. "Someone will be along in a minute, just rest for now", we said.

Shortly after, the naval officer came back and took charge once more. Scrivs and I were relieved of duty and told to get some rest before the landings, scheduled to take place within the next 24 hours.

Back at the storeroom I couldn't rest. Images of the galley and the SAS men were still fresh in my mind. What could have gone wrong for a disaster like this to happen at such a critical stage – just before the landings?

We later learned that the crash could have been caused by a sea bird, possibly an albatross, flying into one of the helicopter's air intakes, causing the engine to stall and sending the chopper into the sea. The raid on Pebble Island had been carried out by D Squadron 22 SAS, who successfully wiped out six enemy Pucara fighter planes and five other aircraft. Of the thirty SAS men who crashed into the sea when cross decking, only eight survived. Many of those lost had been from D Squadron.

CHAPTER SEVEN
Judges

FIRST INTRODUCTION

**Friday, 21st May 1982 (Zulu Timings 4 hours forward –
Greenwich Mean Time).**

Our landing was delayed and, as we waited in the ship's
galley, pictures of the dead men I had seen in there came
flooding back. CSM Weeks hurried between the lads, issuing
two grenades to each man to shove down the front of his
smock, as there was nowhere else to put them. On leaving
Intrepid, we were each to collect two mortar bombs to take
ashore. These would be left on the beach, at a safe distance, for
the mortar platoon to pick up later. Each man must have been
carrying in excess of 120lbs. Bergens were easily in excess of
50lbs – with webbing weighing over 40lbs. My personal
weapon, the SLR, with a loaded magazine of twenty rounds
weighed 11lbs and the bandolier of 200 rounds – 12lbs. This
was without the grenades and the two mortar rounds. I felt
sorry for the lads carrying the GMPG, which weighed 24lbs
and the Carl Gustav anti-tank weapon, 36lbs, and thanked my
lucky stars I was not one of them. To put the weight we were
carrying into perspective, my own body weight at the time
was only around eleven stone – approximately 150lbs.

Harrowing pictures of D-Day landings and visions of

platoons being wiped out by machine gun fire must have been on everyone's mind. Although we had been informed the landing should be unopposed, the word should never instilled much confidence. It would certainly be good to get off the ship and get 'terra firma' under my boots but I wasn't looking forward to the marine coxswain shouting, "Down ramp – everyone out!"

At around 0700 hrs we were called forward to board the LCVP. As we made our way towards the landing craft, one of the surviving SAS blokes stood on the deck of the Intrepid looking out towards the Falklands. Wearing his fur-collared Arctic parka, he stared into the distance, his hands jammed firmly in his pockets. I followed his direction of sight and through the misty half-light could see the Atlantic, and in the distance, land. I returned my gaze to the SAS bloke and wondered what was going through his mind. As I neared him he looked around, noticed me, and gave me an approving nod and wink as if to say, "You'll be alright son." I only wished he was right. He recognised someone behind me and put out his right hand. "You're bloody freezing!" said the Para as they shook hands.

"Tell me about it," said the SAS bloke.

I heard them exchange farewells and the obligatory, "Look after yourself." The SAS man returned to his observation of the landing area and the Para continued on his journey.

As I entered the LCVP I prayed to God the landings would be unopposed and that I would survive the day. Our craft left Intrepid and made its way out to sea where it circled until the other LCVPs joined it. The sea was rough and everybody crouched down as the LCVP rose and fell with the choppy waves in San Carlos Water on the northwest coast of East Falkland. In the distance, and to our left, a fire fight was going on at Fanning Head. Tracer rounds from automatic gunfire cut through the air, concentrating the firepower on a specific area. We looked at each other as if to say, "What the hell is going on?"

We were reassured that the Special Boat Squadron were keeping the Argentine observation post at Port San Carlos busy while we landed. Even so, everybody crouched lower. My heart pounded in my chest and adrenaline raced through my veins while we circled for about 15 minutes until all LCVPs were present. Then we set off for our designated landing spot at Sandy Bay.

As we neared Green Two Beach the fire fight at Fanning Head was now accompanied by a naval bombardment. The tracer rounds, explosions and flashes reminded me of a November Fifth firework display but, being May and almost daylight, it all seemed surreal and unnatural. The radio operator, listening to dozens of transmissions being sent over the radio net, informed us that there was a tent on the beach. "What the hell is that doing there?" I thought.

I checked my weapon's sights and my ammunition pouches to ensure everything was in its place and that the pouches were securely fastened to prevent my magazines from falling out. I am sure this was more nervous behaviour than professional soldiering. Other landing craft were alongside us and, perhaps selfishly, I couldn't help feeling a sense of relief that there were now other targets for the enemy to aim at, other than just our craft, should the landings be opposed.

A Marine shouted, "Prepare to beach!"

The LCVP's engine slowed. I braced myself in preparation for the landing. "Dash, down, crawl, observe, sights, fire", is the standard operational procedure for coming under fire. With the equipment I was carrying this would probably change to "Struggle, fall, sink, be blinded, do nothing, get shot!"

It seemed to take an eternity for the LCVP's ramp to lower. The Marine screamed "BEACH!"

I looked over the shoulders of the men in front of me to the foreground and middle distance. Nothing seemed to be unto-ward. I focused on a spot just above the beach where I would head for before going to ground. I raised my weapon to a makeshift firing position and stepped over the ramp into the sea. The water came just below my knees and was freezing. To my right other lads were landing in waist-high water. With several comical hops, skips and very small jumps I was soon out of the sea and on to the beach. The beach was only about forty feet wide but covered with stones, which made the journey across it with the equipment we were carrying, almost impossible. I left my two mortar rounds at the top of the beach as instructed and continued on, going to ground in a soggy, bog-like patch.

Marvellous, I thought. I've been here two bloody minutes and I'm soaking wet already!

We moved off and our section joined the platoon and company formation advancing up a dirt track towards the Port San Carlos settlement. Forty-odd Argentine soldiers were reported at Port San Carlos but, as we tabbed towards the settlement, news passed down the staggered file formation that they had fled on seeing our troops land. Major Mike Argue, B Company's OC, decided to go straight to the next phase of the operation and move our company to the appropriately named Windy Gap, some three or four miles further inland, while A Company moved into the settlement.

The company now broke down into platoon and, subsequently, section formations for the hard uphill slog towards Windy Gap. The bracken and fern-covered land was boggy, while the absence of trees and rocks made finding cover from enemy fire impossible. Due to the lie of the land, our section commander, Cpl Brian Milne, placed us in arrowhead formation with our gun group up high to our left. Within minutes of starting the tab, "Air Raid Warning Red!" barked out.

Everybody went to ground and within seconds Argentine aircraft screamed overhead towards San Carlos Water where our ships sat. Missiles and naval gunfire rang out from all directions. I lay there feeling vulnerable and useless against the aircraft. Cpl Milne decided he had seen enough and ordered the section forward. As we continued on our way, more and more air raid warnings came, so many in fact that the last few were ignored totally.

Arriving at Windy Gap we paired up and dug in. My 'oppo' or 'buddy' was Ron Duffy. Cpl Milne sited our trench overlooking Cameron's Ridge on the opposite side of San Carlos Water. A reference point, known as The Knob, was ahead of us. The trench is in three parts. The central, chest-deep section is for the soldiers' firing positions. Individual sleeping areas for both soldiers are placed at either end of the main trench. These sleeping bays are not dug as deep as the main trench but still manage to appear grave like. The sleeping areas are then overlapped with a string mesh, held in place with foot-long metal spikes, with a waterproof covering placed on top. This 'ceiling' is then completely covered with earth to give some protection against air attacks. The whole trench and its forward edge, known as the parapet, is then fully camouflaged with flora from the surrounding area. Ron and I cracked on with digging the trench only to find that about four feet down we'd hit the water table and the trench floor filled with water. This did not perturb Ron and he happily carried on digging. Already soaking wet-through from constantly taking cover from the air raids, I could have cried. Cpl Milne had already given us our arcs of fire, which overlapped with neighbouring trenches on both sides. Once the trench had taken shape we set about putting up arc sticks. These stop a soldier's weapon going past the end of the arc of fire during the hours of darkness to avoid shooting each other. We also completed our range cards – brief sketches of the land to our front with various reference points and their ranges. Their main objective of this basic but very effective aid is to help the soldier in concentrating his and others' firepower towards the enemy at a predetermined spot.

Ron wasn't happy with the name Cameron's Ridge. He declared, "The Camerons, like the MacDonalds, can nay be trusted." I think we settled on it being called Scottish Ridge but to be truthful if Ron had wanted to call it Heathrow Airport I wouldn't have argued. Ron still carried his black book and had now been given a bayonet and a loaded weapon!

That afternoon, while we made sure the trench was being camouflaged properly, Argentine aircraft continued their bombing raids on our ships in San Carlos. We could only watch in awe as the ships tried to protect themselves by firing their anti-aircraft guns and missiles in a ferocious and determined manner. Long before we heard them, we would see the glint of the sun reflecting off the sides and wings of the enemy aircraft, as the pilots banked their planes ready for the next bombing run. By the time the engines could be heard the aircraft had long disappeared from view. This was extremely unnerving, because the planes travelled at such high speeds, and you were never sure where they would appear next. My sleeping bag zip broke, marring my first night in the trench in Arctic conditions. I cannot explain how important a sleeping bag is to a soldier in the field. It is a lifeline. The 'doss bag' or 'green maggot' provides warmth and comfort, which in turn provides a night of peaceful rest. Once my zip was broken it was irreparable, and however hard I tried to cover myself the wind always managed to find a gap and keep me uncomfortably chilled. As the night progressed Ron and I took our turn of 'stag' or sentry duty, watching and listening for signs of unusual activity to the front of the section and platoon position, before waking the next trench and handing the duty over to them. Ron made sure my weapon's sights were set to the battle setting of 300 metres and that throughout the two hours of sentry duty I was looking down the sights of my weapon. The night came and went without incident.

The following day we received our first intelligence briefing since landing. A number of enemy aircraft had been shot down with very little damage caused to our own aircraft and ships. At the end of the briefing Sgt McKay commented that if the quantities of enemy aircraft that had been shot down were correct in these reports then the Argentines had run out of Pucaras, their light fighter aircraft. That day the bombing raids continued and Pucaras and Mirages screamed over-head. The intelligence reports were obviously not worth the paper they were written on and were someone's idea of cheering the troops up. The problem was that we had been informed of the total number of enemy aircraft in the Argentine air force prior to landing on the Falklands and our numbers didn't match up to those being shot down. I decided not to take too much notice of intelligence waffle in the future and would conclude for myself how the enemy air force was doing by the daily activity I experienced.

As Ron and I scanned the area to the front of our trench for enemy activity, Ron looked over to me in his familiar, yet intensive way, and said, "Tom, if the enemy come now we will expend all of our ammunition at them. We will then fix bayonets and charge them."

I looked at Ron briefly for some sign of emotion, but he just stared at me, nodding his head in his usual approving manner, as if he had given the matter much thought. He returned to observing the area to our front. I thought to myself, the man has gone f-ing nuts!

The Royal Artillery set up their Rapier detachment just to the rear of our trenches. The Rapier is a guided anti-aircraft missile launcher. A prime target for any aircraft pilot. I thought, thanks a bunch. More attention to ourselves. Still at least if the enemy did come when Ron and I were in mid-charge we would have the support of guided missiles. Unfortunately, or fortunately for us, the thing never seemed to work and each time enemy aircraft came into view we would look towards the missile launcher in expectation only for nothing to happen. People would be shouting at each other and rushing around but that was all that ever happened. In this particular case the Rapier – another fantastic piece of sophisticated equipment that cost millions of pounds to develop – amounted to nothing.

Ron and I would be unsupported once more in our bayonet charge.

The next few days were spent patrolling to the east of the battalion area, trying to survive the onslaught from the Argentine air force. An order passed its way down, small arms fire was no longer to be used against enemy aircraft, as it was felt that this was a complete waste of ammunition. I am not sure what they expected us to do during air raids, just sit around and make a cup of tea probably, but for the most part the order was ignored and small arms fire continued. Ron and I were the obvious exception to this disobedience as we were still working to Ron's agenda of expending all of our ammunition against the enemy, should they show their faces, followed by the absolutely brilliant – don't know why I didn't think of it myself – bayonet suicide rush.

Sleeping in the trench one day, I was woken by a huge explosion. Startled and feeling a little dazed and confused, I quickly scrambled out of the sleeping bay area and into the main part of the trench. Ron was already there, admiring a huge air fight taking place overhead. He pointed to the air fight overhead and then to great plumes of smoke that surged into the sky from where the fleet was located in the Falkland Sound. The Argentines were hitting the fleet with everything they had.

"Why didn't you wake me?" I asked.

"No need", said Ron, "There's nothing we can do and you needed the rest. If you had been needed I'd have woken you."

I could see he was being sincere and that he had my best interests at heart. Ron, I concluded, was a nice man, however crazy.

During a night patrol to clear the ground to the east of our trenches at Windy Gap, our section came across an old farmhouse with several outbuildings and sheep pens. Cpl Milne laid the section up short of the buildings and we spent time observing the area. No movement or enemy troops could be seen so Cpl Milne decided it was time to take a closer inspection of the farm area. Myself and another lad were given the job of taking out one of the small outbuildings farthest from the farmhouse. Memories of the 'garrotte squad' lessons on Canberra came flooding back. We were to get as close as possible to the outbuilding undetected and, if enemy forces were inside the building, I was to release my grenades inside, then follow my 'oppo' in and neutralise any foe. My heart pounded as the section crawled nearer and nearer to the barn. My mind was focused on the task at hand and not on the ultimate consequence. At the last minute Cpl Milne decided the barn was uninhabited and cancelled the final assault. I felt relieved but untested and wondered what the outcome would have been had the assault gone ahead and the barn been occupied. After another period of observation and listening we all nervously entered the barn. No one was inside. The low wooden building had been used to house sheep and I was amazed at how warm it felt being inside, sheltered from the ice-cold wind. The barn provided an excellent observation post for the rest of the farm buildings and it was soon obvious that the whole place had been abandoned. Cpl Milne told the section to get a hot drink, after which we would be leaving to return to the company position back at Port San Carlos.

On the return journey we could hear the distinctive sound of several double-rotor Chinook helicopters flying overhead. The radio net informed us these were not friendly forces. Earlier that day in a television broadcast, a journalist had informed the British public how 2 Para were poised ready to take Goose Green the following day. The Argentines promptly took action and were flying in additional troops. I hated the journalist who had betrayed 2 Para, and wished he could be made to pick up a weapon and face the same fate that awaited our comrades in our sister battalion.

We stayed at Port San Carlos until Thursday, 27th May, when we received orders to tab to Teal Inlet, a settlement some thirty-odd miles away. We learned from that day's intelligence briefing that the Atlantic Conveyor, a cargo ship carrying all manner of supplies, including our issue of Arctic boots and winter clothing, had been sunk. The ship had also been laden with Chinook helicopters, a vital part of the battle plan to leapfrog the troops forward quickly to capture large chunks of no-man's land. With no Chinooks at our disposal we had no choice but to tab to our destination.

"If the Para Reg remains true to form we'll probably end up tabbing all the way to Port Stanley!" said Sgt McKay.

My heart sank like the Atlantic Conveyor. Port Stanley was over eighty miles away.

B Company would lead the battalion advance to Teal Inlet,

which was occupied by Argentine troops. Sgt. McKay informed the platoon that we would be tabbing in light order. Our bergens would be air lifted to us once Teal Inlet had been secured. This posed a serious problem. The Falklands is a cold and wet place with a wind chill factor of up to minus 20 degrees. Our bergens contained all the essential items of spare clothing a soldier needed to stay warm and dry. With a thirty-mile tab ahead of us no one wanted to put on too much clothing as the body would soon be perspiring making the clothes wet and uncomfortable. However, each time we stopped the wind would rapidly cool the body down and exposure could set in. Saying goodbye to my doss bag, as I stowed it away in my bergen, was a painful experience. Without my trusted green maggot and all the other items of spare clothing, a warm night's rest was going to be a thing of the past.

We set off for Teal Inlet at around 1430 hrs. At the same time, 45 Commando were leaving for their destination, a settlement to the north called Douglas. The Commandos had decided to take all their equipment with them and as they marched off or 'yomped' as they called it, a few of them moaned about the kit they were carrying. As I came level with him, one Marine asked me what our destination was. In true Para fashion I simply stared through him thinking, bloody hat, should have been listening at his briefing. I ignored him totally and moved off.

Personally, I would have been happier to have my sleeping bag with me but the powers-that-be had decreed we were to leave all unnecessary weight behind. The initial pace was furious and the Marines, laden like Sherpas about to undertake an ascent of Everest, were soon left behind. As I looked back over the ground that we had covered I could see the battalion stretched out as far as the eye could see, in single-file formation, making the shape of a large letter S over the ground. This was known as the battalion snake, which could be extremely demoralising if you were one of the lads at the back. Each time you looked up, all you could see were countless bodies in front of you for miles, like signposts informing you of the ground still to be covered. Being at the front had the total opposite effect. Not only had you already covered the ground, which gave you a sense of achievement, but you also had the advantage of knowing the sheer force behind you, should you encounter the enemy.

The barren terrain made the initial pace of the tab almost impossible to maintain and after about an hour and a half the pace slowed a little. The journey took us up hills, down hills, through knee-high streams and over boggy marshland. Trousers, boots, puttees and socks were soaking wet and the lads were soon complaining of blisters and sore feet. Every hour we would stop for a fifteen-minute break and Ron would immediately be on my case to take my socks off, wring them out and swap them over from foot to foot. At the time I hated it and wished Ron would leave me alone. All I wanted to do was rest my aching limbs and loosen my equipment but Ron was very persuasive. Begrudgingly, I would remove each boot, cursing him under my breath, and do as he had said, taking a little time to massage each foot to help my blood circulate. The result was amazingly uplifting and I would feel a thousand times better. Ron was right, of course, but a pain in the arse nevertheless. Not that I ever told him.

The tab went on and on for hours, as did the incessant rain. At certain stages of the march we would find ourselves in double-file formation and, as darkness crept in, I looked over to my right and saw 5 Platoon coming up alongside us. My hopes were raised that I would see Stu and have a brief moment of morale-boosting chatter. I kept a sharp eye out but was struggling to identify him through the rain when all of a sudden an image appeared. The soldier was hunched over, face lowered, shielding from the wind and rain. He had his Arctic hat on his head, ear flaps down. Previously when we had been issued the Arctic hat we had all laughed and scoffed at it – a piece of true 'hat' equipment. The Arctic hat was made of camouflage material, quilted with woollen flaps that pulled down over the ears and secured underneath the chin. From a soldier's point of view hearing is essential to be alert to unusual noise in the field. Obviously if a soldier has his ears covered he cannot hear and this places him and others at risk. I was shocked to see Stu's flaps down. As he came next to me I murmured, "How you doing, mate?"

Stu looked over in my direction and said, "F-this – I've had enough."

I didn't know what to say to him. Yes, the tab had been arduous. Yes, the wind and the rain meant we were continuously soaking wet. Yes, the terrain had been difficult. Yes, the streams had been freezing and yes, my feet were killing me but we were Para Regiment and these things never bothered us, did they? Stu tabbed off as 5 Platoon took over the lead and I was left to my thoughts. I hadn't previously thought that much about the tab. We had been briefed to tab thirty miles to Teal Inlet and I had simply resigned myself to it. Also being a 'crow' there wasn't really a lot I could say. Not that anyone would have listened to me if I had anyway. Seeing Stu so hacked off and hearing him voice an opinion, now gave me one. To be honest I could have done without it. The human brain is an amazing thing and when allowed to think for itself will do so. All of a sudden I was aware of my surroundings and became instantly hacked off. The wind and rain ripped at my face like grains of rice, leaving my skin sore and unprotected. My webbing dug into my hips and back and became extremely uncomfortable. My feet were killing me. I was suddenly aware just how wet I was. My feet squelched with every step I took and my boots rubbed through soaking wet socks against my skin, which was now soft due to being constantly immersed in water. I was cold, chilled to the bone. I had chosen to wear a sweat-top underneath my Para smock for the tab. Up till then I had been fine but suddenly I realised I was freezing. My smock provided no resistance to the wind and rain; my sweat-top was soaking wet and I could feel the water running down my chest to my midriff. Suddenly, my situation became unbearable but there was nothing I could do. The tab continued for several more hours.

Eventually we came to a halt in a bog, ankle-deep in water at the junction of wire fences. This doesn't sound an awful lot but in the Falklands the landscape is so barren such things are marked on the map. As we crouched down on our haunches we received the order to change into our warm clothing and rest for a couple of hours.

Where the hell we were meant to keep warm clothing I will never know. Every pouch of my webbing was crammed with ammunition, water or food and the bergens containing our warm clothing were still at Port San Carlos. Nevertheless, the order came. I looked around for a dry patch to sit on but there wasn't one. The water was above the grass and above my boots. I took off my webbing and laid it in the water to sit on and closed my eyes to wish away two hours of my life. Ron was immediately on me. "Take off your boots, laddie," he said. "Swap your socks over."

I could have burst into tears in desperation, my morale was rock bottom, my body ached all over and my feet were killing me.

"Yeah, I will, Ron. Just give me five minutes," I whinged.

"Do it now laddie!" he barked. I wanted to shoot him. My fingers were dropping off and as I removed my wet gloves to undo my puttees and bootlaces, my hands were physically shaking.

What is the point? I thought. I'm going to take these boots off, wring out my socks, put my boots back on and place them back in ankle-deep water! Still, who am I to argue with the mad Scotsman? So I did as Ron had said. As I removed the first sock I could see the extent of the damage to my foot. The complete sole of my foot was white, rather like your fingers get if you have stayed in a bath too long, but this was much, much worse. Where the skin on the sole had absorbed so much water it had swollen to several times its usual thickness. My whole foot looked abnormal. I cupped my hands around the foot to try and put some warmth back into it. I felt absolutely nothing. Ron noticed what I was doing and came over to me. He took one look at my foot and undid his Arctic windproof smock.

"Place your foot under my armpit," he said.

Not wishing to receive the sharp end of Ron's tongue again, I did as he said. After a few minutes I could feel the heat from under Ron's arm going into my foot. Initially it was a tingling sensation, but this soon gave way to a sharp pain as the senses returned to my foot.

"Swap the feet over," said Ron.

I quickly placed my boot back on and removed the other. That foot too was placed under Ron's armpit. For that brief moment the senses returned to both my feet and I felt better. The relief was short-lived as my feet were required back on the ground in the freezing cold, ankle-deep water. We had been tabbing for approximately fifteen hours, my body and mind were exhausted.

At first light the order was given to set off again. As I lifted my webbing from the ground water poured out of every pouch, increasing its overall weight. I clumsily tried to put my shoulders through the straps and got myself all caught up. Everything had shrunk. Annoyed, soaking wet, cold and frustrated, I ripped the webbing from my back and threw it on the floor thinking, if this is soldiering in the twentieth century you can stick it. The line started to move off leaving me behind. Ron looked over at me like a parent sometimes does when their child has just thrown a tantrum for no apparent reason. With numb fingers, I resentfully adjusted and loosened the shoulder straps and belt to their maximum lengths and threw the water-filled canvas webbing over my shoulders and on to my back. Taking my place in line I resigned myself once more to a long hard slog. Ron nodded approvingly.

For hours and hours we continued to tab. Uphill, downhill,

again through bogs and marshland. My feet were in a complete mess by now. I looked like an old man, bent double and hobbling. We eventually came to a wide, waist-deep river. Once across we were told we had made good progress and were ahead of schedule. We would rest by the side of the river for three hours or so. It was now approximately 1500 hrs, some 24 hours since we had left Port San Carlos. As I lay, soaking wet through, on the damp grass by the side of the river I tried to think of home and some of the comforts I was missing. I couldn't visualise it. All that stayed in my mind was how cold and wet I was. My body shivered. My hip bones ached, not from the webbing rubbing against them throughout the tab, but ached from the cold, which was now deep in my bones. The pain kept me awake throughout the two hours we stayed there.

We moved off earlier than expected to catch the last of the daylight. It was still some eight miles to Teal Inlet. The plan now was to get there quickly and set up an ambush just outside the settlement. After another mind-blowing, back breaking slog at a quicker place, we were soon ready to take up our positions in the ambush area. There we lay for hours…waiting. The rain had stopped to be replaced by freezing cold temperatures. Frost lay all around and then, without warning, it snowed. B Company's OC Major Mike Argue, eventually decided to enter the settlement and, with 4 Platoon as his back-up, he went up to the biggest house in the settlement, which incidentally doubled as the pub, and simply knocked on the front door. We, in a huddled mass, stood behind him weapons at the ready. A woman cautiously opened the door and peering out enquired who was there.

"Major Mike Argue, B Company, 3rd Battalion Parachute Regiment," he said in his best official-sounding voice.

"There's no one here," came the reply and she tried to close the door.

"No, you don't understand," he said. "We're from Her Majesty's Forces. British Army, we've come to liberate you!" he stuttered.

"Oh, in that case then you'd better come in."

The door opened and Major Argue entered followed by the whole of 4 Platoon. We were shown into a large front room that had a huge table at one end. At the other, armchairs were arranged around the large, open fire, which provided the chief source of light for the room. My eyes were drawn to the fire and for a few moments I stared blankly into it enjoying the patterns of the flames and the warmth they gave out. It reminded me of my father's pub and the inglenook fire he would light every night prior to opening for the evening session. For a brief moment I was back there, warm, safe and without a care. My back rested against one of the front room walls by the door way and my feet took root. I wanted to become part of the furniture, unnoticed, left alone. I knew that in a short while we would be ordered outside to dig defensive positions in the snow until a decision was taken as to where the battalion would head for next. But for now I was inside, near a fire and staying put.

Major Argue and the NCOs spoke with the family who told them the Argentines had left the settlement some hours before, taking several of the islanders' Land Rovers with them. The lady who had originally opened the door explained that on hearing the knock, she had thought the Argentines had returned and had not wanted to converse with them. She apologised for her actions and seemed genuinely embarrassed. To rectify the situation, she quickly set about making pots of tea, which she brought out accompanied by the biggest selection of home made cakes I have ever seen. At first I didn't want to take a cake or a cup of tea, fearing that this would bring attention to myself and result in my early departure from the house but as time went on and she passed me through the door way for the umpteenth time my resistance caved in. The brew was strong, sweet and hot, and the cake surprisingly filling. Her smile, hospitality and compassion were weakening. I suddenly forgot all about my hardships and the long hard tab we had endured to get here. I wanted to live the moment and stay in these surroundings. She rearranged the furniture and beckoned a few of us over to the fire. The lady told us to remove our wet clothing and boots and dry ourselves as best we could. She then left and reappeared with an armful of towels. Not giving a second thought to the rest of the battalion, who had by now been ordered to dig trenches around the settlement, I stripped and dried myself in front of the fire. The hours passed and it became obvious that Major Argue was going to allow us to stay in the house until first light. My clothing, boots and equipment were by now spread out around the fire drying and I, unashamedly, dozed off.

Just before first light, Major Argue told everyone in the house to dress and take up defensive positions outside. Slowly and despondently we started to get ready. My boots were now rock hard from being force dried by the fire and my feet had swollen to several times their normal size. At first I couldn't get my feet into my boots and began to panic, fearing chastisement from the NCOs. Others were having similar problems and some, no matter how hard they tried, couldn't get their boots on. After several attempts and much manipulation I managed to cram each foot into its respective boot. Walking was now impossible.

4 Platoon formed en mass outside the house and waited to be informed of where to take up our defensive positions. Major Argue came out and discharged a barrage of abuse. Some of 4 Platoon would have to remain behind in the house as they had been unable to put their boots back on. He told us to get a grip and reminded us that we had a job to do. My feet were in agony and I was concerned that this would be seen as a weakness. So, ignoring the pain, I followed Ron to the spot where our trench was to be positioned. After clearing the snow we set about digging the trench. The ground was solid and the digging back breaking.

That evening, trench by trench, we could go to the house, get a cup of tea and warm ourselves in front of the fire. As our turn came, Ron declined the offer preferring to stay in the trench. I accompanied Tony Evans the Section 2 I/C. The front room was filled with people I didn't recognise. Ignoring them, we pushed our way to the front, by the fire. There we sat staring into the flames. After a short while four lads came into the room dressed in black. Their equipment was also black and they had ropes draped over their shoulders.

"SBS," whispered Tony.

I looked over and was amazed at how small and young one of them looked. The others seemed to fuss over him ensuring that he got a spot next to the fire and helping him to remove his heavy equipment.

"He's a youngster?" enquired Tony to one of the older lads.

"Yeah, just nineteen. We call him Titch, but he's a good 'un," he replied.

I stared in disbelief. A nineteen-year-old in the Special Forces? How could he cope? The SAS would never consider one so young. Ironically, I never thought of my own age, just seventeen, or how young I appeared to others. Tony and I stayed in the house all night chatting with the SBS lads and left prior to stand-to at first light. Other than Ron, no one was any the wiser.

After stand-to Major Argue got the company together in front of the house and went off on one again. He said we looked liked a dejected rabble and that he was appalled at the numbers of lads who had dropped out from the tabbing due to foot complaints. It was time to 'Wake up and smell the coffee' and get on with the job in hand. He had received orders that we were now to tab to Estancia some twenty to thirty miles away and he wanted everyone at their best for the march. The lads were more interested in the fact that someone might be brewing coffee than anything else the Major had to say. To be honest, he probably should have chosen a better phrase because from the moment he mentioned coffee everyone's mind was elsewhere.

"Get your kit packed and get a f-ing grip, you're members of the Parachute Regiment and this is what we do!" he concluded.

As the company disbanded, mumbles of "Where's the coffee?" and "Who's got the coffee then?" could be heard. Major Argue was not impressed.

News of 2 Para's success at Goose Green filtered through to

us. Initially we were euphoric – ecstatic that a battalion from the Regiment had achieved so much against such over-whelming odds and that Regimental pride and tradition had been upheld. Soon though details of the fifteen losses, thirty-seven casualties and the fatality of Lieutenant Colonel 'H' Jones came through. Stories of 2 Para lads being shot while advancing to secure enemy positions flying white flags of surrender enraged us. I hated all journalists, blaming them wholeheartedly for the additional Argentine troops that had been flown in and wondered whether our battalion would suffer a similar fate due to a journalist seeking fame and fortune for himself. Sod the Press, sod the news-hungry British public sitting at home warm and dry ignorant of the sacrifices being made and the daily threat we experienced. The war was now personal. We were here, alive and surviving and that was all that mattered. No one else did.

Jas was not going to be coming with us to Estancia. His feet were in a complete mess. Trench foot, immersion-foot and frostbite were all mentioned. When I went over to see him he looked in agony and I felt for him. Jas, as was his way, put on a brave face and joked, "Well at least I'll get a lift." It turned out that Mortar Platoon had commandeered a tractor with a trailer, on which to load their exceptionally heavy base plates and mortar tubes and Jas would be going along for the ride. Lucky bastard, I thought and bade him farewell for now.

The battalion snake was awoken and as we set off from Teal Inlet one of the locals stood at the edge of the settlement and shook everyone's hand as they passed him. He said a few words of appreciation and encouragement to each individual, thanking me personally for what I was doing and wishing me good luck for the future. Believing the islanders wanted our intervention and assistance gave me a good feeling. It convinced me at the time that what we were doing was correct and right, however painful. The feeling was short-lived and evaporated after a few more miles of tabbing leaving me again with the harsh reality of battling against the hostile weather and unforgiving terrain.

The tab was similar. Bog-like marshes that clung to your boots not wanting to release them and long tufts of grass that would collapse to one side when your body weight was transferred to that foot. The grass was painful to walk on twisting the ankles in all kinds of awkward positions and, however you tried to estimate the way the grass would tilt, it always seemed to do something totally unpredicted. Occasionally we would be treated to the odd pothole or puddle and at one point Ron disappeared up to his chest. All that could be heard was a loud "Yippee!" as Ron entered the freezing cold water. The rest of us couldn't believe his attitude and burst into laughter. Ron was unfazed. He simply climbed out, shook himself off and carried on. Ron was an inspiration to us all, but definitely mad.

Every now and then we would come across what we called 'rivers of stone', large rocks and boulders that spread across the route for what seemed miles. There was no way around these 'rivers', you simply had to cross them. The huge grey rocks and boulders made the tufts of grass experience seem like walking across a bowling green. Crossing the rivers of stone could sometimes take an hour and my feet and ankles ached with every demoralising step. Total concentration was required on each step and when eventually you looked up to view the route ahead, progress never appeared to have been made. I placed these rivers of stone just below the journalists on my most hated list.

At midnight we stopped and 'bashered up' for the night. Mount Kent was to our front where the SAS along with 42 Commando would be dealing with any hostile forces in situ. We were told to minimise unnecessary movement, as we were now within range of the enemy's artillery. The advice was welcomed because, with the exception of a two-hour break just before last light, the battalion had been continuously tabbing since leaving Teal Inlet. Everyone was exhausted and tempers were short, as were our rations. We stayed there until the following afternoon without our bergens and the warm kit that would have made the stay more bearable. At around 1600 hrs we set off for Estancia. The SAS and 42 Commando did secure Mount Kent, experiencing little resistance as the majority of Argentines had been transferred to Goose Green some days earlier. We, the pack animals of the British Forces, continued to tab, 'march-or-die' style towards the settlement of Estancia which could just about be made out, far away on the horizon. We moved into the settlement during the early hours of the morning and sought refuge in one of the large outbuildings. The rest of the battalion joined us some hours later. Finally, helicopters brought in the bergens and everyone set about changing their clothing and socks, and getting a much-needed hot meal. One of the locals hung up a raw sheep's carcass and within seconds the lads had helped themselves to it. Nothing was left. The RSM went berserk and everyone was reminded that although they were fighting a campaign, discipline was to be maintained at all times.

The Battalion Medical Officer set up shop in the main house and started to inspect the feet of the troops, half a dozen or so at a time. I was sceptical about seeing him, fearing that he would say that my feet were in too bad a condition for me to continue. So I stayed, hidden from view, in the outbuilding. After a while the medical staff realised that many of the lads were hiding and so they and the MO came over to the outbuilding. We were all ordered to remove our boots and socks so each soldier could be inspected. When the MO saw my feet he confirmed my fears.

"Your feet are in a bad way, you need to rest up so they can repair," he said.

I was gutted. I had tabbed all that way without interference from anyone and now, suddenly, someone had decided I was unfit to continue. I felt I had let everyone in the platoon down and would be branded 'a waste of rations'.

B Company was ordered to set up their positions on the slopes of Mount Estancia. Along with several others, I had to remain in the settlement until my feet had repaired. Watching the lads set off up the hill, I wished I was with them. As they disappeared from view the Battalion Quartermaster started shouting at me, "What the 'f' are you doing standing around? Get yourself cleaned up and shaved!"

I looked at him and wanted to tell him to go 'f' himself but obviously couldn't. He ignored my insolent glare and turned his attention to some other lads standing over by the newly-created latrine.

I retreated to the outbuilding thinking he was a complete prat. The hierarchy were making their presence felt, not giving a thought to the hard endeavours of the troops. I was in no mood to be lectured by some REMF, rear-echelon mother f-ker who had probably been enjoying a tour of the Falklands by helicopter, or worse still, he may even have had his own Land Rover. Either way I felt he hadn't endured the same hard slog I had. I returned to my bergen and sleeping space to find someone had placed a blue British Forces Post Office letter on my sleeping bag. I had intended to pack my kit and join my platoon on the mountain, leaving the Quartermaster and the RSM to their own devices, but a letter from home was just the escape I needed.

I immediately sat down and opened it. The letter was from my fiancée Laura, telling me what had been happening at home, how she was involved in saving a children's play-group from closure. The group was struggling to make ends meet and she and her friends had organised a sponsored walk to raise funds. She had even enclosed the front-page cover from the local paper with a photograph of a variety of women, all dressed in Saint Trinian's uniforms, complete with short pleated hockey skirts, stockings and suspenders, carrying buckets with official-looking notices saying, "Save our Playgroup". Laura was in the centre of the photograph displaying her wares. Surrounding the women was a large crowd of men and boys, mouths agape enjoying the moment. I looked up and surveyed my own surroundings. Men in various stages of dress and health hobbled in front of me trying to put on brave faces and mask their discomfort. The wind-driven rain pounded against the tin sides of the outbuilding and leaked through its roof. The ground to the front entrance had turned into a quagmire through overuse and, like most of the surrounding area, resembled a scene from the First World War trenches. I looked back at the photograph, at the happy smiling faces. People of my age and older who hadn't a care in the world other than raising a few bob for a playgroup that was probably a complete waste of time, run by unqualified hands with nothing better to do than help Johnny with his potty training. I cursed Laura for her ignorance of my situation and cursed the blokes in the photo, wishing I could wipe the smile from each of their faces. Packing my kit I went over to the medic and informed him that I would be making my way up the mountain to join my Platoon.

"Any chance of a lift by tractor?" I asked.

"No chance. If you want to go up there you will have to walk!"

The lads' bergens had been taken up the hill by tractor. I, on the other hand, would have to carry mine if I wished to restore some personal pride and join them. Screwing up the letter and photograph, I walked over to the latrine and dropped them both unceremoniously into it, then started the long hard climb up the slopes of Mount Estancia.

The mountain seemed to go on forever, the slopes appeared vertical. Within fifteen minutes I was soaking wet-through, thanks to a combination of the weather and perspiration. The heavy and cumbersome bergen made the climb even harder. My temper grew shorter with each step. My feet were killing me once again and, as I looked back towards the settlement, I cursed the medic's nonchalant attitude and my own stupidity for attempting the climb in my condition. An hour and a half later I reached the summit of Mount Estancia, a thousand feet above sea level. As I trudged off towards the platoon position,

Grose appeared in front of me, happy and smiling. "You're in a state Tom," he said. "What's up?"

I glared at him unable to catch my breath. He came over to me to assist with my bergen.

"Leave me alone, Grose – I'm not in the mood!" I snapped.

Grose looked at me and I felt guilty for shooting the messenger. "Sorry, but that was one hell of a climb and I'm goosed," I said.

"That's all right, mate, your section is over there. Come on I'll show you."

I followed Grose to the spot where our section was bashered and apologised for ripping his head off.

"You're okay, Tom, you can buy me something special for my birthday next week – coming to my party?" he asked.

I looked at him and laughed. There we were in the middle of nowhere, on top of a mountain, soaking wet-through and exhausted, joking about his eighteenth birthday party.

"Wouldn't miss it for the world," I said and Grose left with a huge smile on his face.

My section had found a disused peat pit to set up their bashers. The high wall of the pit provided excellent cover from the wind and, as I approached, Jas called out, "Over here, Tom".

I made my way over to the spot Jas had set up his basher. En route, Cpl Milne asked me how I was doing and I quickly relayed the story of the Quartermaster and RSM to him. "You're better off up here with us away from all that bullshit", he said. "Get your basher set up and get in your doss bag. We could be here a while". Ron bid me a warm welcome and seemed to respect my decision to be with the platoon at the front line. Ron also appreciated the climb I had made with the bergen and enquired about my feet.

"Oh, they're okay," I said.

Ron knew I was lying and gave me a drink of his whisky. How Ron managed to get regular supplies of whisky I will never know, but in the two weeks we had been on the island, Ron's hip flask had never run out. Ron had whisky with everything: tea, porridge, stew, fruit salad, biscuits. Nothing passed his lips without having been flavoured by some of the best double malts Scotland had to offer. I often wondered how better our re-supply would have been if Ron had been in charge. Or, if the Atlantic Conveyor had been carrying a supply of Ron's whisky, whether the Argentines would have got anywhere near the ship.

Rumours abounded of an attack on Mount Longdon, which lay four miles west of the capital, Port Stanley. The height advantage from the castellated summit of Longdon meant any attack on Stanley would be vulnerable from the rear, unless the mountain was taken. No one was sure when the attack would happen but we knew it was coming. D Company had already undertaken several recces of the mountain, gleaning intelligence of the Argentine positions, numbers and weapons. These probing patrols had been supported by members of the Mortar, Anti-Tank and Machine Gun Platoons. Within the first few days of arriving on Mount Estancia, the battalion set off to assault Mount Longdon, only for Brigadier Julian Thompson, Commander of 3 Brigade, to fly in personally by helicopter and stop the advancement. A rumour circulated that the Brigadier was extremely upset with our CO, Lieutenant Colonel Hew Pike for advancing under his own steam. The Brigadier apparently wanted a brigade assault comprising of several units with several objectives being hit at the same time. The problem was no other unit involved in the brigade assault plan was battle-ready or was as far forward as we were. Our CO didn't want to wait for the 'hats' and was keen to get on with the task but Brigadier Thompson was having none of it and halted the advance there and then. So we trotted back to our positions on the forward slopes of Mount Estancia and waited for the 'hats' to catch up.

To pass the time waiting for the 'hats' we undertook daytime patrols and, at one point, 4 Platoon found ourselves at Murrell Bridge. After setting up a temporary defensive position, the platoon relaxed to enjoy an unusual bout of dry weather and observe the area to our front. We could see Two Sisters Mountain to our right, probably less than a kilometre away, and in front of us the start of a man-made road that ran for about ten miles into Port Stanley. It felt good to have advanced so close to the capital. At this rate of advancement, the end of the campaign was in sight. During the early after-noon a Scimitar tracked combat reconnaissance vehicle from the Blues and Royals accompanied us. Through the telescopic sights on our weapons, we watched Argentine soldiers queu-ing up for scoff on Two Sisters summit. They were out of range of our own mortars so we called in a fire mission only to be told the artillery were in the process of moving positions. There was little else we could do, so we sat enjoying the scenery when suddenly, the Blues and Royals' commander said, "I'll have a go with my gun. They're in range."

He gave the command and a salvo fired from the barrel on

his vehicle. Within seconds, we could see the Argies running for cover as shells exploded around them. We were all highly amused, pleased with the chaos we were inflicting. Minutes later the ground in front of our positions was ripped up with the response from their artillery. That well and truly wiped the smiles from our faces. The Blues and Royals commander decided the engagement wasn't for him, firmly battened down the hatch on his vehicle and retreated, with much haste, towards the safety of Estancia. We foot soldiers were left shell-shocked and wondering what to do next. Lt Bickerdike gave the order to 'bug out'. In a flash our kit was packed and we were ready to go. I watched Scrivs and one or two others in a small cluster of rocks to our left scrambling to collect together kit they had left out airing while shells landed all around them. Although later we all laughed about it, we were extremely lucky not to have sustained any casualties.

On 11th June, we learned the Battalion would be attacking Mount Longdon that night. Earlier in the morning Scrivs, Jas and I went over to Grose's basher to wish him a happy eighteenth birthday. We all shared a brew together and agreed that his party would have to be postponed until after the attack on Longdon. Grose found the whole thing highly amusing and was in a great mood. It was undoubtedly the best day he'd had since being on the island. It was great for us all to be together. Although we were in the same platoon we were in different sections and because of the tabbing and the tactical operations we had been unable to communicate. In fact, it was probably the first time we had managed to get together since leaving the Canberra. We all relayed our stories of the 'march from hell'. With the exception of Jas, whose feet had been in a complete mess at Teal Inlet, everyone had tabbed the total distance. We had all done extremely well, proving our fitness and determination. We were all proud of our achievements to date but wondered how we would fare in the heat of battle.

That afternoon Cpl Milne handed out BFPO letters for everyone to write home. I decided not to as I had only recently written home. I was also concerned that with the battle pending, I might write something that would worry Mum. Writing to Dad didn't cross my mind. I handed Jas my BFPO and he wrote a second letter home. We spent the rest of our time cleaning weapons, checking equipment and talking about the long leave we'd be entitled to when we returned home. We also discussed how we were going to spend the money that had been accumulating in our bank accounts while we had been away.

The CO gathered his company commanders together and issued them with the Battalion Battle Plan, which trickled down the ranks until Cpl Milne informed us. We all listened intently as he went over the Battalion Battle Plan, the company's mission and the platoon's objective.

A Company would advance, on the left of B Company, to the north of Mount Longdon, clearing the ground until it could occupy a spur of high ground there. The high ground had been given the code name 'Wing Forward'. Once completed, they would be able to further advance to Wireless Ridge.

B Company would assault Mount Longdon towards its summit. The summit had been given the code name 'Fly Half'. We would then continue along the ridge to the second peak, on the leading edge of Mount Longdon, facing Port

Stanley. This second peak had been given the code name 'Full Back'.

C Company would be held in reserve and deployed as deemed appropriate – code named by the blokes in B Company 'Lucky Bastards'.

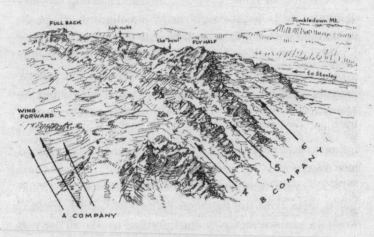

Mount Longdon: The initial battle plan. (Graham Colbeck)

The Company's Mission: To secure 'Fly Half' and 'Full Back'.

4 Platoon would advance through the clear ground along the northern edge of Mount Longdon to a central area, where we would move south to the halfway point known as 'Fly Half'. There we'd join forces with 5 Platoon and continue the advance towards 'Full Back'.

5 Platoon would advance up Mount Longdon's central ridge to 'Fly Half', join forces with 4 Platoon and advance towards 'Full Back'.

6 Platoon would advance towards the summit of Mount Longdon and secure 'Fly Half'. Once secured, they would hand-over to 4 and 5 Platoons who would continue the advance towards 'Full Back'.

4 Platoon's Objectives:

To clear the ground on the northern slopes of Mount Longdon and join forces with 5 Platoon at 'Fly Half'.

To secure 'Full Back'.

To aid the element of surprise, the attack would be silent, which meant that prior to ground troops going in Argentine positions would not be bombarded by our artillery or Royal Navy gunfire. It was anticipated there would be approximately one battalion of Argentinians – about 800 men – in situ. Their morale was expected to be low and their resistance weak.

In the early evening, just before setting off for the start line, code name 'Free Kick', Major Argue called us all together. Standing at the top of Mount Estancia he pointed towards Mount Longdon and said, "That's where we will be this evening." Then, pointing towards Port Stanley, added, "And that gentlemen, is where we are ultimately going."

We all peered into the distance to Mount Longdon. To me it looked like any other mountain, huge, grey and unwelcoming. I wondered what secrets it held. To its left I could just make out Stanley and beyond, the sea that led to home. Switching my focus back to Longdon I reminded myself to take one step at a time and not be distracted by thoughts of a homeward journey. Major Argue continued, informing us of the attachments that would be supporting us throughout the assault. From within the battalion, there'd be support from the Mortar Platoon, the Milan detachments of the Anti-Tank Platoon, the GPMGs of Machine Gun Platoon in the SF – sustain fire – role plus snipers from Patrol Company. Externally we would have support from the Royal Artillery and naval gunships. Casualties would be cas-evaced immediately, taken by helicopter to the hospital ship SS Uganda – a journey time of less than twenty minutes.

Major Argue assured us that, from briefings and intelligence gleaned from D Company's recce patrols, there were no land mines on Mount Longdon. I looked around at B Company, formed in a circle around the OC, and could see Stu with the boys from 5 Platoon. I wondered what he was thinking. Turning back, I caught the OC's last words, "And may your God go with you."

I stared at Major Argue for a moment in disbelief as the lads drifted back to their positions to kit up. What the hell did he say that for? I wondered. His intelligence reports were telling him a slightly different story to ours. He must know people are going to die tonight, I concluded. I looked past the OC to Longdon once more and thought, "This is serious shit".

As I turned to leave I caught Baz Barrett's eye. We just stared each other, raised our eyebrows simultaneously and both gave a puzzled expression. I wanted to say, "What the f- is happening here?" or "Jesus, I wish I was back in Juniors – having a laugh," but it wasn't the time. Instead, I turned away and while walking back to my basher said a prayer for all of us.

For me the Sermon on the Mount was over.

CHAPTER EIGHT

Ruth

Ruth and Naomi

We were soon on our way towards the start line and our objective, Mount Longdon. The intention was to complete the eight to ten mile tab within three hours, crossing the start line, code name Free Kick, at around 2200hrs on the 11th June 1982. This supposedly 'leisurely' pace was to assist the support platoons, who were required to manhandle their heavy equipment, like Milans, mortar tubes, base plates, machine guns and tripods, from Mount Estancia to their positions on the flanks of Mount Longdon.

Once again the tab was hard going and, in those initial stages, Mount Longdon never seemed to get any closer, always looming in the distance. When we eventually got off the forward slopes of Mount Estancia and on to the lower levels, Longdon looked daunting against the skyline. Although not as high as Mount Estancia, it appeared to go on for ever and I became concerned I would never get to see its forward slopes. As darkness fell, I wondered if I would die that night. Would my death be quick and painless? If not, would I be able to cope with my inevitable drawn-out fate. I hated being in this position, faced with the thought of dying before my eighteenth birthday, the fact I wasn't officially old enough to sign-on with the Army, and might never get the chance to. I hated the fact that I wasn't even old enough to vote for the Government that had sent me miles from home to my possible death on foreign soil. I wasn't even old enough to see an X-rated film or to buy a drink in my local. I might never get the chance to marry or have children of my own. I felt sad for Mum and my sister Jo, and wondered how they would continue to live their lives on hearing the news of my death? Would they would fight to bring my body home, to rest in a place I had lived and loved, rather than leave me on this cruel island – a place I felt nothing but contempt and disdain for. 'The Soldier', Rupert Brooke's famous war sonnet didn't sit well with me. I hungered to make the journey home one way or another – dead or alive.

The Soldier

If I should die, think only this of me:
That there's some corner of a foreign field
That is forever England. There shall be
In that rich earth a richer dust concealed;
A dust whom England bore, shaped, made aware,
Gave, once, her flowers to love, her ways to roam,
A body of England's, breathing English air,
Washed by the rivers, blest by suns of home.

And think, this heart, all evil shed away,
A pulse in the eternal mind, no less
Gives somewhere back the thoughts by England given;
Her sights and sounds; dreams happy as her day;
And laughter, learnt of friends; and gentleness,
In hearts at peace, under an English heaven.

As my head raced, doubt set in. I realised I was thousands of miles from home and the people I loved, the people who had protected me as a child. I missed them terribly. For the very first time I felt 17 years young, not old, and extremely alone.

To get to the start line we had to cross a wide stream. The Royal Engineers had put a plank of wood over the stream to help us cross and then put a ladder on top of it, which created a massive bottleneck and caused a delay in reaching the start line. In the pitch darkness, it was hard to pick out the rungs of the ladder. Placing my feet between the rungs, the plank beneath bowed with the weight and became unsteady. If the Engineers had placed the plank on top of the ladder things would have been easier, but they hadn't, so B Company ground to a halt while everyone crossed the makeshift bridge. The delay only served to exacerbate the doubt running through my head.

Reaching the start line, on the other side of the stream, we immediately fanned out in an extended line. As I crouched there waiting for the other members of my section and platoon to join the formation – I knew this was it. There was no turning back now. Come what may, very soon all of my training, nerves, courage and determination would be put to the ulti-mate test. I looked up at Mount Longdon, now just a few hundred yards in front of me and wondered whether this would be my final resting-place. Through the darkness I could make out its rough outline and the highest peaks. I had a fairly good idea of the terrain between the start line and the moun-tain; prairie-type grass with the odd dip, waterholes and the occasional lonesome peat pit. Very much like the isolated areas in the highlands of Scotland. My whole body shook and although it was said to be more than minus ten at the time, I knew it was not due to the temperature. I tried to control my breathing as best I could but the anxiety I felt was too great. My heart pounded in my chest as I waited for the command to advance, which would put an end to my anguish.

Finally, everyone was crouched in position and the whispered order came to move forward over the start line, depicted by white mine tape placed there previously by one of D Company's recce patrols. I stood up slowly, rifle at the ready and moved forward. I could see men to my left and to my right advancing in a continuous straight line, not dissimilar to those seen in the battles of the First World War. It seemed ironic that, despite all our modern technology and sophisticated weaponry, in the end it all came down to men fighting each other, face to face, hand to hand, yard by yard.

The CO of 3 Para had decided that the mountain would not be bombarded prior to our attack, preferring to benefit from the element of surprise. This meant our Harrier jump jets, naval guns and the Royal Artillery had been left out of the battle preparations to ensure the Argentines did not anticipate a follow-up assault by foot soldiers. Now, as we slowly advanced, I couldn't help but wish the mountain had been bombed to hell for a couple of days prior to our attack. A huge crater would have been a far better sight than the dark, unwelcoming mountain range that loomed before me.

Soon the order came to break down into section formations. With Cpl Milne at the front on the right, we adopted a staggered file. Ron Duffy took up the front left position with Jas directly behind Cpl Milne. I followed Jas.

I can clearly see the moon on the horizon. The evening air is crisp, the night sky, unclouded. Away from artificial light and air pollution, the moon is sharp and bright, creating a brilliant aura around the mountain. A sudden explosion followed by screams of pain breaks the silence as Cpl Milne steps on an anti-personnel mine. Immediately machine gun tracer rounds rain down on us. Flares light up the sky. Spontaneously, I go to ground through instinct and training. Mount Longdon, previously cold, dark and still, has come alive.

The mountain and our initial objective 'Fly Half' are still some 100 yards away to my right. Our section, now compromised and out in the minefield, is vulnerable to the enemy gunfire, exposed like rabbits caught in a car's headlights.

Cpl Milne's screams are now muted. Instead, we hear the horrendous groans of a man in serious pain – shock is setting in. For a few brief seconds we lie there in the cold damp grass, doing nothing, taking stock of what is unfolding before us, knowing there to be land mines all around. The enemy continues to fire automatic weapons in our direction. It will only be a matter of time before they have us firmly fixed in their sights and we are annihilated. We must take action.

Still lying on the ground, Jas turned to me and said, "I'm going to Cpl Milne to inject his morphine."

Jas edged slowly towards to him. No one else moved, said or did anything, anticipating Jas to initiate a second explosion. Moments passed while the enemy continued to fire. Eventually I crawled forward to Jas. Cpl Milne was in severe shock.

"I've injected the morphine," said Jas, "but it doesn't seemed to ease any of his pain. I'm going to give him mine."

This may have seemed the correct and Christian thing to do but, as any infantry soldier knows, the single morphine syrette you wear around your neck, taped to the cord of your dog tags, is for personal use should you require it. The way things were unfolding it would be a very brave action at this early stage of the battle. Jas didn't see it that way and injected his morphine into Brian. Ron crawled over to us.

"I think he's lost the lower part of his leg," whispered Jas.

"Okay, don't tell anyone else what you have seen, lads," said Ron. "Bad for morale."

A decision is taken to leave Ron attending to Cpl Milne, while the rest of the section continue through the minefield towards the enemy gunfire. I survey the ground that I must cover, knowing there are land mines ahead. But as I slowly raise myself from the ground, I cannot move however hard I try. I tell myself time and time again to take a step forward but my legs ignore the order. I stay motionless contemplating the unthinkable. I pray to God to give me strength and take an initial stride but nothing happens. Then a thought enters my head. If I want to see Mum and Jo again I've got to move forward. Suddenly I do. Fearing that each step I take could lead to the loss of a lower limb or even death, my weapon visibly shakes in my hand. The lads behind shout at me to slow down. They are placing their feet in the footprints I've left on the frost-covered ground. Resentfully, I comply and my momentum is stifled for a brief moment. The enemy's accuracy increases as they fire down at us from a number of bunkers higher up the mountainside. In minutes it's a free-for-all as our section disperses, seeking cover from the onslaught.

The enemy fire is more intensive now that we have gone to

ground. I'm alone, lying flat on the slight up-slope trying to make myself invisible as the rounds from enemy guns zip through the air just above my head. There are no foxholes here. I look up and can make out the large dark boulders, pitch-black crags and light grey rock faces from where the enemy are firing. I can see other members of the section slightly ahead of me to my right, in what appears to be a disused peat pit, a far better place to seek safety than the open space I'm in. They are older, more experienced soldiers and I dare not presume I can join them. With the enemy fire continuing in my direction, they seem to appreciate my predicament and gesture towards me. Within seconds I am with them, unified, accepted, a comrade.

"What were you doing out there?" asks Geoff Logan. He was a tall, thickset lad, from the Bethnal Green area of east London. He was the platoon's machine gunner and carried the GPMG. He was also much older than me and had been in a lot longer. I think it was the first time he had ever spoken to me directly. His number two Taff – John Wynne-Jones – was with him.

"I didn't think there was room for me," I say, not wishing to tell him that I'm too afraid to ask whether I can join them. I was still a 'crow' after all.

Suddenly there's a huge explosion, followed by a great plume of white smoke, as a 66mm anti-tank missile rips into an enemy bunker. 5 Platoon is clearing the ground in front of them on their way to the rendezvous point at Fly Half. The enemy position falls silent and for a few brief seconds the barrage of gunfire is halted as the other enemy positions switch their attention to 5 Platoon.

We seize the opportunity and break-free from our cover and make it to the foot of the mountain to join the rest of our platoon. By now all hell has broken loose on the mountain above us. I see shadows and blurred images of 5 Platoon. For a moment I think of Stu and hope he is okay. Lt Bickerdike has re-organised the platoon and we start to make our way up the mountain to join 5 Platoon. Explosions and gunfire are going off in every direction. It is impossible to identify friend or foe. Dark, unidentifiable figures dart from rock to rock. It is only really possible to determine a definite enemy target when an image is firing at you or in your direction. In such instances it is acceptable to respond instantly with as much firepower as you can muster. The situation is further complicated by the occasional sky-lined or silhouetted shape. Everyone's instinct is to immediately take out the target but 5 Platoon are now advancing well into the enemy position and no one wishes to be responsible for shooting a colleague. Confusion adds to the anxiety. Men are shouting at each other, "Move left," or "Take out the bunker on the right!" Chaos reigns. Argentinians bark out counter orders, followed by bursts of automatic gunfire, tracer rounds and explosions, which light up the darkness.

Each round makes a 'zipping' sound as it cuts through the air on its deadly journey. As rounds bounce off the rocks, the smell of flint burning fills the air. Red tracer rounds acting as 'spotters' can be seen heading in one direction, ricocheting off something in their path, heading skywards or in a completely different direction, it all seems surreal. We all know each tracer round is closely followed by three more rounds, invisible but just as deadly. The sheer volume and speed of the automatic gunfire on the hillside means tracer rounds appear to have no gaps between them. The streams of red and green gunfire appear to be continuous. Dark crevices provide the enemy with a variety of hiding places. Areas that were cleared are soon reoccupied by enemy troops being fed from a maze of rat-runs. At one point, I thought we had been surrounded because I could hear gunfire, movement and foreign voices all around me.

Our advance came to a halt just before Fly Half. Waiting for the next order, Jas and I crouched down beside the body of a dead Argentine. He had been shot several times and obviously discarded from a position above us. From his profile it would appear that he had broken an arm and a leg, probably sustained in the fall down the mountainside. Feeling no remorse whatsoever, Jas and I sat on his corpse, our backs against the grey hard stone of the mountain and waited. As the moonlight increased we were able to see each other a little more clearly. There was a downside to this. We were also able to notice shadowy figures lurking and moving across the ground we were still to take.

Lt Bickerdike and Sgt McKay were in conference with Cpl Stewart 'Scouse' McLaughlin, who had led the bulk of 5 Platoon's assault on the ridge above us. From his position in the rocks on the higher ground, Cpl McLaughlin was informing our platoon commander and sergeant where the enemy positions were located. Every now and then a loud thumping sound could be heard, 'boom-boom, boom-boom'. Finally Sgt McKay came over and crouched down by me.

"What's that noise?" I asked.

"That's a .50 Cal., son," he said.

Being none the wiser I said nothing. Later I'd find out 50 Cal meant a .50 calibre anti-aircraft machine gun, a huge beast of a weapon designed not to kill soldiers, but to rip aircraft apart in mid-flight. The enemy had found a new purpose for the weapon. Us!

Lt. Bickerdike peered around the rock face leading towards the enemy's .50 Cal position, contemplating the platoon's next move. One of the lads shouted to him to take care he wasn't shot by one of the covering enemy positions.

"They won't shoot me I'm an Offi..." A round ripped into his leg, he spun round and collapsed on the ground.

"You were saying, sir?" someone shouted sarcastically.

There seemed little we could do to advance. It had become a stalemate. Sgt McKay decided to take a closer look at the area we were to cover and, in particular, the bunker housing the enemy's .50 Cal. Fixing his bayonet to his weapon and taking Cpl Ian Bailey, Private Roger James, Jas Burt, and one other, I beleive, he set off to recce the enemy positions. We could hear Sgt McKay talking to Scouse McLaughlin as the recce party crept towards the enemy bunker.

"There's two of them to your right and some others to the left," said Cpl McLaughlin.

Their conversation was often interrupted by smatterings of Spanish from the Argentines. All of a sudden it fell quiet. Cpl McLaughlin called out to Sgt McKay. Nothing came back. Moments passed; again he called out, still nothing. Then a burst of machine gunfire. Loud thumps from the .50 Cal. A spat of semi-automatic gunfire. Two explosions. Silence fell. From just around the corner groans could be heard. Sgt McKay could not be seen and did not respond to Cpl

McLaughlin's repeated calls. Cpl Bailey and Private James
had both been shot. After a short period, Jas returned to our
location and sat down by my side. He did not want to talk
about what had happened or what he had seen. 4 Platoon was
now without its platoon commander and platoon sergeant
and we no longer had our section commander. Sgt Des Fuller,
attached to B Company Headquarters, was sent forward to
take command. After a brief catch-up conversation, he gave
the order to fix bayonets and prepare to move.

Jas turned to me and said, "I'm not fixing my bayonet."
Referring to the men who had been on the ill-fated recce, he
added, "So far everyone who has fixed bayonets has been
shot."

We were told to move around the corner of the rock face
and form up by a small, rocky ridge one hundred feet or so
from the front of the main enemy bunker. Once in place, the
order would be given to charge head-on towards the enemy's
.50 Cal position. Without hesitation, 4 Platoon moved round
and crouched down behind the ridge to avoid being silhouetted against the backdrop of the minefield. There, in the darkness, we crouched huddled in a close group for what seemed
an eternity, waiting for the order to charge. Men from my
platoon were behind me and to my left, their fixed bayonets
occasionally glinting in the moonlight. Jas was to my immediate right. The atmosphere was tense in apprehension of what
was to come. We could see our breath on the cold night air as
we panted those last few minutes away. In the First World
War the order to charge was given by the sounding of a whistle, whereupon the soldiers would climb out of their trenches
and run self-sacrificingly across no man's land towards the

enemy's line. More than sixty years later we were doing basically the same thing – but without the whistle.

Moments passed, nothing but tension, and then Sgt Fuller gave the order – "Charge!"

As we clambered over the damp rocks of the ridge Jas slipped, lost his footing and stumbled. Other members of the platoon, yet to break cover, urged him on from behind and he quickly recovered. As I cleared the ridge and ran towards the enemy's position, firing my weapon, I thought of nothing. No doubt, no fear. Nothing. It was robotic. Adrenaline raced through my veins and my heart pounded. As I crossed the ground in front of their position they fired at me. I continued to charge, unstoppable, unperturbed by the pounding gun. I took cover at the forward edge of the enemy's gun position and crawled through a gap in the rocks just short of the leading edge of their trench, to allow others to take cover where I had first gone to ground. Rounds zipped over me. I pushed my head into the earth and small rocks trying to make myself as small a target as I possibly could, all the time the rounds continued to be fired at me. The Argentine soldier firing was adjusting his position to try to get the rounds lower to the ground where I was lying, but he couldn't. Possibly he was restricted by the height of the rocks in front of his trench, possibly it was just my good fortune. Either way, the shots continued over my head. Due to my prostrate position I couldn't return fire and decided it would be best if I crawled back to the spot where I had initially taken cover, to the front of their position. As I inched myself backwards, keeping as low to the ground as possible, I felt a bayonet jab me in the back between my shoulder blades. I froze. The bayonet pressure released. I yelled at the individual to move back and allow me to do the same. As I scrambled back behind the rocks, Private Dave Wakelin, an attachment to our section from Motor Transport Platoon was there. He looked at me and burst out laughing.

"F-ing hell," I said angrily. "First that gunner nearly had me and then I thought you were going to stab me!"

"So did I," he replied, with a huge grin. "That was a bit hairy though."

Making myself comfortable behind the rock I felt for my ammunition pouch and changed the magazine on my SLR. Better to have a fresh twenty rounds than run out in a time of need.

Within seconds the intensity of what had happened unravelled itself in my mind. I looked back through the dark over the ground that I had run across. As my eyes regained their focus, there was most of the platoon, wounded, taking cover or lying motionless. I recollect breaking cover and the initial charge, and vaguely remember Jas, who was to my right, going to ground mid-charge.

"Jas?" I called out. Nothing came back.

"Tom is that you?" a voice asked.

"Is that you Scrivs?" I said.

"Yeah, I'm over here with Grose. He's been shot and in a bad way."

At that moment all the adrenaline in me subsided. Small infrequent bursts of automatic gunfire continued to spit out from the enemy trench. What was left of our platoon returned fire in a desperate attempt to silence the guns.

Taff Wynne-Jones crawled to where Dave Wakelin and I had taken cover. He had the section's GPMG with him.

"Geoff's been shot," he said. "Looks like I'm the gunner now."

While he settled the machine gun into a firing position on the rocks to our front, I crawled back to look for Jas. I spotted him lying face down about thirty feet from where I had taken cover. I called to him but he didn't answer. As I drew nearer I feared the worse.

"Jas?" I said, hoping he would answer. Again nothing. Grabbing his smock I turned him over to face me. Jas's body slumped unnaturally towards me and one of his arms fell to his side. A round from the .50 Cal machine-gun had penetrated his head and killed him instantly. I stared at Jas unable to let go. As the blood flowed over his face, it reminded me of one of the many streams I had seen at night in the Brecon Beacons, glistening in the darkness as the water passed over the rocks, purposeful yet incredibly peaceful. Jas wouldn't have felt a thing. We had always sworn that should one of us be killed, the other would remove his dog tags and hand them to his parents as a keepsake, a reminder of a brave, unselfish and final act. I braced myself but I couldn't bring myself to do it. Mentally and physically the task was just too much. Under my breath I apologised to Jas for not being able to keep my promise and laid him gently back down.

Crawling back to Taff Wynne-Jones my anger raged.

"Act as my No.2 will you?" asked Taff.

"Jas Burt is dead," I said through gritted teeth.

"I'm sorry," he replied.

As I removed my bandolier and placed it on the gun, I wanted to kill everything and everyone still inside the enemy's position.

"Grenade!" shouted someone twenty or thirty feet to our left.

Wynne-Jones and I shielded ourselves as best we could as fragments from the grenade flew everywhere. "Jesus Christ!" I shouted, "we're over here, you're going to kill us!"

A burst of enemy fire came from the trench towards the direction the grenade had been thrown from. Wynne-Jones nodded to me, we both sat up and took up a firing position. I fed the belt as he let off a burst of about a hundred rounds. The other members of the platoon on the other side of the trench took advantage of this burst of fire and also let rip and in that moment the enemy position went silent. With the machine gun recoiling violently in Wynne-Jones' shoulder, loudly spitting out its rounds, we were too engrossed to notice Cpl McLaughlin coming up behind us. He had been shouting at us to cease firing and to conserve our ammunition but we hadn't heard him. With some force, Cpl. McLaughlin whacked Wynne-Jones on his helmet.

"Stop f-ing firing!" he shouted.

Immediately the gun stopped.

"What the 'f' are you doing?" he screamed. "We need that ammunition, the position has been taken!"

Wynne-Jones and I said nothing. Cpl McLaughlin was not in the mood for excuses.

"Here," he said, throwing down another bandolier for the gun. "Take this".

Wynne-Jones and I looked sheepishly at each other after 'Scouse' had left to distribute more ammunition to the others. Cpl McLaughlin was simply beyond belief. Walking from position to position, he was totally unfazed by the mayhem or the gunfire. He appeared to know exactly what was required of us soldiers and how to effect it. His professionalism was unrivalled and his bravery without constraint. He was an inspiration to all around him. He continued on his way, giving out orders and instructions to everyone he came across. If anyone was to be commended for their bravery in the honours roll for the future, he certainly was going to be the prime candidate. Thank God he was on our side, I thought.

"I'm going over to help Scrivs with Grose," I said to Wynne-Jones.

Grose was lying on his back with Scrivs to one side.

"I think he's been shot in the chest," said Scrivs like a surgeon diagnosing a patient. "But I can't find the exit wound."

Scrivs removed his glove and once more tried to feel for an exit wound around Grose's back. Each time a shot rang out Scrivs, without any hesitation or a thought for his own personal safety, would lie over Grose to protect him. An incredibly brave, unselfish and unambiguous act between friends. "That poxy sniper has been shooting at us all the time we've been here," he complained. "How's Jas?"

Not wishing to distress Grose any further, I simply looked at Scrivs and slowly shook my head from side to side. Scrivs closed his eyes for a second in acknowledgement. I was grateful for Scrivs' simple expression of sympathy and thankful I was with him at this time. His mental strength, just like his physical, was always evident.

With the enemy gun position now silent, around us other members of the platoon who had been hit could be heard groaning in agony and calling for assistance. Scrivs and I removed Grose's webbing and discarded it. Grose was not impressed at being disturbed and told us so. I then checked that the dressing Scrivs had put on the chest wound was firmly sealed around its edges. Grose was in pain and complained that he was struggling to breathe. "Let's get him on to his injured side," I said to Scrivs.

Grose screamed in discomfort and begged us not to move him. Scrivs and I succumbed to his pleading. The problem we faced, with a wound to the chest, was that the lungs could fill up and Grose might drown in his own blood. He had to be placed on to his injured side so any internal fluids could drain, or flow into his damaged lung, leaving his uninjured lung to function without restriction.

"Grose you must move on to your injured side," I said, trying once more to reposition him.

"Don't move me, don't move me," he screamed.

Feeling nothing but total compassion for Grose's pain, I again gave in. As the immediate firing from the enemy position had stopped, other members of B Company were now attending to the 4 Platoon injured. Taking a moment to assess the situation Scrivs doubled over and, with his hands cupped acting as shields, lit a cigarette. A few puffs later the fag was extinguished and Scrivs turned his concentration back to Grose.

"How're you enjoying your birthday party, mate?" he jokingly quizzed Grose. "You certainly know how to have a do. I think the neighbours will be upset with all the noise though."

Grose tried to laugh but the pain was too much. "Don't make me laugh," he pleaded. "We're going to have to move him," I said to Scrivs. "We can't stay here out in the open." I placed my hand on Scrivs' shoulder to beckon his head nearer to mine. At that very moment a single shot rang out. Scrivs fell across my lap and fluid splattered on my face. I pushed Scrivs off me with an instinctive jerk and, all in the same movement, moved a few inches back, wiping my face and staring in disbelief. Scrivs lay motionless in a limp, crumbled heap.

Pte Simon Ward, who was just a few feet away, asked me to check his pulse. I looked at Scrivs and then at Simon and said, "There's no need." Scrivs was dead.

I sat there not believing what had happened. One minute I was talking to Scrivs with my hand on his shoulder, the next – ZAP he was gone. A shudder went up my spine. Grose groaned. What the f- am I going to do now? I thought. When is it going to end? I glanced around. Everywhere I looked soldiers lay wounded, murmuring, some screaming. I thought, "I'm not going to make this."

Grose groaned again and snapped me out of my personal thoughts. I returned to his side. "I'm here, mate," I said. "You all right?"

Grose looked at me and asked, "Where's Scrivs?"

I looked at him not wishing to tell him but he could see it in my eyes. Grose screwed up his eyes, not in physical pain but the pain of losing a friend and tears fell. I couldn't help but let the tears fall too.

"You'll be all right, mate. I'll look after you, I won't leave you," I said.

"Where's my helicopter?" he asked. "They promised us twenty minutes and we'd be on the hospital ship."

"It's coming, Grose," I lied. "It's coming. Just stay with me."

The CSM came over. "Who've you got there?" he asked.

"Grose, sir," I replied.

"Not his last name you knob, what's his first name?".

"Neil, sir, but we call him Grose," I said.

The CSM knelt down by Grose's side and talked to him for a moment, reassuring him that all was going to be well.

"Right, let's move him back to the RAP," he commanded. "Use a poncho as a stretcher and carry him out of here."

We immediately placed a waterproof poncho on the ground and Simon and I tried to get it under Grose. Shots from the sniper continued to ring out. With the CSM overseeing the evacuation, 5 Platoon's commander, Lt Mark Cox, Pte Mick Swain, Simon and I all grabbed a corner of the poncho and lifted it to carry Grose to the makeshift Regimental Aid Post (RAP) about fifty yards away, tucked among the rocks.

A shot rang out and Mick Swain went to ground. "I've been shot," he said calmly. "In the buttocks."

More shots, and everyone took cover. Grose screamed in pain.

"We've got to move him." I reiterated.

We tried once more with Lt Cox holding two ends of the poncho. The weight was too much for him and Grose crashed to the ground, screaming in agony.

"F-ing hell, sir!" I yelled.

Without thinking I placed my weapon to one side and removed my webbing. Going around to Lt Cox's side of the poncho, I grabbed both ends. Lt. Cox swapped places and the three of us started to slowly move Grose towards the RAP, keeping as low as we possibly could. Every few feet we would stop to rest and I would talk to Grose, who, by now, was

becoming extremely distressed. The Argentine sniper continued to fire in our direction. Other wounded members of the
platoon were also being escorted back to the open-air RAP.
Cries of distress could be heard everywhere. Carrying Grose
over the rocks was very hard and my arms ached with his
weight. Nearing the RAP, Grose cried out in pain and we
stopped in our tracks. A single shot ricocheted off the rock
above our heads.

"I'm sorry, Grose, but we have to keep moving," I said.
"The sniper still has us in his sights."

Grose begged us to leave him there.

"Out of the question," I told him. "We're going to the RAP
together."

More shots zipped over our heads and it was obvious that
if we stayed there it would only be a matter of time before the
sniper picked us off one by one. We pressed on with Grose
moaning in discomfort. Just short of the RAP, located in one of
the passageways between hug rocks on the northern slope of
Longdon, just fifty yards or so from where we had taken the
Argentine position we took cover and rested. Lt. Cox went off
to assist another injured lad, so Simon and I pulled Grose into
the makeshift 'hospital' and were directed where to place
him. Injured lads lay all around. Cpl Bailey who had been
shot several times on the initial recce with Sgt McKay was
placed on his own some way from the other injured lads,
though his moans could still be heard. Although he had been
given medical attention and his wounds dressed, the medics
thought he may not survive. His isolation, although harsh,
ensured that those also injured would not be adversely
affected by his fate. Making Grose as comfortable as I could

on the short trodden grass passageway, I lay down beside him and re-assured him that all would be okay. "The next time we'll be moving is when I'm carrying you to the helicopter," I told him. He seemed to take comfort from my words. He knew his condition was slowly deteriorating but fought against it all the time. I checked and rechecked his dressing and adjusted his clothing so he could feel my touch and know I was constantly with him. We talked for about an hour and I listened as he told me about his family, how much he loved them and how he wished he was with them. I never allowed him to doubt that he would see them all again. We took comfort in the cold and dark with warm thoughts of home and family. At around 0300 hrs, Grose began to lose consciousness. I was afraid he was slipping away and started to reposition him to keep him awake. Grose complained he wanted to sleep. "Keep your eyes open," I told him. "If you fall asleep we'll miss the chopper and we don't want to do that."

Grose looked at me and said, "It's all right Tom, I know the helicopters aren't coming." I looked into his eyes and could see that he had resigned himself to not getting off the mountain.

"That's not true, Grose!" I said. "They're just waylaid. In a couple of hours you'll have nurses all over you, you lucky sod." He forced a smile and I knew he wanted an end to his pain. I needed to act fast to rekindle his desire to live.

"Wait here, don't go anywhere," I smiled. "I'm going to try and find a medic. I won't be long."

Leaving Grose for a few brief moments, I scurried around the RAP looking for a medic, conscious that Grose was alone. Against a rock face next to a group of injured lads was the company medic, head in hands, totally exhausted. He looked older than his years and desperate.

"I'm with Grose, just up there a bit. He has a chest wound and is losing consciousness. Come and have a look at him will you?" I asked.

The medic looked at me and I could see he was mentally and physically shattered. In those last few hours his eyes had seen so much pain, grief and mutilation. Everyone around him wanted and expected him to perform miracles – myself included.

"I've got nothing left," he said. "No bandages, no drips, no morphine. Nothing. Everything has gone!"

Welling with anger, I glared at him and snapped back, "Just come and give him some reassurance will you? Check his dressing. Tell him he's going to be alright. He's heard it from me for the past couple of hours and needs a fresh voice!"

Grudgingly, the medic followed me to where Grose lay. He inspected the dressing and shone his small torch into Grose's mouth to check his airway. Grose coughed up a blood clot. The medic cleared it, turned to me, shook his head and sat back, resigned to the fact there was nothing more he could do for him. For that single moment and incorrectly, I hated him more than I hated the enemy. I took up a position by Grose's head and held him. Clearing a second blood clot from his throat, I cradled him for a moment like a brother.

"Don't leave me, Grose," I whispered.

Grose fidgeted in a final and desperate attempt to fight against his injury.

"Thanks, Tom." He lay in my arms for a moment, before releasing his final breath. I couldn't release him from my grip, hoping he would feel me still there with him, and by doing so would come back to life. With the medic's assistance I tried to revive him, but to no avail. Eventually I stopped trying. Tears formed in my eyes and then an overwhelming surge of emotion hit me and I cried uncontrollably. I cried for Grose, I cried for his parents, I cried for his brother and I cried for his sister. I cried that he was too nice a lad to have died in such a way, and I cried for not being able to save him. Being unable to compose myself I lent over him, readjusted his clothes and closed his mouth, in some feeble attempt to remove the reality of the situation. I still held on to him throughout. Several moments passed and I ignored the sniper's unrelenting pot shots. Holding Grose firmly for one final time I pulled his head to mine, kissed my friend on the cheek and said good-bye. Laying his head down I used the poncho to cover his body and face and crawled a few feet away. There I sat, alone, back to the rock-face, staring back at him, recounting the last moments of my friends.

All hope of getting off the mountain alive has now abandoned me. My one and only hope is that when I am shot the end will come swiftly. In the darkness, the groans of wounded men are all around me. Shots ricochet off the rocks just above my head, as the sniper continues to prey on any sudden movement. Minutes pass like hours as I sit there in the dark without moving. I am now absolutely freezing and incredibly thirsty.

Sgt Fuller and Cpl McLaughlin come to the forward edge of the RAP and rally the remaining uninjured men to advance once more up the dark passageway back towards the area from where we had just brought the wounded. The land we'd fought over and won had now been re-occupied by Argentine troops. Cpl McLaughlin ushers me into a leading position. Unarmed, I search for a rifle to go back once more to the ground where our platoon had been wiped out. I can't find one. A private from 5 Platoon, who has been shot in the back, offers me a 9mm Browning. I take the pistol ungratefully. This weapon only holds nine rounds and is useless in such circumstances. Advancing up the passageway in a leading role, with only this weapon would be suicidal and meaningless. I woefully regret discarding my rifle, believing it will lead to my demise but feel guilty that I could think badly of a lost friend for being in this predicament. I see a few members of what is left of 4 Platoon sheltered in the rocks at the forward edge of the RAP, near the spot where Grose is laying. Men pass them and advance with stealth along the passageway, rifles at the ready. Immediately, shots ring out followed by a barrage of gunfire. The leading soldier is killed. Other casualties are sustained in the onslaught of gunfire that follows. The advance is halted. We are losing the fire fight. The advance is pushed back down the passageway towards the RAP. I crouch for a while by Mick Cullen, 4 Platoon's radio operator who had continued with his duties throughout the assault although having been shot in the mouth. Another brave unselfish and unrewarded act. Groups from Support Company reinforce the attack with Milan missiles and GPMGs from Machine Gun Platoon. Once more B Company surges forward in an attempt to obtain the advantage. The Argentines are repelled. Quickly the decision is taken to bring A Company across from their position on the western spur of Mount Longdon, known as Wing Forward, to reinforce and revitalise the advance. As A Company cross the open ground to join us on the northern slopes, they attract Argentine gunfire. A Company return fire. Complete chaos ensues as fire from our own troops ricochets off the rocks where we are seeking sanctuary. Screams directed at A Company to "Stop firing!" ring out everywhere.

From their higher position on the hillside, 5 Platoon give covering fire as A Company take over the assault. The Argentine counter-attack is halted, quashed and pushed back towards Full Back. A Company move forward into the Argentine positions.

Fighting continues for several hours throughout the early hours of the morning until Full Back is eventually taken. At last, B Company is ordered to extricate its casualties from the makeshift RAP in the rocky passageway on the northern slope down to a more secure First Aid Post at the foot of Mount Longdon. From there, the casualties will be evacuated to a rendezvous point at a safer distance from the battle, where they will be documented, processed and airlifted to the hospital ship SS Uganda. It has been over six hours since they crossed the start line, a far cry from the twenty-minute evacuation that had been promised in the orders we received before the attack.

Initially, I helped carry Cpl Bailey down to the FAP. While making my way back up the mountain to help further, I was asked to assist Cpl Ned Kelly, who had a stomach wound. By now, tracked snowcat vehicles were being used to evacuate the casualties. I helped Colour Sgt Brian Faulkner load Cpl Kelly on to the back of a vehicle, which already has two other casualties onboard. The corporal was in a bad way and C/Sgt Faulkner told me to escort him to the helicopter pick-up site and not to let him fall sleep at any cost. Thoughts of Grose come flooding back and I resented, once more, being responsible for another man's life or subsequent death. I wished I was back up the mountain on my own. Cpl Kelly was renowned for having a short temper and I recalled the 'garrotte squad' session on Canberra where he threatened to fill Jas and I in for messing around. I feared I might f- up and end up being shot by him. I checked to see whether he had a weapon with him. Luckily, he didn't.

Cpl Kelly could not get comfortable in the back of the snow-cat. He was constantly fidgeting, which caused him pain. He winced, not wishing to show any discomfort. He was a hard man and I admired his courage. I felt useless and alien in this environment and found I was without conversation. Cpl Kelly stared at me and I could not look away. Without saying my name, he directed me to look at his wound. In a split second, thousands of thoughts rushed through my head. What if half his stomach is hanging out? What do I tell him? What if I can't help him? What if…? I braced myself and cleared my head. Moving nearer to him, I could see a tattoo on his neck – someone's name. For the first time I considered Cpl Kelly as a family man and appreciated his obvious concerns.

In the swinging light in the back of the lunging vehicle, I started to undo his smock but he told me, "Leave it – just lift it up."

As I lifted the smock I could see his Army jumper had a hole in it and the surrounding fibres were laddered like a stocking. Blood bordered the laddering. I raised the jumper and his under garment and got a first glimpse of his wound.

"Everything is fine, Corporal," I told him, trying desperately to sound confident and convincing. The entry wound was like a small tear, approximately one to two inches wide, with part of his gut pushing through it. We had always been told that in such cases we were to push any protruding parts of the stomach back inside the wound, to reduce the chances of further damage to the internal organs. I told him what I'd seen and asked whether he wanted me to do it. Cpl Kelly didn't say anything. He looked at me menacingly. Once more I wished I were somewhere else. Finally, he nodded his head and looked up at the vehicle's green canvas roof. Removing my blood stained gloves I pushed the protruding stomach back inside, devoid of any emotion. Cpl Kelly nodded in approval.

"I can't dress the wound, my field dressings have been used up."

Again he nodded at me and I gently lowered his clothes to cover the wound.

"Shall I look for the exit wound?" I asked.

"It's been attended to," he replied.

I knew the closeness was over. Sitting back on my seat I looked at him, making sure his eyes were open. He stared at me.

"Don't let me fall asleep," he said.

Once more the burden of an unwanted responsibility had fallen on me.

We soon arrived at the disembarkation area. Other snowcat vehicles were already there and the walking wounded stood chatting to one another. As we offloaded the casualties I felt the air of relief from the wounded. All were happy to be alive and on their way to the hospital ship. I envied them.

I was alone in the back of the snowcat on the return journey to Longdon. Small pools of blood covered the seats and the floor. The left arm of my camouflage smock was soaked in blood; there were smatterings on the front. It smelled of death, acrid and stale, which lingered in my nose and throat for an eternity. I thought about Jas, Grose and Scrivs. The reality of never ever seeing them again hit me. My mind replays the events since crossing the start line, taking me back over the battleground. I concluded the only reason that I had survived the initial charge was the arc of fire from the .50 Cal. On seeing our charging platoon fanned out on the skyline in front of him, the Argentine gunner must have swept the gun's massive barrel from his left to right side. I, luckily but quite simply, had run between the spread of the rounds as he swung the gun in a desperate attempt to inflict as many casualties as he could. A huge wave of depression filled me as I thought about my friends who weren't so lucky. I felt guilty for not removing Jas's dog tags and for not checking Scivs. I felt responsible for not being able to save Grose's life. All in all I felt I had let my friends down; friends who had believed in me and trusted me.

I could not counsel myself. Our platoon has been virtually wiped out and, although I had not been close to the majority of older lads, they were familiar faces. With the loss of Jas, Scrivs and Grose, the only person on the mountain I could possibly say I knew well and trusted was Stu – and I hadn't a clue whether he was alive or dead. I hated my situation and my feelings of guilt. I wished I was dead by whatever means fate might bring. At least in death I would be resting peacefully somewhere, away from this turmoil, this hideous violence and this mental torture.

My thoughts drifted to Stu. If he was dead, I certainly

didn't want to survive a minute longer. Throughout the campaign when writing to our mothers, Stu and I had always taken the time to include one another in our letters. That way if one of our letters didn't get through, or was lost in the post, the other letter would inform them that both of us were okay at the time of writing. As our mums lived six doors apart in the same street, which ever of them received the mail could walk down to the other with news of our situation.

If Stu was dead I didn't want to bear that news. I already had enough bad news to contend with and wasn't coping well. I certainly didn't want to walk down the street knowing Stu's mum had lost her beloved son. Knowing that as time went by her eyes would look at me and wonder why it had been him and not me. I didn't want to live that way and wouldn't. As soon as I was back on the mountain I would find out if Stu was alive or dead.

If he was dead I would make my way to the forward positions of Longdon, where fighting was continuing and accept any fate that awaited me. I wasn't scared or frightened any more, more simply resigned to the inevitable fate that awaits us all. What I was doing, I consoled myself, was bringing it forward to a time of my choosing. If everyone I knew and trusted was already dead I'd prefer to join them than face a lonely, guilt-ridden future.

The snowcat pulled up at the foot of Longdon and as I raised the rear flap to de-bus I noticed daylight had broken. Artillery shells and mortar rounds still rained down on the hillsides. Explosions could be heard continuously. As I walked through the FAP area I saw blood stained field dressings littering the site. I noted that the grass was no longer

green but red. Although visually I saw these things, emotion-
ally they did not register. It all meant nothing to me any more.
My purpose was to find Stu, hopefully still alive and if not, to
put an end to my misery.

Leaving the FAP and making my way to the passageway
that led up the mountain to where A Company were clearing the last of the Argentine positions, I spotted Steve
Richardson from 6 Platoon. He had often been in pubs in
Tottenham where Jas, Graham Collins and I would go drinking when on leave. He knew Jas was dead and shook his
head in disbelief.

"Have you seen Stuart McAllister, 5 Platoon?" I asked.

He shook his head again and replied, "No, I haven't mate.
I'm sorry."

I interpreted this to mean Stu was dead and walked past
Steve, resigned to my next action. The rest of the journey up
the mountain is hazed. I cannot recall my path or the total
number of Argentine or British bodies that I passed. I just
know there were many.

I arrived at the spot where I'd left Grose's body and knelt by
his side. The poncho still covered him, his Army boots stick-
ing out of the end. I stared at the poncho, removed from the
situation, unable to relate to my friend. Needing to see him for
a final time I lifted the poncho from his head. Nothing had
changed – Grose was gone.

I lowered the poncho and started walking forward towards
the leading positions. I felt the presence of someone to my
right. I turned to see a paratrooper with a sub-machine gun in
his hand. Not registering the individual, I walked on before
being grabbed by the sleeve. Stu held my arm and looked into

my eyes. I still did not register that it was him. Somehow faces had changed. Everything was different.

"Tom it's me," he said.

I now knew it was Stu but I could not snap out of my mental state. He took me to his position in a crevice at the forward end of The Bowl. I crouched on my haunches with my back to the rock staring in a trance at Stu, who was facing me. He put on a brew and made some porridge, which he flavoured with drinking chocolate. We both ate and drank – nothing was said.

Warning cries of "Incoming!" could be heard every few seconds and shells continued to pour down.

I fell asleep. I don't know how long for, an hour maybe two, but I fell asleep on my haunches. When I woke, Stu was still there watching over me. He put on another brew. I told Stu of the events that had led to me making my way to the forward positions. He listened and eventually said, "The first thing we must do is get you another rifle and some webbing. When you're ready we'll go forward and get them."

I looked at him, grateful for his friendship; I trust him implicitly and knew he had rekindled my spirit to want to live. After another brew, and much attention from Stu in the form of easy tales of the previous night and a desire to get home, we venture forward. Blood, bodies, carnage, weapons and equipment lay scattered all around and I soon replaced my weapon, ammunition, webbing and rations.

A Company had now occupied Full Back and were attracting Argentine artillery fire from Port Stanley and mortar fire from Mount Tumbledown, across the valley to the south. My mind was now clear. I moved with ease around the positions, taking cover as artillery shells and mortar rounds occasionally landed around us. My instinct to survive was back. We ventured to the forward positions in search of food. Several rounds landed too close for comfort, so Stu and I took cover by some rocks. As I crouched down to view the immediate area, the grass was covered with blood. Looking down, my gloved hand supporting my body was in a huge pool of thick, clotted, red-black blood. A used field dressing lay abandoned a few feet away.

I looked at Stu and we decided to take our chances with the incoming rounds and change our position. Once again the horrendous nature of what we had been doing and the ultimate consequences hit home. We made our way soberly and carefully back to the safety of our position.

After a while, we again ventured out of the position and returned to the lower slopes, near the FAP. Enemy artillery shells still pounded the higher peaks. The pattern was always the same. First they fired a few shells, waited to see the landing point. Then they would fire a salvo, the shells creeping forward from the initial landing spot, obliterating anything in their path. The routine was then repeated on yet another reference point high on the mountain. The 'crump' shells could be heard in the distance, followed by shouts of "Incoming!" Everyone sought refuge. The shells whistled as they cut through the air nearing their target, and then screamed into their final impact point. As the shells landed and exploded, the affected area became vacuumed as all the air is sucked out. Sods of turf, pieces of rock and scorching hot fragments of the shell were sent flying in all directions. Their devastating and terrifying impact was often followed by cries of "Medic!"

When fired, Argentine mortars make a totally different sound to the artillery shells. There's a dull 'thud' on being fired and they make no other noise that may warn you of their intended impact point. They are, however, just as devastating as the artillery shells.

As Stu and I made our way back to our crevice in The Bowl, we passed the CO, Lt Col Hew Pike, talking with the RSM. Both men stopped and looked towards us.

"What platoon are you?" the CO asked.

"5 Platoon, sir."

"4 Platoon, sir," Stu and I replied respectfully.

The CO and RSM both looked at us for a moment, nodded their approval and both said in unison, "Well done, lads".

We responded with a courteous nod and continued on our way.

Back in our position we sat, retracing our steps and recalling our observations of the battle. Throughout our conversation we could hear an Argentine, not far from us, moaning, calling out for assistance, pleading for water. His distressed state became disturbing and, however hard we tried, it was impossible to ignore his groans. Finally, Stu jumped up and declared that he could not bear the noise any longer. Grabbing his SMG he went off to end the Argentinian's misery. Alarmed, the Argentine soldier raised his voice and begged for forgiveness. I closed my mind to his pleas and waited for the noise of the executioner's shot. Moments passed and silence fell.

"I couldn't do it," said Stu as he returned. "He's in a right old state. I gave him some water and told him to be quiet or I'd shoot him."

I smile at Stu, not bothered either way. At least, though, the Argentine had shut up.

The battalion sustained several more casualties and fatalities from the constant bombing of the mountain. Tempers were short, the lads' feelings disassociated. Occasionally, we heard single shots and short bursts of gunfire around us as positions still found to be harbouring armed enemy troops were cleared. No one batted an eyelid unless one of our soldiers was injured and then assistance was swift and attentive.

Throughout the morning, the fallen were removed to a mortuary area, adjacent to the FAP. Stu and I watched as the lads were collected and carried down to the mortuary, where the Padre checked the pockets and clothing of each victim, removed and bagged up any personal possessions.

During the afternoon, the Argentine prisoners were organised into groups to collect their dead and a mass grave dug to for them. Stu and I did not get involved with this, although when venturing forward we did see the bodies of the Argentinians who had been responsible for so many of our platoons' casualties and deaths.

Two of them had been removed from the main bunker and temporarily placed against each other on the ground. They had both been shot several times. Their boots showed signs of grenade damage. The toe part missing from one and the boot ripped from the foot of the other, exposing his bare skin. Their uniforms, dirty, blood stained and crumpled, no longer promoted the sense of pride, cleanliness and discipline normally associated with a soldier. Their clothes, no longer needed for the parade-square would now act as a shroud when these soldiers were finally laid to rest.

My initial reaction on seeing them was of revenge. The feeling that they'd got their just desserts. This soon subsided as I wondered whether they had been friends in life as Jas, Scrivs, Grose and I had been.

For the first time I found myself respecting them as people, lads in their prime like us. They were no longer the elusive, untrustworthy and grotesque enemy that had been portrayed by politicians and the media's propaganda. I did not see the young conscripted soldiers, considered incapable of putting up a fight against a professional army. No, what I saw before me were men who hadn't wavered when attacked, who had held their position to the very end, inflicting as many casualties and deaths as they could. Contrary to popular belief, it is not a soldier's job to die for his country. His job is to ensure someone else dies for their country. Like us, these men had done that and had paid the ultimate price. Their age was of no consequence. After all, everyone on the mountain appeared to be older than me, and at just seventeen with Jas and Scrivs now gone, I was probably the youngest soldier, on both sides, to be left on the mountain.

Later, Major Argue gathered B Company together and informed us that the remnants of 4 Platoon would join with 6 Platoon. The battalion's next objective would be the heavily-protected airfield in Port Stanley, at a date and time yet to be confirmed. Stu and I replenished our magazines and filled our webbing pouches with as much ammunition as we could find.

As the evening drew near, Stu and I moved position, back towards 6 Platoon, above where the mortuary was sited and set up our basher. We found Ron Duffy there. It was the first

time I'd seen him since he had been left in the minefield to
attend to Brian Milne. Ron had heard about Jas, Grose and
Scrivs and passed on his condolences. While Stu went off to
collect water from a puddle, I set about putting up the basher
with Ron who told me of his experience in the minefield. Ron
had laid next to Brian for several hours before a snowcat
could get near to remove Brian from the area. When the snowcat eventually turned up Ron rolled out of the way. The driver
had stepped out of his cab, straight onto a land mine planted
where Ron had been lying. Ron then had two casualties to
evacuate.

The Argentines had most probably used Elsie mines, a
small, green plastic anti-personnel land mine with a mush-
room-shaped plunger at the top. When trodden on, the
plunger collapses into the main body, detonating the charge.
These plungers have a small plastic rim around them, as do
the main body. With the high water table in the Falklands, the
space between these rims had been filled in time by water
from the ground. With temperatures down to minus ten, the
water between the two rims froze and turned to ice. Ron
thought that we may actually have trodden on many mines
during the advance that did not detonate because ice stopped
the charge going off. I shuddered at the thought. Ron's body
heat could well have defrosted the ice trapped in the mine
below where he laid, hence the second explosion.

Jesus Christ, I thought. How lucky were we? As I continued
setting up the basher, I thought of Stu out in the open land
below the mortuary, collecting water. I looked up and could see
him out there. I wanted to scream out, "Mines!" but couldn't.
Grabbing my weapon I started to make my way down to Stu.

Before I got to him he had finished and was starting to make his way back. When we eventually got to one another I relayed the story. Stu looked back over the open ground and said, "Sod that! – for a game of soldiers."

We returned to the basher and vowed not to take any more unnecessary risks. Water after all could be taken from the fallen. We collected Argentinian blankets along with some Argentine bully beef from an enemy sangar, and started to make a bully beef stew.

Looking back down the grassy slope to the mortuary we saw several body bags had now been tagged and laid out in a row. In a strange, but non-macabre sense, it was good to be near the lads, all of us reunited once more.

Pouring some of the water that Stu has collected into the mess tin full of Argentine bully beef, we added whatever rations were in our pouches, including broken biscuits and a packet of powdered oxtail soup. It was the first meal of substance we'd had since leaving Mount Estancia, twenty-four hours previously. Stu, Ron and I were so hungry we devoured the meal before it had even come to the boil. Taking turns to act as sentry, we cautiously settled down. Throughout the night the shelling continued, although more sporadically than during daylight. The temperature once again fell below zero. Stu and I had difficulty keeping warm. Our bergens had still not been brought forward from Estancia. Laying under the basher with the Argentine blankets over me I could not remove the previous night from my mind. Flashbacks of the fighting startled me from my dozing. I tried to discipline my eyes to stay open to counter the flashbacks but my tiredness overwhelmed me and, as my eyes closed, the flashbacks reoccurred. I got up from under the basher and stood with the blankets wrapped around me, looking down at the lads in the mortuary. I stared at their body bags, convincing myself that I'd combated my mental relapses. Then the images of the dead and mutilated reappeared and there was nothing I could do to remove them. The grizzly and gruesome sight of young dead Argentinian men, unnaturally twisted in their last moments of pain and torment, revisit me without invitation. Some have their eyes open, dull, lacking the glint and sparkle of the living. Others have closed their eyes in death. The colour has drained from their faces, leaving a pale yellowish grey. Some express their torture through their open mouths and wincing eyes. Others show panic and fear. Their expressions leave you contemplating how they met their end. Were they startled in their position? Taken by surprise? Or, on first being injured, had they thought they would be all right, and then later realised that a slow death was to be their fate? Most of their faces are splattered with a dark, reddish black. This is the colour of dried blood, not the scarlet red romanticised in Hollywood films. The blood is broken into ugly patterns, solid towards the centre, broken and dotted around the edges. The blood patterns have lines through them, where the soldier has changed his facial expression throughout his dying moments. Often those expressions are exaggerated by the positions of their hands and fingers. Some clutch at their wound in desperation; some support their head, as if in a final resting position or mimicking a foetal position. Others have their hands in front of them, fingers curled, as if reaching out for something or someone. All of the dead, British and Argentine have one trait in common, none show expressions of happiness – that expression is only for the living, those people miles away from here.

As I stood staring into the distance during the early hours of the morning of 13th June, it began to snow. Failing to remove the images of death from my mind, I crawled back under the basher next to Stu and watched the snow fall and settle. My mind drifted and I realised that since being on the island I had constantly been wet and freezing cold. To add to this I had been frightened, lonely and devastatingly sad. I promise myself two things: should I survive the next attack on the airfield and eventually get home, I would never return to this God-forsaken place; and when I am eighteen, back in barracks and required to officially sign on the dotted line, I will not do so. If this is life in the Army, then I have already seen too much for my liking.

Just before first light, we were packing everything away when my stomach started somersaulting and I was in desperate need of relief. I told Stu I needed to relieve myself and asked him to stand post while I did. Taking our weapons, we walked round to the south side of the mountain, all the time I was holding my stomach. Mount Tumbledown lay ahead in the distance. With Stu standing guard, I tried to settle into a position to get on with my ablutions. My stomach didn't appreciate my predicament and, like a tap on full flow emptied its contents. At the very same time I vomited violently. Spray from my mouth shot out ten feet in front of me and steam rose as it hit the ground. Stu rushed to my aid. There was nothing I could do to stop the flow and I retched in agony, my windproof trousers still around my ankles. To a civilian the moment would have been extremely embarrassing, but to me and Stu it was just one more 'shitty' situation.

As I lay on the snow-covered ground, clutching my stomach still trying to retch, I started shaking uncontrollably. Stu helped me regain my dignity and coerced me back to our basher area. With the basher now packed away I lay on the ground shivering; like a malaria sufferer, my head was burning. Stu and Ron considered their options. First they covered me with blankets to maintain my body heat but, still shaking violently, I could not regain control of my body. In the end they took me round to the RAP, where a medic placed me in a sleeping bag with my weapon, telling Stu he would keep an eye on me. The medic expected to see an improvement in my condition within a couple of hours. I lay there semi-aware of my surroundings. From time to time I felt the medic check my temperature, my forehead and my pupils. After a while he stuck a drip into my arm. I still had violent shakes and my temperature rose even further. The medic called for stretcher-bearers and I was carried to a snowcat. Stu had not left my side. The next thing I remember, I was in a tent with an Army doctor looking over me. A large brown Paddington Bear-type label had been attached to my smock. It had an outline figure of a person on it, detailing where a solider has been wounded. Mine had the letters D & V (Diarrhoea and Vomiting) written across it in black felt tip pen. I felt very weak and very stupid as I listened to them talking about the battalion's casualties.

From the tent, I was taken to a field medical centre in Fitzroy I think, although I cannot be certain. I also cannot recall the onward journey. The medical centre was filled with self-important non-combatants, parading around in their crisp clean uniforms. I felt foreign lying there in my blood-stained uniform. I had been placed on a camp bed in isolation in an outbuilding. I disassociated myself from these 'hats', feeling nothing but contempt and resentment towards them. Their Army, just like their uniforms and 'war zone', was very different to mine. After several hours I regained my strength and asked to go back to my unit. No one seemed to be able to make a decision. I waited for hours before someone in author-ity came over to me.

Again, but probably disrespectfully this time, I repeated my request to be transported back to my unit immediately. My patience was wearing thin. I was instructed that nothing would be moving until the following day, where depending upon logistics I might be able to go back to my unit. I felt cheated and dejected and wished I was back with Stu in the company of Paras. The 'hats' didn't understand my frustra-tion and kept advising me to enjoy the rest and build up my strength. I felt like a schoolkid being mollycoddled by his parents. I wished I could tell them all to go to hell but I needed their help to get back to my unit at the earliest opportunity. I lay in isolation, resenting every minute and every person who passed by.

Next morning, 14th June, I discovered nothing was moving due to the forward units pushing their way towards Port Stanley. I thought of Stu. I'd let him down not being with him when the battalion assaulted the airfield. I looked around at the 'hats' in the outbuilding, all warm, dry and self-apprecia-tive. I resented them bitterly. Time passed painfully slowly. Finally, late in the afternoon I was informed that a chopper was coming in to take me back to my unit. With no friends made and no goodbyes to be said, I sat at the entrance of the medical centre to await its arrival. Hours passed by – no chopper. Suddenly a huge cheer went up in the outbuilding. The 'hat' who'd told me about the in-coming helicopter walked over smugly and shook my hand.

"The Argentines have surrendered," he said. I stared at him in disbelief.

"What about the chopper?" I asked.

"En route now, mate," he said and walked off, probably to change into a fresh shirt or to open a bottle of Champagne he'd tucked away in his fridge somewhere.

I'm not your f-ing mate! I thought – and turned away to stare at the rain. The surrender was for real mates to share and savour. For fighting comrades to pat each other on the back and congratulate each other on surviving: For reflection upon those friends who hadn't made it; for an understanding and appreciation of what each had been forced to undertake and experience. It was a 'brothers in arms' moment, a memory that would live long in one's mind, to be told years later to inquiring grandchildren. Instead, here I was forced to share it with a 'hat' who probably hadn't even seen an Argentinian and who, as soon as it was declared safe, would be arranging a battlefield tour to get an Argentine souvenir to take home. Standing in the doorway I looked out at the helicopter landing-pad. The rain was lashing down.

A short while later a helicopter landed. As I clambered into the back, which already had a cargo of Special Forces personnel, the pilot asked me where I was heading for.

"3 Para. We were on Mount Longdon, but I not sure where

they are now!" I shouted to him over the noise of the helicopter's blades.

"They're in Stanley," he replied as the chopper lifted itself from the ground and set off.

The rain was now sheeting down, visibility minimal. Every now and then the pilot would land the helicopter hoping for a break in the weather but it never came. As we leapfrogged forward I was concerned the pilot would give up and return to the medical centre. He persevered and eventually the helicopter landed at a small grass racetrack behind the houses that border the main road leading into Stanley. Rations and equipment were being off-loaded from other helicopters. I ran over to one of the men responsible for incoming stores.

"Where's B Company?" I asked.

He pointed to the houses in front of the track and said, "In and around this area."

I walked out of the racetrack towards houses, where I saw members of 5 Platoon.

"Has anyone seen Stu?"

They pointed me to a house where I found Stu in the front room. We stared at each other without saying anything. The moment for celebration had passed. Stu smiled. "What's happening?" I asked.

"It's a free for all. Bloody impossible to find anywhere to sleep!"

We left the overcrowded house and decided to enter every house along the street until we found somewhere comfortable to sleep. Every bit of desirable and available space had already been taken. With the night drawing in, the C Company Colour Sergeant offered us a space.

"It's not much", he said with a broad smile, "but it should do you for the night."

Stu and I followed him to a small kitchen at the rear where C Company's 66 mm anti-tank rocket launchers, grenades, flares and various other forms of explosives were stockpiled.

"You can keep an eye on this lot for me," he laughed.

Stu and I quickly checked every single grenade pin and each 66mm rocket launcher was securely closed and fastened. We then rechecked each other's allocation before settling down for the night. It would be disastrous to have survived the last few days only to be killed or maimed by a faulty pyrotechnic. Tomorrow we would explore Stanley.

CHAPTER NINE

I Samuel

The Childhood of Samuel

We rose early and went back to the houses B Company were occupying. The CSM gathered us all together and allocated each platoon a house, which meant the company was now centralised and re-organised. The bergens were eventually brought forward. As we collected them we could see those belonging to the fallen, a sobering sight.

I joined other members of 4 Platoon in a garage to the side of a house. Wynne-Jones, Dougie Fields, Simon Ward and myself cleared the floor and arranged individual bed spaces. We spent most of the morning wrapped up in our doss bags keeping warm. During the afternoon we were told to keep off the gardens to the front and rear of the houses – mines had been found in some of them. Vehicle mines that had been made safe lay discarded to one side of the driveway to our garage. We were also informed not to go rummaging for souvenirs as booby traps had also been found.

Later Wynne-Jones, Dougie and I sat in the back of a white civilian Land Rover, chatting. The rain was again pouring down as I told them of the doctor's conversation I had overheard, talking about the casualties from our battalion. I was certain he had said Tony Kempster's brother, Dave, from 4 Platoon, who had been shot several times when attacking the

.50 Cal position, had had his arm amputated. I didn't know what to do. Should I inform Tony or not? It might not be accurate and could lead to unnecessary anguish for Tony. If it was true, surely Tony would want to see his brother at the first available opportunity? Wynne-Jones reckoned Tony had the right to know. I felt awful but knew I must tell him. Wynne-Jones went off to find Tony while I sat in the back of the Land Rover waiting. After a short while Wynne-Jones climbed into the back of the Land Rover, leaving Tony Kempster waiting outside in the pouring rain. I got out and stood by Tony's side, half expecting him to punch hell out of me at any minute. The atmosphere was tense.

Tony was shaking. "I understand you have some news for me," he said, emotion in his voice.

"I don't know how to say this," I said. Tony didn't move or say anything, so I continued tentatively. "I overheard two medical staff talking and they mentioned your brother – one said that he had his arm removed due to his wounds." I stopped ready for an onslaught but Tony turned to me, tears filling his eyes. For a moment nothing was said. We stood facing each other in the pouring rain and then he said, "That must have been hard for you. I appreciate it, thanks."

With that, he walked off. I stood for a while watching him go, feeling desperately sorry for him and his brother. I then returned to the Land Rover and watched the rain run down its windows. Hours passed.

The following day, Dougie Fields returned to the garage with a ten-man ration pack he had swiped from the racetrack when the storeman's back was turned. We devoured its contents and then all returned to the racetrack to see what other goodies were being brought in by the constant stream of helicopters. All of us managed to get an Arctic sleeping bag and one more ten-man ration pack. Our spirits lifted.

That afternoon everyone was allowed down to the Post Office to send a telegram home. As Stu and I walked down the main road into Stanley, near the War Memorial we noticed some lorry containers dumped in a lay-by. The first was a container full of green Wellington boots. We weren't interested. The second container was full of coffee and at the back of it – chocolate. Stu and I sat inside cramming dark chocolate down our throats until we were sick of the sight of it. We filled our pockets with as much as they could take and continued into Stanley. As we neared the post office, we spotted a small, detached building with Georgian-style windows. Inside we saw pieces of army equipment, webbing and several weapons. Stu climbed through the open window and retrieved one of the weapons, a 9mm Browning pistol. Walking over to the post office, the dustbins were overflowing with Argentine grenades. They were black with a white timing device dial on the top. It was unnerving to be surrounded by so many temperamental explosives. We entered the post office and both sent a telegram home to our mums. Due to the restriction on words we did not mention each other in our telegrams, which read along the lines of: IN STANLEY SAFE – STOP – HOME SOON – STOP.

We had a brief walk round but were soon bored. and ventured back to our respective houses. That evening the padre gathered B Company together at the racetrack and held a private memorial service to remember the friends we had lost with prayers and solemn hymns.

The following day, Friday 17th June, the battalion held a formal memorial service in the church at Stanley. We formed up in three ranks and marched as a battalion for the first time since leaving Southampton. We stopped outside and filed into the small wooden church, which was soon overcrowded, Some stood at the back while others crammed the aisles. I was seated in the rear pews. The atmosphere was sombre as the padre read out the names of the Battalion dead:

Private Richard Absolon	aged 19
Private Gerald Bull	18
Private Jason Burt	17
Private Jonathan Crow	21
Private Mark Dodsworth	24
Private Anthony Greenwood	22
Private Neil Grose	18
Private Peter Hedicker	22
Lance Corporal Peter Higgs	23
Corporal Stephen Hope	27
Private Timothy Jenkins	19
Private Craig Jones	20
Private Stewart Laing	20
Lance Corporal Christopher Lovett	24
Corporal Keith McCarthy	27
Sergeant Ian McKay	29
Corporal Stewart McLaughlin	27
Lance Corporal James Murdoch	25
Lance Corporal David Scott	24
Private Ian Scrivens	17
Craftsman Alex Shaw	25
Private Phillip West	19

| Corporal Scott Wilson | 24 |
| Private Craig Jones | 20 |

In all, twenty-three men from the 3rd Battalion, Parachute Regiment had lost their lives during the battle for Mount Longdon. It was to be the highest number of fatalities during any land battle for the Falklands. Some of them husbands, some of them fathers, some of them brothers, all of them sons, each an individual. To Joe Public they would be just names, unidentifiable soldiers killed in action. Three of them were my friends; the best I could have ever wished for. Each with their own very special personality, wants and desires: Jas, the cheeky cockney, who had an eye for the girls, the patter to go with it and change in his pocket for the fruit machines; Grose, the quiet, dark-haired, dependable man, who adored his family, and was a naturally talented marksman; Scrivs, the overseer, the sensible one, with a maturity beyond his age and a presence to match. Although each soldier would never wish to admit it, it all seemed such a waste. Such tragic loss of life for such a desolate, wind-swept island that no one prior to the invasion had ever heard of or cared about. "Theirs is not to make reply: Theirs not to reason why; Theirs but to do and die", those words of Lord Tennyson's would be the politician's response. My reply to that would be unprintable.

The padre finished the service with the reflective words of Lawrence Binyon:

"They shall grow not old as we that are left grow old:
Age shall not weary them, nor the years condemn.
At the going down of the sun and in the morning,
We will remember them."

There and then, I swore I always would.

The battalion filed out of the church without anyone talking and was marched back to our respective areas. It was time to start thinking about going home but unfortunately for us the Argentine prisoners, having been employed clearing up Stanley, were to be taken home first – nearly 13,000 of them.

Next morning C Company and several Royal Marine units embarked from Port William on the SS Canberra, with more than 4,000 prisoners on board. Their destination was Puerto Madryn, in the south of Argentina. Eventually C Company returned with a story of one Argentine prisoner who carried his army issue sausage bag with him everywhere he went. When the lads tried to take the bag from him he went berserk. A further investigation revealed he had a body in the bag, believed to have been his brother. His explanation was simple; he didn't want to leave him behind. Argentine losses during the campaign amounted to 755 dead with 1,053 wounded. The sinking of the General Belgrano was a major contributor to the numbers of the dead. It is believed at least thirty Argentines were killed on Mount Longdon, with sixty or so wounded and fifty taken prisoner, although these figures have never been verified. Total British losses were 255 men killed and 777 wounded. In addition, three civilians, Mrs Doreen Bonner, Mrs Mary Goodwin and Mrs Susan Whitley, lost their lives.

As soon as the SS Canberra returned, we would be going home. The journey would be by sea to Ascension Island aboard the MV Norland. From there we'd go by plane to Africa and onward to Brize Norton, in Oxfordshire. I couldn't wait to get off the island. The landing craft seemed to take an eternity ferrying us out to the Norland, where we would join our sister battalion, 2 Para. The Marines would be kept away from us and would be going home on the Canberra, not that anyone gave a damn what the Marines were doing. Once everyone had boarded, we were told to report to the cookhouse for a 'Scale A' parade. Stu and I grabbed a bunk on one of the lower levels and quickly showered before going to the briefing. It was the first shower we'd had since leaving the Canberra five weeks earlier. The cookhouse was already packed when we arrived. Everyone waited impatiently expecting a briefing on good behaviour during the homeward journey.

To our amazement Brigadier Julian Thompson, Commander of 3 Commando Brigade, wanted to address the two parachute battalions. As he walked through the masses to gain a central position, my first impression was how small he was. Who says size doesn't matter!

My second observation was that he was wearing his chief-of-staff badge in a 'cabbage hat'. From that moment I lost all interest in anything he had to say. Regardless, he waffled on about how new links had been forged between the men of the red and green berets. I stared in disbelief as this man tried to relate to members of both Para battalions. He eventually stopped amid murmurs of "F-off, you hat" and "When's scoff?" It wasn't a good speech at all. In fact the Brigadier probably would have gained more respect if he'd stayed out of sight, anonymity giving him a greater presence and standing. Still, anyone who stands in front of more than five hundred paratroopers wearing a green beret deserves all he gets. After his speech and departure we were given our first hot meal that had not been part of a ration pack. We queued up with great expectation only to be disappointed. What a homecoming – boiled rice with stew.

The next event on the Norland of any significance was my 18th birthday, Wednesday 30th June 1982. Stu had managed to swipe some Jacob's Cream Crackers, a tin of salmon and a jar of Heinz Salad Cream from a container on one of the upper levels. We enjoyed these together in our bunk, with a black plastic webbing mug full of hot drinking chocolate. It doesn't sound much of a party, and probably only lasted for about ten minutes, but it was fantastic at the time, a meal to remember for ever. The following day, the Princess of Wales's birthday, our toilet overflowed, and everything that anyone had passed on our level seemed to reappear in our cabin. Stu and I woke to the sounds of water splashing against the sides of our cabin and a smell any pig farmer would have been proud of. The floor had disappeared beneath scenes not dissimilar to a bad day on Margate beach. Climbing out of the bunk very carefully, I told Stu I would go and get a mop and bucket to help us clean up the mess. Stu set about the task and I left and made my way to another cabin occupied by people from our platoon. There I made myself comfortable and fell asleep for a couple of hours. When I returned to our cabin, minus the mop and bucket, Stu went mental. The floor was now sparkling clean and only a little of the smell lingered.

"Don't think you've got away with not doing your share!" he moaned, "I've left you the toilet area."

I opened the door to the toilet to find at least six inches of solid sewerage, being held in place by the toilet step.

"I'm not bothered about this shit!" I said, plunging my

hand into it. I grabbed a handful and presented it to Stu, who promptly threw up everywhere and left the cabin. I cleaned up the remaining mess.

That weekend both battalions celebrated Airborne Forces Day. ABF Day is usually the first Saturday in July and gives past and present members of the Airborne Forces a chance to celebrate their membership. Normally one of the three Para battalions does the formal parade in the morning. The rest of the day, together with Sunday, is spent on the piss. On this occasion, there being no requirement for a parade, both battalions went straight on the piss. The Other Ranks' mess was packed with lads from both battalions all swigging merrily from cans of lager. Stu and I sat with my old corporal from Juniors, Cpl Tom Camp, who had returned to 2 Para from the depot. We chatted about our experiences on the island and the lads who had been lost. Suddenly the singing changed to soccer-style chanting, and within seconds it kicked off – 2 Para versus 3 Para; the usual routine for all Regimental get-togethers – drinking, singing, fighting. Tom Camp stood up wished us well and advised us to join the blokes in our battalion. As we said our goodbyes the OR's mess turned into a free for all. Bodies and punches flew everywhere. After dodging the beer cans and the odd wild flung punch, Stu and I made our way through a maze of corridors to get to our bunk. Fighting had now spilled to these areas and it became an escape and evasion exercise to get back unscathed. Eventually, and after splitting up, we did manage to rendezvous back at the cabin. Locking the door behind us, we left the remainder to continue fighting well into the early hours.

Our impending leave was to be in the region of eight weeks; however there were conditions to this. On arrival at RAF Brize Norton everybody was to be searched. Anyone found in possession of firearms or pyrotechnics would lose their leave, forfeit their pay and spend their leave in the battalion jail. Stu and I did not relish the prospect of losing our leave if we were found in possession of the 9mm pistol he had commandeered in Stanley. So we went to extra lengths to conceal the offending item. We sawed one of Stu's water bottles in two. The pistol barrel was slightly longer in length than the water bottle, so the barrel was placed in a plastic bag and inserted inside the water bottle, which had been lined with a second plastic bag. The two halves of the water bottle were then taped together with black masking tape. The water bottle, complete with plastic lining, was refilled just in case the contents were investigated. After much messing around and far too many spillages, we decided it was too much effort for too little reward. Instead of risking our leave we would throw the pistol over the side of the ship and forget the whole matter. It seemed the rest of the battalion had decided to do the same and up on deck all kinds of souvenirs were being thrown overboard!

Eventually, the MV Norland anchored off Ascension Island where we were ferried by helicopter to await the aeroplanes that would take us, initially to Africa, and then home. As we stood in the dark at the airfield, we each received 200 Silk Cut cigarettes as freebies and were asked whether we'd like any duty free. It seemed like we were returning from a cheap package tour. Sod your drink, I thought, just get me home!

The flight was unremarkable, as were most of the air stewardesses. Making myself as comfortable as I could, I slept until landing in Africa. On arrival we were allowed to stand outside on the apron while the aircraft refuelled for the final part of the journey home.

As our plane touched down at RAF Brize Norton and taxied to its final resting place the Regimental band stood in formation ready to strike up a tune. One or two officials paced up and down on the tarmac. Stu and I felt relieved that we had discarded the pistol. The passenger steps were brought forward, the front doors of the plane opened and the cabin crew beckoned us out into the daylight. I would have been the very first member of the plane to disembark but as I reached the door and the band struck up the Regimental tune "Ride Of The Valkyries", a huge cheer went up and I couldn't face it. I withdrew and allowed others to walk off ahead of me. After a few deep breaths and one or two slaps on the back, I walked through the aircraft door, down the steps and across the concourse to the arrivals building, where our families were waiting.

As Stu and I neared the gangway leading to Arrivals, an RAF Regiment soldier stood there looking very sheepish. Everyone else was being cheered at and receiving welcoming pats and slaps on the back but this poor 'hat' was on duty and not part of it at all. I looked at him, nodded and said, "Looks like you joined the wrong regiment mate." He smiled at me and returned an appreciative nod. As I walked through the doorway, I realised the moment I'd been dreading was upon me. It would be stupid to say I wasn't looking forward to seeing my family or Laura. It wasn't that I hadn't missed them; that was not true. It was more to do with the onslaught of tears and emotion that would inevitably come my way. Tears that I felt were not due for me. I had returned home safe and sound. The tears were for those who had been lost and for those who would now be dealing with wounds that would affect the way they lived for the rest of their lives.

As my eyes regained their focus, I could see Mum, Jo and Laura standing together. I made my way to them through the other families who were enjoying their own private moments and stood in front of them waiting for their reaction. All three cuddled me together and of course their tears started to flow. I hugged all of them at once and wanted to apologise for the pain they had been through since my departure but I couldn't. Their pain seemed irrelevant to what some families had and still were experiencing. My mouth felt dry. I wanted and needed the moment to pass. Eventually Mum informed me that Dad was in the airport lounge as well. I turned just as Dad came up to me; he shook my hand, told me I looked smart and said that he would be in the pub if and when I needed him. I noted his distance; it seemed that not even a war could close the divide that my parents had established. Dad then left.

Returning my attention to Laura, looking into her tear-filled eyes, I reminded myself how young, bubbly and happy she was and wondered whether I would ever be that way again. She wore a white, short, summer dress covered with different coloured spots. A tight belt accentuated her petite figure. I held her against me and kissed her. I could feel her through the delicate dress she wore and could smell her perfume. She felt soft and warm to touch. Her fragrance was sweet and flowery. It all seemed so foreign and unreal after the hardness and violence I had known since leaving and I felt alien and uneasy with it. Laura had not changed; she was the same young, fun-loving girl she had always been. I on the other hand had and didn't want my life, at this moment in time, to be overtaken or controlled by the soft touch or sweet smell of a woman, especially one that I felt no longer knew the man who was in her arms.

Releasing myself from her embrace I looked around the arrivals lounge. Families, at first glance, appeared to be enjoying their reunions, and tears were flowing everywhere. On closer inspection though, I noticed the lads seemed dazed, confused, and unable to interact comfortably with the people they had known for years. It all seemed so awkward and false. Stu brought his family over to mine and we all hugged and wished each other well before eventually saying our goodbyes. Stu and I made our way to a side exit where the search tables and Army vehicles were located. Everybody seemed to just walk past the tables and the officials, who were ineffectively asking whether anyone had any firearms or pyrotechnics on them. We sat on the back of a wagon waiting to be transported back to camp when someone came round and told us that we could make our way back to camp with our families. Stu and I jumped off the wagon and went back to our families. Stu's sister Margaret, who was living in Swindon at the time, said she and her husband would take us back to camp and so off we went. We stopped in a local pub, where the landlord bought us a drink and congratulated us on a job well done. Not wishing to get too involved Stu and I thanked him for his kindness and distanced ourselves by sitting on a table away from the bar. It was a beautiful summer's day with the sun high in the sky and not a cloud to be seen. It was good to be back in England.

The journey from the pub back to camp was slow, frequently interrupted by non-committal conversations about family and friends. As we neared camp, along one of the narrow country lanes, I could see the yellow fields of rape stretching for miles, all gently swaying in the warm summer breeze. It was the first real colour I had seen since leaving the Falklands and it looked beautiful. I lost myself for a moment remembering the island's muddy tracks, freezing cold streams, tufts of grass and the barren landscape that went on for miles. Why had we fought for such a god-forsaken place? Good old Blighty was beautiful with its counties and metropolis, but the Falklands was one large sheep pen, complete with sheep shit. What a waste, I thought.

Margaret and her husband dropped us back at camp and Stu and I made our way to our block. The camp appeared deserted. I wondered where everyone else had got to, probably still making their way back. Walking into my room, Grose's bed space was the first thing I saw. His locker was wide open. The contents had been removed and his mattress was folded over. I threw my kit on to my bed and walked over to Grose's area. I stood there not believing the harshness of it all. Grose had gone and within hours the Army had sent 'strangers' to break into his locker, remove his Army and personal possessions and prepare the bed space for the next candidate. I couldn't believe the coldness of it all; surely the Army could have waited until we had arrived back. What was the rush? As his friends we would have ensured everything due to the family would have been checked and packed compassionately. Items that Grose may not have wished his family to see would have been removed. We all had one or two of those items! But also silly things, like the red socks he superstitiously wore each time he parachuted, meant something to Grose and may have had sentimental value to his family. Consumed by emotion I left Grose's bed space and walked into Scrivs' and Jas's room. Their bed spaces were exactly the same. I walked out onto the veranda and took in a few deep breaths to compose myself. My head was spinning with memories of when we were all last on the veranda being briefed by the CSM for the impending transport to Southampton. The whole Company grouped together listening intently to what the CSM had to say. All of us smiling and laughing in naïve excitement of what adventures lay ahead. A lot had happened since then and the boyish eagerness to fight for one's country had been replaced by a veteran's understanding and wisdom of the true horrors of war. As I stood there with echoes of the lads' conversations pounding in my head someone came up to me and asked what I was doing.

"We were told to report back to camp," I said.

"Everyone else has gone straight on leave," he replied. "I suggest you do the same".

I shook my head in disbelief. What a cock-up.

I grabbed my kit, nodded to Grose's bed space area and went to find Stu.

"Where do you want to go?" Stu asked, as we sat in his car. "Home?"

Staring out the window I thought back to the arrivals lounge and Laura. "I don't think I could face it just yet," I said, telling him all about the lads' bed spaces and the lack of compassion demonstrated by the battalion. "I know it sounds silly but all I want is a good night's sleep in a bed with clean sheets. I'm not ready for tears and families." We sat for a moment unsure what to do. Finally Stu started the car and said, "We'll go to Margaret in Swindon. It's just down the road, she'll be all right."

Once more I was thankful for Stu's understanding and company. To be perfectly honest I didn't think I could cope with anyone else. Stu and I had shared the Falklands together and only he and I knew how things were. I was not ready or able to share that experience with anyone else.

Margaret was surprised to see us on her doorstep but without fuss made us both welcome, vacated her house and went to stay with friends. Stu and I sat in the front room with cups of tea and chatted about nothing. The golden rule went without saying; we never talked about the Falklands, only the good times. I must have slept for hours for the next thing I knew it was morning and Margaret had returned. Stu and I walked around Swindon town centre for most of the morning and early afternoon. I was amazed at how normal everything seemed. People going about their business as if nothing had happened; not that there was anything they could do to change it. Nevertheless they all appeared so engrossed with the basics of life, buying bread, the daily newspaper, weekly shopping. I couldn't believe it. They didn't seem to care that people had actually lost their lives fighting in a campaign miles from home. They just went about their normal routines. I resented them. I saw teenage boys, no younger than me, leaning against walls smoking and chatting to girls trying to look as cool as they could while trying frantically to arrange the next date. Giggling, the girls tried to ignore their come-ons. I considered them to be kids and wondered what they had all been doing on the night of 11th/12th June. The night that I changed from a boy to a man who now understood how precious life was and how quickly it could be taken. Although I was still their age I felt no affiliation with them. Their lives were unfolding and being wasted. Suddenly I felt like my father observing his son's early teenage years. My, how the world turns.

Stu and I left Swindon later that afternoon with every intention of making our way home. The journey was easy as we talked of nothing and listened to his cassettes. Somewhere along the route we again decided we weren't ready for the closeness of our families, so we took a detour and ended up at my Dad's pub. It was now late evening and the Wheatsheaf was packed. Dad was pleased to see us but did not make any fuss. He allowed Stu and me to sit outside in the garden unhindered. We talked for hours and when the pub closed, Dad eventually joined us and we sat for a while sharing brief experiences of the cold and wet. We slept at the pub that night and decided that in the morning we would return to Hoo.

As we turned off the dual carriageway on to the road into the village we saw Jackie McCoy, a girl I had dated for a while when I was in Junior Para. We stopped the car and she jumped in the back. After exchanging the usual pleasantries, she enquired, "What was it like returning and seeing all the street banners and stuff?" Stu and I looked at each other and said, "What are you you talking about?"

Jackie seemed puzzled and then said, "You haven't been home yet, have you?"

We smiled and replied, "No, not yet!"

She couldn't stop apologising as if she had let some great surprise out of the bag. We told her not to worry and dropped her near her home. After Jackie disappeared, Stu and I sat in the car contemplating our options. Street banners meant fuss and attention, something neither of us wanted. However, we had to see our families and the longer we left it the worse it would appear. We decided to go into the village and have a quick drink to give us Dutch courage before venturing home, and so we popped into the Five Bells.

Eventually the time came to face the music. As we pulled into our road, we saw some of the posters Jackie had been talking about, hanging from the windows of our houses. It was nice that our families had made the effort but it was the total opposite to what we had wanted. Returning from a conflict is awkward to say the least. Mentally you are exhausted and confused. Emotions lurch within seconds, from anger to tremendous feelings of guilt and depression. The slightest thing can bring them on. Anger towards those that weren't there and haven't a clue, especially if they ask, "Did you kill any Argies?" Guilt for what you were made to do and have done. Guilt for your initial naïve 'gung ho' attitude for the war before being awoken to its true horrors. Worst of all guilt for surviving the campaign without a scratch, while others didn't return or are hobbling around on newly-acquired prosthetic legs, or learning to tie their shoe laces with only one hand. Depression often follows the guilt and the problem was that Mum, Jo and Laura couldn't relate to this feeling. It was not because they hadn't been to war. It wasn't quite that simple. Women dealt with things in a maternal way. Tears, cuddles and the need to keep asking if everything is all right is not something we men do. What we need is to be left to our own devices for a while until we have made sense of our woes. Solitude or an area away from the limelight is what I really sought. Being paraded with banners seemed more like a celebration of a child's birthday than a homecoming for someone who has seen his friends shot to hell. It seemed immature and inappropriate. To someone who had been to the edge of all reckoning, where it was better to end his life at a time of his choosing than have it snatched away, the banners seemed wrong. Unfortunately, those around me didn't understand the pain and guilt I was feeling, as each day I grew older when others I had known didn't.

A few hours later I was out of the house and back in the pub with Stu. After a few days of spending as little time as possible at home and as much time as I could on one of the stools in the public bar of the Five Bells the inevitable happened. Joanne came into the pub and, in front of everyone in the bar, let rip. I was selfish for not spending time at home with Mum; for not contacting Laura since my return; life had not been easy for them back here while I had been away. Initially I ignored her, looking at Stu as if to say, "Want another drink?" but as Jo ranted on I could no longer control my anger and replied with venom. Jo left the pub in tears and I decided that this would be the last leave I would spend at home with a family who no longer knew me. It was time to establish my own life and move on. That evening, while washing and preparing to go out with Stu, Mum shouted up that Laura was on the phone. She had apparently called every night since my return only to be told I was already out or not available. I told Mum I was going out and that I'd ring her the next day. Of course, I had no such intention. Mum informed Laura of the situation then came into the bathroom where she told me of the calls and the tears. After a lecture on the mistreatment of girls, something Mum felt I had obviously inherited from Dad, she asked me to call Laura and arrange a date to end the relationship, if that was my intention. "Laura deserved that at least," said Mum. I called Laura straight back and arranged to take her out the following night.

I suppose my intention had been to meet Laura and end the relationship, believing that for the immediate future I was best left alone to deal with the aftermath of the Falklands and not expose anyone else to the Dr Jekyll and Mr Hyde character I had become. The best made plans of mice and men have a funny way of being altered when they do not take into account someone else's involvement. Laura proved to be good company, medicine for the mental torment I was putting myself through. Her understanding of the Falklands campaign and what I had experienced was minimal, as was her desire to know, which made a welcome change from the constant barrage of enquiries from other acquaintances. Laura simply wanted our relationship to return to what it had been before; the dates, the late night conversations, the fun. Nothing had changed for her. Where I took offence to this naivety from others, with Laura I enjoyed it and allowed myself to relax in her company. Our dates became personal, without other company and our conversations became longer. Throughout the leave I sought sanctuary with her.

ABOVE: Junior Para: Mark Robert Jason Eyles-Thomas reporting for duty. 'With a name like that you ought to be an officer,' a Corporal said sarcastically. After that Mark always introduced himself as Thomas.

ABOVE: 476 Pltn Passing out: Back row - Neil Grose, far right; Jason Burt, second right; Centre - Steve Jelf, third left, Mark Eyles-Thomas, eighth left. Front row - Ian Scrivens, second left.

ABOVE: Steve Jelf, left, Jason Burt, centre and Stuart McAllister onboard SS Canberra

ABOVE: 4 Platoon, 3 Para onboard SS Canberra.
Back row: L-R Ron Duffy, Andy Stone, Neil Grose, Steve Jelf, Mick Cullen, Jason Burt, Mark Eyles-Thomas, Mick Swain, Tony Barlow, Dave Kempster
Centre: Cpl John Lewis, Cpl Brian Milne, Cpl John Balmer, Lt Andy Bickerdike, Sgt Ian McKay, Cpl Ned Kelly, L/Cpl John Hedges, L/Cpl Tony Evans, L/Cpl John Goreing
Front row: Ian Scrivens, Geoff Logan, Craig Harrison, John Wynne-Jones, Keith Parry, Simon Ward, Mark Eisler, Steve Playle

ABOVE: Steve Jelf, far left, Steve Playle second left, Neil Grose, centre and Jason Burt, right. Ascension Island (April 1982).

ABOVE: Jason Burt, front of picture, Andy Stone, back to camera. Ascension Island April 1982.

BELOW: 4 Platoon on SS Canberra (Ascension Island in distance)
L-R Geoff Logan, Cpl Brian Milne, Steve Playle, Lt. Andy Bickerdike and Cpl Ned Kelly.

ABOVE: Scrivs, left, and Mark Eyles-Thomas, right, on SS Canberra. Night before transferring to HMS Intrepid.

BELOW: On Ascension Island; Mark Eyles-Thomas, centre with Sgt Ian McKay, bending over, Cpl Lewis, left, reading a book.

ABOVE: Landing craft training off Ascension Island. Lt. Bickerdike, right with radio ear-piece, Steve Jelf, centre with Scrivs in front of him. The SS Canberra's life-raft can be seen at the top right of picture.

LEFT: This is part of the letter Mark (known to his family as Jason) wrote home from the Canberra before cross-decking to HMS Intrepid prior to landing on the Falklands at San Carlos.

Dear Maria Jo,

Well this will probably be the last letter. I'm not sure for how long but I'll write every chance I get.

I've taken out an insurance policey but you can also take one out on me if you want.

I'm not saying that I'm doomed, cause I've got no intentions of going just yet. So don't flap and write to the Commanding Officier or Sergeant Major, you'll just drop me right in it.

I can't see us sustaining heavy casulties but we'll just have to wait and see. Please don't start to flap I can look after myself.

Anyway theres weeks yet,

See ya soon

lots of love.

Jason.

Mum & Jo,

        Just a line to say that we deploy tomorrow onto the islands. I hope you never have to read this letter but just in case anything does happen to me I want you to know that I do and always will love you both. Love to Laura and apologise to her from me.

        <u>Your</u> ever loving son.

                    Jason. xxxx.

ABOVE: The short note Mark wrote to his mum and sister, Jo, just before landing on the Falkland Islands. It was to be opened if he did not return.

BELOW: Mark Eyles-Thomas in a trench above San Carlos Water.

ABOVE: Tiny figures of soldiers show the scale of the rocky outcrops on Mount Longdon where 3 Para fought with bayonets against Argentine .50Cal guns. Photo Vince Bramley.

ABOVE: 3 Para treat their wounded in a makeshift First Aid Post at the foot of Mount Longdon. The Paddington Bear Style label can be seen on the casualty's smock. Photo: Tom Smith

ABOVE: Evacuating casualties in tracked snowcat vehicles.

ABOVE: June 12, 1982 Mount Longdon is retaken. Photo: Graham Colbeck

ABOVE: Argentine dead killed in a grenade attack. I saw not useless conscripts but brave men who didn't waver when attacked, who had held their position to their very end. Grenade damage can be seen on the boots of both soldiers.

BELOW: The British fallen: Helmets and rifles jammed into the ground to mark where paratroopers died. Photo: Graham Colbeck

ABOVE: 3 Para reach Port Stanley. Photo: Vince Bramley

BELOW: The letter Mark wrote to say Stuart and he were safe and well.

Dear Mum and Jo,

Well writing this in Port Stanley, and its good to know thats its all over and im in one piece.

Hope you'll all OK at home. Me and Stuart should be home soon.

Have had a fierce battle on Mount Longdon and have had heavy casualties and lost some very close friends. Thank god me and stuart are O.K. and will both definately be coming home in one piece.

Will close now.

love you lots

Can't wait to be home.

Jason xxxxx

ABOVE: Fallen heroes return; The Paras' military funeral held at Aldershot in November 1982. Photo Brian Bramley, Aldershot News.

BELOW: A quarter of a century after the battle for Mount Longdon, Mark Eyles-Thomas with his 17-year-old son, Dominic, who plans to join the military. Photo: Dale Cherry, Mail on Sunday

Being on my own often meant being swamped by feelings of guilt and depression. Everything would be fine as long as I didn't see a newspaper, watch the news or get into conversations about the Falklands. If I did, rage would engulf me. It appeared to me that the media coverage was biased in favour of the Marines, and conversations, however discreet, always led to the ultimate question, "Did you kill any Argentinians?"

Things were as normal as could be until I went with Laura to a party in Hoo. The party had been good fun and we had laughed and danced the night away with friends from the village. People had been briefed to leave me alone and not mention the unmentionable. Laura and I had stayed the night having been given a room to ourselves while other rooms were packed with anything up to five couples. In the morning I went down to the front room to thank the host for a great night to find everyone around the television watching the SS Canberra dock at Southampton. The 'Great White Whale', as she was affectionately known was escorted into the harbour surrounded by tugs. Water boats, with plumes of water jetting into the air, announced the ship's arrival for miles. Civilian vessels swarmed round her like bees to a honey pot, creating an entourage worthy of any royal visit. Nobody noticed my presence as I stood in the doorway watching the broadcast and listening to the conversations. As the Canberra docked and the Marines disembarked, they were led by the youngest Marine on board. I cringed as the 18-year-old lad was ceremoniously met, kissed on the check and given a red rose to welcome him home. The surrounding dockside was packed with families, friends and members of the public all cheering, waving flags and singing along to the Royal Marines' band, playing on the quayside. This momentous occasion, on the scale of Charles and Diana's wedding, was being enjoyed by a jubilant British public as they welcomed their homecoming heroes. To me it was just another scene contrived by the Government for the unsuspecting public. The Marines had, to all intents and purposes, surrendered the Falklands to the foreign invaders. It had not been a battle that would go down in the annals of Marine history as a last man, last round stand, far from it. For the hard talking British Government it could be seen that part of its armed forces, and an elite part at that, had gone soft. After all, when was the last time British Forces had surrendered without anyone being killed? In my eyes it appeared as if the Marines had been sheltered throughout the initial stages of the campaign, ordered out of the limelight until the generals had decided what kind of foe Britain was up against. The Paras had been used as a screening force, sent out miles in advance of the rest of the units, clearing the ground prior to the arrival of the commandos. The political dilemma faced by the Conservative government at the time was how the public would react to the Marines losing a land battle in their struggle to recapture the islands. Better to be safe than sorry, and so the Marines, through no fault of their own, were held back. They landed after us, and I include both Para battalions here. They arrived in settlements twenty-four hours after we had cleared them, and were promptly swamped by the media ready to take film footage and photographs of them hoisting up the Union Jack for speedy transmission back to the UK. Worse still, during the final surge towards Port Stanley after the surrender, they were championed by the powers-that-be as the first unit to enter Stanley, while others including 3 Para were ordered to "go firm and let them through". Now, on their homecoming, they were once more receiving the full attention of the media and the British public, while the rest of us had been swiftly and unceremoniously shipped back, and flown into Blighty through a back door.

It made me sick. I was annoyed a Government would play such games. The partygoers, however, were mesmerised by the coverage and lapped it up, feeling extremely patriotic, believing they had done their bit by listening to the evening news and buying the daily newspaper to keep themselves abreast of events. Before their cheers had subsided and their song 'Don't Cry For Me Argentina' had faded, I had left them. My experiences of war were real and my homecoming was most definitely very different to the one being televised. Laura joined me outside and our relationship took a step backwards. I blamed her for trying to return me to a normal way of life while I still had so much to deal with. I blamed her for allowing me to laugh and dance the night away, while my friends lay in foreign soil, their relatives still unsure whether their bodies would be returned home and I blamed her for my aggressive state of mind. It all ended in tears. I took her back to her mum's and went to find Stu.

For a while Stu and I returned to going out alone, sitting for hours staring into our drinks while the evening hours passed slowly. On one occasion we found ourselves back in the Command House, in Chatham, the place where I'd first dated Laura, listening to a Royal Marine spout off about his antics down 'South'. It was early in the evening and we were sitting in chairs by an upstairs window, enjoying the summer breeze.

The Marine was at the bar with one of his friends and, unfortunately for us, in earshot. At first I ignored his boasts, preferring to stare out of the open window enjoying the scenery offered by the pub's garden and the River Medway in the distance. Before long he became impossible to ignore. Stu shot me a look that said the time had come to enter the conversation. As we rose from our seats, the Marine's friend left unsuspectingly, heading for the toilet. Stu and I joined the Marine at the bar and informed him that we couldn't help but overhear his conversation. We told him that we were both members of the 3rd Battalion, Parachute Regiment, and like him had just returned home from down 'South'. We enquired where exactly he had seen so much action. The chap weighed up the situation and realising emotions were probably running a trifle high, caved in. He was not a Marine at all. To call him one would be an injustice to all those who achieve the green beret. He was just another 'hat', attached somewhere down the line to the Marines. He had spent most of the campaign onboard the Canberra, and for the last week at Port San Carlos. He hadn't even seen an Argentinian nor fired his weapon. He was "simply spinning yarns to my civvie mate". Staring at him in disbelief, I was angry this man could allow himself to 'spin yarns' about his so called 'experiences'. His yarns would eventually be found out through their inaccuracies, tarnishing the reputations of all those men and units who had served so bravely. Initially he had been oblivious to our resentment, believing us all to be 'brothers-in-arms' but, realising the matter was of great importance to us, he had changed tack. As his friend came back from the toilets, he introduced us as heroes of the campaign, front-line soldiers who had seen far more than he had. His friend looked bemused. Stu informed the 'hat' that there had already been enough talking on the subject. No doubt feeling a little foolish, the 'hat' made his apologies and left with his friend.

Stu and I returned to our chairs by the window. As paratroopers we had been inundated with people who had "nearly completed the training if it hadn't been for my knees" or "Yeah, I was in Para Regiment – 6 Company." As there is no such company you always knew they were lying. And knees? Give us some credit, please! Now we could see the next trend had already started, "Yeah, I was down 'South'…" A decision had to be taken. Would we become involved in every yarn we overheard, or simply become immune? The decision wasn't hard to make. After all who wants to get involved with every low life who needed to impress friends with tall tales of derring-do? Far better to ignore it and get on with the problem of rebuilding our own lives.

That night I rang Laura and we spent the last few weeks of my leave together, until I had to return to camp. Stu and I organised a few parties for everyone in the village to enjoy, including an engagement do for Laura and me. In the main, though, the parties were superficial, as our relationship with the members of the old gang was never going to be the same. I took to spending most afternoons in the Bridges pub, down in the village. I was not drinking heavily. I'd just sit with an orange juice or a glass of Coke listening to records from the jukebox without interference from anybody. Noel, a quiet, unassuming landlord allowed me to sit at the bar without having to enter into a conversation, and I felt safe and comfortable with the arrangement. I even took to reading the newspapers again. The major story at the time was of the battle the families of the fallen were having to bring their bodies home. I couldn't understand why there was so much fuss. If a man has given his life for his country and his family would like his body returned to be buried, or cremated, at a place of their choosing, why not grant that wish? It would seem to be the obvious and most compassionate thing for the Army to do. But no, they were embattled with the bereaved families. The official line for the time being was that the bodies of the fallen would remain where they were. From time to time new stories about Jas, Scrivs and Grose would appear. One day The Sun's front page even called for them all to be awarded the Victoria Cross. I suppose that's when the phone calls started at home from the Press. They would ask me for a comment on a certain story that had been published or ask to interview me about my experiences down 'South'. I always politely refused to comment or declined the interview, but as time went on the requests changed to demands, informing me that the British public had a right to know and it was my duty to inform them or correct any previous inaccuracies. The last straw came when I overheard Mum, who was struggling on the phone with a local reporter, all the time trying to protect me from his vulture-like enquiries. I took the phone from her and couldn't believe what this man was saying about the fallen and their 'supposed' right to be repatriated. His approach was controversial. Let them lay where they had fallen; what the public really wanted to know was had any atrocities been committed? And the inevitable – "did I kill any Argentinians?" At one point I even thought of agreeing to meet him on the pretence of an interview to punch the living daylights out of him. Common sense prevailed and I replaced the receiver and then left the phone off the hook. From that moment on I vowed never to talk to the Press.

Throughout my leave I had been in contact with Jas's mum and dad, Syd and Terry Burt. I met with Syd during the early weeks of leave and took my Dad to meet him. Graham Collins was on leave from 1 Para and also came along. Dad, in fairness, was useless as a Samaritan, not knowing what to say or when to say it. He drank heavily, leaving Graham and me to comfort Syd as best we could. After leaving the pub we went back to Jas's home to meet Terry. Syd out drank my father and the visit came and went with both dads enjoying a little too much to drink. Syd gave me a Du-Pont tortoise-shell cased lighter and a Swiss Army knife with 'Jason' written on it. Both were to be 18th birthday presents for Jason along with the Ford Capri car Syd had promised him. I never got the Capri but that was to be expected because Syd was Jewish and made all Scotsmen look generous! It was a joke that Jas and I would often relay to him when we were on leave together.

It would be an understatement to say both Syd and Terry both found the grieving process extremely hard. Their house, once full of laughter and Jas's dirty Army clothes, was now like a church, a shrine to their lost son. Jas's bedroom was full of framed photographs of him, depicting his early and teenage years. Unopened 18th birthday presents and cards from friends and family carpeted the floor. Chelsea scarves and posters punctuated the framed photographs that hung on every wall, a true testament to a much-loved son, if a little unnerving for the onlooker.

As we left their house, I agreed to help Syd with his market stall in Wentworth Street, east London, just as Jas would have done had he returned. During my leave, I did work with him on a couple of occasions. After the lunchtime trade had bought most of the cut-price food and household goods on the stall near Aldgate, Syd would take me to West Ham baths, where we would enjoy a sauna, a cold dip and something to eat. Our days always ended in the bookies, although Terry was never informed of this unless Syd had backed a winner. We even spent an afternoon at Walthamstow dog track, where Syd introduced me to the delights of leaving the racetrack penniless!

I enjoyed my time with Syd, although I was aware that his enquiries about his son's death left me in an unhealthy frame of mind. Stories abounded in the Press. Some said Jas was with Sgt McKay on the recce and was killed alongside him. Others promoted or championed him for an award for brav-ery. Each time a new story was printed, Syd and Terry would be pulled from pillar to post, unsure of the truth. My problem was I didn't want to talk about it at the time but felt obliged to do so. When asked, I always told Syd the truth, never embel-lishing the story in an effort to comfort him. Unfortunately, others hadn't been so truthful, telling 'harmless' white lies or relaying stories in line with his beliefs, in a naïve attempt to aid his grieving. My story would often contradict these tales and those circulating in the newspapers. I told Syd that when he was killed, Jas was not with Sgt McKay even though this wasn't what he wanted to hear at the time. I also told Syd about the dog tags. However, each time I told Syd or contra-dicted a story or a newspaper article I felt isolated, as if I was decrying Jas's name or actions. As we spent more time together and Syd's enquiries became more and more demanding and personal, I'd console myself that it was a small price to pay as I had returned unscathed and he had lost his son. The truth was I couldn't cope with Syd's constant and unrelenting quest for information and the unwelcoming emotions it brought me. Tears, feelings of guilt and days of deep depression would often follow my visits to him.

In my efforts to return to normality, I took driving lessons and managed to pass my test after only six lessons. The fact I'd been driving Stu's yellow Ford Cortina for well over a year obviously had something to do with it. Nevertheless, it was a relief for Mum to know that her son was now legally entitled to drive alone. I bought a blue Vauxhall Cavalier for £900. Stu and I promptly set about installing the correct sound system and speakers ready for the journey back to camp.

Throughout my leave I had been plagued with severe pains in my feet. My soles still looked abnormal. They were pure white, badly swollen, and pitted like an orange peel. As they warmed up in bed at night, horrendous needle-like pains would shoot through my toes and feet. The pain was excruciating and I'd scream out in frustration and anger. The remedy was to leave the bedroom window open with my feet outside the blankets, to maintain a more comfortable low temperature. However, each time the temperature rose and blood started to circulate below the ankles the pain would return. I can remember Mum coming into my room one night and seeing my feet for the first time, she cried as she held them. Again, I would console myself that it was a small price to pay. Nightmares and replays of the fighting are stereotypical of a soldier's return from battle. Unless you have been there and experienced it for yourself you cannot imagine how vivid and real these uninvited intrusions are. They take over your life and you become a slave to them. Initially, you fear turning the light off, or closing your eyes, knowing that as soon as you relax, the mind will wander and you will be thrown headfirst back into the deepest depths of the battle. I would often wake in the middle of the night startled, covered in sweat or shouting. Then, once the moment had passed, and the realisation that it was just another bad dream hit me, the tears and sobbing would start. Tears for the fallen and injured. I also sobbed for myself. When, if ever, would the battle end for me? At one point I thought I was losing control of my mind and took steps to change this. Instead of going to bed at night I would stay up until the early hours, preferring to catnap during the day. It worked at first until Mum woke me from a sleep on the settee. Startled and unsure of my surroundings I nearly attacked her. This experience frightened us both. I returned to sleeping in my room. The problems it brought were another small price to pay.

The time soon came to return to Tidworth Barracks. Determined not to sign on and quit, I was a little unsure of what the future held. The Army, on the other hand, knew exactly what was in store. On returning to camp we were informed that the battalion would be moving immediately 'lock, stock and barrel' back to Aldershot. We were to be housed in Normandy Barracks, Montgomery Lines, next door to our sister battalion 2 Para. On completion of the move, 3 Para would begin funeral duties to bury their fallen. The Army had, at last, succumbed to the families' demands to bring the lads home.

Before finally leaving Tidworth, I drove across to Brize Norton to see Jas's girlfriend, Clair. I met her in the Spotlight Club and after a few drinks the initial awkwardness subsided. I told her how Jas had died and gave her some of my photographs of him. Returning to camp, my head tormented with emotion, I crossed a hump back bridge where the road veered sharply to the right. Unfortunately, I continued straight on through a privet hedge, and parked the blue Cavalier in someone's front room. A vicar who lived there immediately came out, arms flailing, ranting and raving at me. Patience not being one of my stronger virtues, I informed him there were two passengers in the car and that the Christian thing to do was for him to enquire about their health. I then politely told him to piss off. The police arrived shortly afterwards. After passing a breath test, the police told me my car was most probably a write off and they would arrange for it to be towed away. One of my passengers went to hospital in an ambulance, suffering bruising from his seat belt. The other lad and I spent the night in the RAF cells in Brize Norton until a driver from 3 Para could come down and collect us. The night passed slowly.

Once entrenched at Normandy Barracks, Aldershot, the time came to visit the pay office and sign the official Army papers for my term of serving, from a minimum three years to a maximum of twenty-two. Confident of my decision to leave the Army, I swaggered over to the pay office to be greeted by an overweight Pay Corps Sergeant. "You have some papers for me to sign, I believe?" I said, leaning on the counter in a nonchalant manner knowing that I was about to burst his bubble at any moment. The Sergeant rummaged around his desk and produced the necessary forms. "I have no intention of signing these," I said. "I wish to leave."

The Sergeant smiled at me as if I was a comedian, then realised I was serious. "One for you, sir!" he yelled, and a Pay Corps Major came over to join us at the counter. He explained the facts of life to me. I had already given the Army an undertaking to complete a minimum of three years, which was why they had trained, housed, fed and developed me throughout my training. He then showed me a number of official-looking documents. They were all signed by me, promising the Army a minimum of three years service on completion of my training and/or my eighteenth birthday, whichever was the latter. A lecture followed on taking the 'King's shilling', after which I signed the papers and returned to my block, this time without the swagger. Well, that's the next three years sorted, I thought. I can't wait.

The next period of my Army life was spent attending the private memorial services that were organised independently by the families of the fallen. On these occasions we had to organise our own attendance and transport, with little assistance from the Army. I always felt the Regiment let the families down on these private memorials. Getting a number of lads off together to attend a midweek service was not always easy. Other commitments meant only a handful of us made it to Grose's memorial. After the planting of a tree at his old school and a brief chat with the family, I had to shoot straight back to camp. I felt terrible for doing this, although everybody seemed to understand the Army way of life. What would it have hurt for the Army to give the lads a few days off to spend time with the parents? It seemed as if the Army was simply going through the motions, and that the grieving families and the veterans were a pain in the backside.

I did however manage to spend time with Grose's mum, Anne, the morning before the service. Anne took me up to his bedroom and we sat on his bed chatting for a while. Grose's bedroom walls were covered with football posters and she told me I had been an influence on him in this. It made me smile. Grose was very much his own man and I'd have enjoyed taking the mickey out of him about the decoration of his bedroom. As we sat, comforting each other, our chat obviously wandered to our experiences of the campaign, mine as a soldier and hers as a mum who had lost her son. I cannot begin to describe the emotions that rage when you have experienced the loss first hand and you sit in your friend's house, on his bed, with his mum in tears. How does anyone begin to counsel such a loss? I would have happily swapped my life for his. If I could have given my life there and then to bring him back so his mum could hold her boy one last time, I would have. I felt useless and betrayed by the Battalion. I wasn't qualified to deal with such emotions and yet, I wanted so much to help her and remove her grief. I felt desperately for her. Our tears continued for some time before we composed ourselves and joined the others downstairs.

Once I'd said my farewells, I gave Grose's brother, Mark, a lift to the railway station, as he also was due back to his regiment. Our conversation was general, having little in common other than his brother. I was surprised how little he knew of his brother's achievements with the Regiment. He maintained his 'big brother' attitude for most of the journey and I politely acknowledged his status, not wishing to upset the apple cart, believing that I would never see him again.

The Parachute Regiment and Airborne Forces' memorial service was held at Aldershot Football Stadium on Friday, 1st October 1982.

I had written to Roy and Rosemary Scrivens to see whether they would be attending. Rosemary wrote back to say she and Roy were going but Scrivs's little sister, Victoria, would not be there as they felt the day might prove too long for her. I must admit to feeling slightly disappointed that I wouldn't see Victoria, as Scrivs had often talked affectionately of her. I was keen to tell her this and just how brave her big brother had been. That conversation would now be for a later date.

The day was warm and sunny. Both parachute battalions were present, as was the Regimental Colonel-in-Chief, Prince Charles, the Prince of Wales. The streets of Aldershot were lined with people cheering us on as we marched through Aldershot to the football stadium. It felt somewhat contradictory that people were cheering us as we went to remember our dead but at the same time I cannot deny feeling warmth and pride that people held the Regiment in such high regard.

It was a day of compassionate speeches, prayers and a lesson read by His Royal Highness from Ecclesiasticus 44, verses 1-15. Kneelers, or prayer cushions, that had been beautifully embroidered each with the name of the fallen were lined up to be blessed before being placed in the military church in Aldershot. Another military spectacle went superbly.

Once the bodies of the fallen had returned to the UK, we

were required to undertake funeral ceremonies in several home towns.

The Battalion practised its funeral duties with coffins supplied from a local funeral director. Each burial party was required to retrieve their coffin from the back of a Land Rover, acting as a hearse, and carry it to the Motor Transport yard. There the coffins were lowered into the workshop pits to give everyone practise on lowering a coffin using the burial strops. It was a demoralising time for all.

Eventually we were given the details of the burials we would be undertaking. I attended a number of private burials in the north of England and, of course, the main military burial at Aldershot Military Cemetery.

At my first funeral the family had requested to have the body of their son brought to their home prior to the burial. This would allow them a private moment with their son, where the family could say their personal farewells. The burial party were to meet the hearse at the home address, where we would carry our companion into the front room and lay his coffin, covered with a Union flag, on two easels. It all sounded pretty straightforward. Of course, everything was to be conducted with military precision and compassion. As the hearse pulled up the family came out to watch the proceedings. The burial party marched to the rear of the hearse to collect our companion. As we neared the path leading into the front of the house it was quite obvious that both sides of the burial party, three men either side of the coffin, were not going to be able to get on to the path. One side was going to have to walk on the recently dug up earth. This is not usually a problem for your average hardened paratrooper, but when you have spent the past two weeks bulling your boots to make them look like glass, dirty boots meant sacrificing a night out on the town. So a push and shove ensued, with both sides ending up in the mud. Entering the front door it quickly became apparent that because the hallway was so small, the coffin was not going to be easily carried into the front room.

It would have to be manipulated up the stairs and edged carefully into the room, requiring the coffin to be placed into awkward positions and even upended. The family were asked to go into the kitchen while we manoeuvred the coffin into place. At first they refused but, try as we may, and with as much decorum as we could muster, we were unable to position the coffin into the front room. Finally the sergeant's patience ran out and the family were escorted into the kitchen and the door closed firmly behind them. What followed next is best left to the imagination but there were cries of "Mind my f-ing fingers," and "Jesus, I can't hold him". Eventually the coffin was in its correct position and draped with the Union Jack. As we stood to attention, either side of the coffin, we bowed in respect before departing. Everyone was actually thinking can't we just pass him out a front window when the family have finished? Of course, no one said it and so the same fiasco ensued when the time came to leave.

On another occasion at a crematorium, the hearse pulled up and as we went to collect the coffin we were overtaken by odours. However hard we tried we couldn't ignore the problem. Eventually the hearse was called back and the coffin taken a safe distance away from the onlookers where the Union flag covering the coffin was sprayed with incense before the hearse returned for us to complete our task.

At a cemetery in Manchester we were told they had taken to burying people three deep. How true this is I do not know but when it came to lowering our coffin into the earth, the eight feet long burial strops that we had were far too short. With heads bowed on both sides of the coffin, the burial party lowered the coffin into the earth in time with the vicar's words, "Ashes to ashes, dust to dust..." Unfortunately in this instance when the vicar's last words had been said, the coffin still had some four feet to go but we had run out of burial strop. Raising our eyes to our colleagues on the other side of the coffin, there was very little any of us could do but let go of the strops in unison allowing the coffin to make its own way to its final resting place. This was not a practised drill moment and ended up with everyone letting go at different times. The coffin bumped off the sides of the grave before crashing to its final destination. I think all us could have jumped in after it but, to be truthful, there was very little else we could have done.

Funerals are very sombre and compassionate occasions for all involved though some however, do have their lighter moments. With no disrespect to our fallen comrade I attended one such funeral. The service had been beautiful and the burial process had gone well, right up to the point were the bugler sounded the Last Post and the firing party fired shots over the grave. On this day, which was a very cold day indeed, the bugler couldn't hit the right notes. The tune coming out of his bugle is probably best likened to Les Dawson playing the 'Entertainer' on his piano at the end of one of his shows. It was dreadful, wrong notes everywhere. Stood around the grave, we cringed each time he hit a wrong note. But as the bugler persevered, struggling desperately to hit the right notes, it got worse and we couldn't help but giggle. That was the start of it. Family and friends saw the lighter side of the burial party's shoulders going up and down in a vain attempt to control our giggling, and they burst out laughing. That was it for us and we all joined in. Later the family thanked us for giving their son a 'good spirited' send off. The CO who had attended the funeral was not as impressed and ordered the bugler jailed. From that moment the Last Post was sounded at all burials by a trumpet, to ensure that the right notes were hit.

The main military funeral was held at Aldershot Military Cemetery on Friday, 26th November 1982, when sixteen lads were to be buried. The night before we had been sitting over in the NAAFI when a Sergeant came in and told us the hearses were arriving bearing our comrades. It was the first time I would be together with Jas, Scrivs and Grose since leaving Mount Longdon. Everyone hurried outside. Each of the sixteen immaculate, highly polished, black hearses carried a coffin draped in the Union Jack. Led by a man in morning dress, they drove slowly past the main entrance to Normandy barracks before coming to a halt a hundred yards short of the sports hall. Fumes from the exhausts gave a weird dramatic effect to the proceedings and the dimmed lights of the vehicles cut through the darkness like huge cat's eyes. The leading man continued walking until he was outside the sports hall, where he turned to face the hearses, and with a respectful nod, beckoned them forward one by one. With incredible dignity and decorum, civilian funeral directors, dressed in top hats and tails, carried their passenger from the rear of their vehicle into the sports hall, where each coffin was positioned. I watched as each one was carried in. It felt good to see them home but difficult to comprehend. Everyone was mesmerised and stood transfixed, not moving or muttering a word. Respectfully, those lads who had not served 'down South' gave way, allowing those who had been there the primary positions.

I didn't return to the NAAFI that night but instead went straight to my bed, knowing that in the morning I would be carrying Jas to his final resting place. The lads, thank God, were finally home.

Aldershot Military Cemetery was packed with families, friends and the media. Burial parties formed up at the lower end of the cemetery by the main road, waiting in the sunshine for the hearses to arrive. As each hearse pulled up, the burial party marched forward, retrieved their companion and slow marched him to his allotted resting place. Evenly spaced, soldiers from the Battalion lined both sides of the cemetery's winding narrow pathways. These custodians stood motionless at 'present arms' but as the fallen were carried forward, and came level with each soldier, he slowly and individually changed from being at 'present arms to 'on reverse arms rest'. This deliberate drill movement requires the soldier to turn his rifle away from him so that the muzzle is on the ground. At the same time, the soldier bows his head in respect, and with his hands on top of each other, rests them and his chin on the butt of his rifle. Nobody in the world carries off the pomp and circumstance of a military procession like the British – and this was no exception.

Graham Collins from 1 Para and Ray Ratcliffe of 2 Para, friends from our depot training days, had requested to join

Jas's burial party. For me, it was an honour to carry Jas, but extremely emotional. I would, of course, have been honoured to carry any one of my friends to their resting place. Weeks before the ceremony I had been placed in the impossible position of electing which friend I would carry to his grave. After hours of deliberation, even at one point considering not being involved with any one friend, I chose to carry Jas with Graham and Ray. I chose Jas because I had been with Scrivs and Grose at their final moments of passing. Jas, like the rest of us in the platoon, had run forward as ordered and met his end on his own. It seemed the right decision for me to make.

As we collected Jas and carried him past each custodian to the area of the cemetery assigned to the Falklands fallen, I talked to him. Not always out loud, but in my mind – nevertheless I talked. Like all others in our burial party, I greeted him warmly as we lifted him from the hearse. From then on, I narrated to him the events as they unfolded. I told him about the families, the friends, and the members of the public who were present. I told him about the cars that had stopped on the main road, causing a temporary gridlock, so their drivers and passengers could get a better look at the military spectacle. I described to him the custodians, as we slow-marched down to meet with Scrivs and Grose, who were to be buried alongside him. As we stood over the grave, with Jas's coffin supported by two planks of wood waiting for the others to make their positions, I told him of the weeks I'd had at home and of Laura.

As the service started I drifted off to happier days when we had all been together in Junior Para. I thought back to the tough training and hardships of Recruit Company and of our pride in reaching the Battalion. I thought of the time we were in a cafe at Waterloo station with Syd, and Jas had unscrewed the top of a tomato-shaped ketchup container. We'd all watched as an unsuspecting civvie unwittingly released the top and dumped the entire contents of the ketchup dispenser on to his food. How we'd all laughed, just as Jas and I had laughed on the Canberra when sending Graham Collins our letters about going South; and sending back his action man's flag, along with photos of it stuck up Jas's bum. I thought of his perseverance with his feet and his determination to be with his platoon during the fighting. I thought of his courage in the minefield, being the first to move forward to assist Brian Milne. And I thought of his unwavering 'charge', worthy of the highest military award, which had led to his untimely death.

As Jas was Jewish, a Rabbi performed his service. None of us understood what was said but it all seemed genuine and sincere, so it didn't matter. As the Rabbi started to speak I relayed to Jas the events following his death; of how the position had eventually been taken. How Scrivs had bravely thrown his body over Grose to protect him from any further injury, as the sniper had continued to take pot-shots at the platoon. How Grose had persevered with his injury, however painful, never once complaining that he shouldn't have been there or that his luck was running out, or blaming anyone for his situation. An incredibly brave, unselfish, and self-restrained demeanour not usually associated with someone so young or at such a self-preserving time. Finally, I told Jas how proud I had been to have them all as friends and that I missed them.

Then the final words were spoken. We raised Jas a few inches from the ground as the supporting planks were removed, before finally lowering him to rest. The Last Post sounded and a bagpiper played a lament. The burial parties were then instructed to clear the way to allow the families and friends their personal moments. As the crowds dispersed I went back to the foot of his grave and said goodbye. I did this with Scrivs and Grose as well.

For a short while I sat on the small grass mound where the families and onlookers had stood, looking back at the sixteen now-deserted holes in the ground. The new shiny South Atlantic medal with its rosette on my left breast sparkled in the sunlight. The same medal had been given to those who had stayed in the United Kingdom but had aided the campaign efforts of those who had been at Ascension Island. The tiny rosette sewn on to the medal's ribbon was the only way of identifying that I had entered the exclusion zone. How one small chunk of metal could ever express my experiences throughout the campaign was incomprehensible to me. Also, I didn't feel the need to parade the fact I had served and survived. The campaign may have been won and seen by many as a tremendous victory for Britain but in truth we were all losers in the end. I removed it from my chest and placed it in my pocket. The time had come to go, to join the families and friends who had made their way back to camp.

To leave felt like a betrayal. As I walked out of the cemetery gates I was in tears.

CHAPTER TEN
II Samuel

The Second Book of Samuel

Once the funerals had been completed life back at camp soon changed. Lt Col Hew Pike moved on to be replaced as CO by Lt Col Rupert Smith. The RSM, Lawrie Ashbridge, and many other senior figures also went. In his first address to the Battalion, the new CO informed everyone of his intention to rebuild 3 Para starting afresh. He had no time for despondency or for veterans with complacent attitudes. 3 Para was a fighting unit and had to be ready to serve anywhere in the world at a moment's notice. He ended his speech with the proposition that should anyone wish to leave, he would happily sign their 'demob' papers or words to that effect. As the parade dispersed from the parade ground many muttered that they'd had enough and were leaving. Battalion morale hit rock bottom. It is said that within the first year of arriving back from the campaign, sixty per cent of those who had served with the battalion in the Falklands had left. Many went of their own free will, others due to their injuries sustained during the campaign, but the remainder, I am sure, were prompted by the new CO's unsympathetic address. The loss of those experienced men was an unnecessary waste of a valuable asset but to the new regime it was a definite strategy for rebuilding and refocusing the battalion.

The bullshit inevitably followed. Battalion sweat tops were no longer to be worn during PT sessions, replaced by Army-issue red PT vests, which were worn by day-one Recruit Company candidates. Instead of being championed as professional soldering, the individual tailoring of webbing belt order was now frowned upon. Area cleaning became a twice-daily event and fights with the 'hats' down town, once accepted as an approved pastime, became punishable by court martial. Shortly after, Stu told me he'd had enough and was transferring to the Royal Engineers.

Finally, I decided to make the next few years of my life with the Regiment as enjoyable as I could. Although I had been made to sign for three years against my will, there was nothing I could do about it. I could, if I wished, mope about feeling sorry for myself or become a type of pacifist but that would simply make battalion life harder. Like it or not, for the next three years I was a soldier in an elite regiment so I might as well commit myself to that fact and to everything the Battalion had to offer. I viewed the weekly training programmes as an opportunity to improve my personal soldiering skills, my leadership ability and my fitness. I took an eight-week paramedic course, becoming qualified to administer drips and to suture. The Battalion could be called upon at any time to face an enemy anywhere in the world, as the new powers-that-be were preaching, so it was in my own best interest to learn as much as I could and become as professional a soldier as my ability would allow. I knew the horrors of war although I didn't relish the thought of ever witnessing it again; I now had the advantage of experience over most of my peers. If I could just channel this in the right direction it could only assist me with my future. My intention was still to leave in three years' time but in the meantime I would focus my energies on being a professional paratrooper.

In November, Laura informed me she was pregnant. I was having a drink in the Queens Hotel, in Farnborough, and used the public telephone to call her. Her announcement came as a surprise but, nevertheless, it made me happy to feel I would be starting my own family. Marriage was the obvious answer. I rang Mum but this news was not received well. The conversation ended with us agreeing to discuss the matter further when I was on leave in December.

Laura and I married in January, 1983, at Allington Church, Maidstone, with Stu as my best man. I was eighteen years old and Laura was nineteen. We spent our honeymoon in a hotel at the bottom of Blue Bell hill, which has since been razed to the ground. I was called back to camp early on stand-by for Northern Ireland followed by a second tour of duty at Hythe and Lydd. We moved into married quarters in Ramilies Park, North Camp, and our daughter, Leanne was born on 16th June 1983, in the Cambridge Military Hospital, Aldershot.

Army life was difficult to say the least. Having spent numerous years' budgets during the Falklands conflict, the Army had little or no resources available. Ammunition was at an all-time low, rations not used during exercises were collected and passed back, to be re-boxed for future ration packs. On several occasions, when ammunition wasn't available, we were expected to complete our battle drills by running around the woods shouting, "Bang, bang, you're dead". It was a complete fiasco. Some soldiers took to writing slogans on their camouflage helmet covers. A favourite of the time was, "It's all b*ll*cks", which summed up the mood of the blokes nicely and mocked the establishment as puppeteers. In March, 1983, B Company were invited to complete the French Para course. We were housed in French barracks around the Toulouse area, not too far from the ancient town of Carcassonne. It was the first time a company from 3 Para had been back to France for about three years. A Company had been the previous visitors and had fallen out with some of the locals, after a heavy dispute in a red light establishment. This dispute had ended with the death of one of their lads and a French local. Thereafter, it was thought best, for diplomatic reasons, to keep the Paras away from France. It was now thought that enough time had elapsed for relationships to be rekindled and we went off to assist with this. Arriving at their camp late the first night, we were gathered together by our OC, Major John Easton. Major Easton had taken over command of the Company from Major Mike Argue, who had been awarded the Military Cross for his command of B Company on Mount Longdon, and had since moved on. Major Easton or 'ET', as he was affectionately known, was a huge man, with hands like shovels, a no-nonsense soldier's soldier and was much respected by his troops. ET recapped the history of the previous visit, followed by the obvious political lecture, saying we were ambassadors of Britain and should be on our best behaviour at all times. He then handed over to the CSM Johnny Weeks. The CSM spoke with his usual candour, informing us not to go down town and order the cheap local plonk that would get us out of our heads. Should anyone get into trouble in the mess he would personally come down and beat the shit out of them.

Everyone understood that the CSM meant what he said about beating the shit out of people but no one realised that he had such a good knowledge of the local wines. So, once the bags had been dumped on to the beds in the blocks, everyone headed down town to order lots of cheap local plonk, as recommended by the CSM.

The following morning the Company formed up outside the block awaiting the CSM, who arrived sporting a black eye. Further investigations discovered the CSM had gone into one in the French Sergeants' Mess and, after much 'cheapo wino', had laid into one or two of the French sergeants. The CSM couldn't be controlled, which had led to the OC being called from his bed to take control of the situation, hence the black eye. All in all B Company was quite pleased with itself. We had managed to last three hours on French soil before things had kicked off. Surely the powers-that-be would be pleased with this achievement?

The second night was worse. We had been housed in barracks that were well past their sell-by date. There was no running hot water and the toilet was a hole in the floor. The French were, of course, housed in brand new barracks next door. During morning parade we marched on to the square and were made to wait for the French troops to arrive. This they did in dramatic style. Their slow marching pace, being exaggerated by their swaying and their low deep singing. Mutterings of "Get on with it," could be heard in our ranks. When they eventually formed up, both national flags were hoisted to the top of their respective flagpoles. This started in unison, with both flags ascending at the same time, but the French flag party raised their game and the Tricolour pipped ours to the post. Mutterings of "Did you see that?" and "French bastards," could be heard from the lads. That set the tone and the second night was spent in a bar arguing with several French troops. Small scuffles broke out and a phone box was wrecked. On the third morning they beat us once again to the top of the flagpole. By now tempers were fraying. That night we housed ourselves in one of the local bars and proceeded to drink everything on the shelves. Everyone was very drunk, singing, and a few of us were dancing on the marble tables. The owner and his staff retired from behind the bar, allowing the lads to help themselves as they pleased. One NCO declared that once the bar had run out of booze it would be trashed. All of a sudden the marble table beneath me gave way and I crashed to the floor. Composing myself, I tried to get to my feet when someone noticed blood was pouring from my right leg. Lifting my trouser leg I saw a five-inch gash across my shin, which eventually needed ten stitches. With my leg bandaged to immobilise it, I was given a set of crutches and returned to camp. The following morning I watched from the parade-square sidelines as the Union Jack won the battle of the flags. The lads were jubilant. The French took it badly and from that moment on the flags were raised independently to avoid further confrontation. On the final passing out parade, when the lads received their French Para wings, I again looked on from the sidelines. The British Military Attaché was present and with our OC came over to ask as to how I had received my injury. "Parachuting?" he enquired, nodding his head in the direction of my leg. The OC stood behind him nodding his head urging me to reply in the affirmative.

"No, sir," I replied. "Fell through a table down town pissed as a newt."

The Military Attaché looked bewildered and the OC shot me a look that said if he hadn't been in distinguished company he would have broken my other leg.

The rest of that year was spent on fitness, battle lessons, parachuting, exercises, and numerous visits to the American Air base at Greenham Common, where anti-nuclear protestors were gathering and demonstrating. The weeks spent at Greenham Common were mind-numbingly boring. Together with the Thames Valley Police, we were positioned inside the perimeter fence line, to ensure that none of the protestors broke into the camp. Stag duty could last up to six hours and comprised of standing in one place, with a colleague ten feet away on either side of you, looking through the chain mail fence at makeshift camp sites and some of the ugliest, dirtiest women that I had ever seen. The highlight was using catapults to smash the mirrors they had positioned on their tents facing into the camp to deflect evil spirits. Immature I know but mirrors and evil spirits – please!

On several occasions they tried to break through the fence and seemed genuinely dismayed when the paratrooper on the other side of the fence, who had been on stag for five hours, would beat the living daylights out of them with his cosh. They would then be penned-in with barbed wire awaiting the arrival of a policeman to arrest them. The police would then charge them with breach of the peace, or whatever, bail them and within a couple of hours they would be back on the other side of the fence, shouting obscenities and spitting in our faces. The best incident occurred after a prolonged attempt at breaking through the fence and Para reinforcements had to be called for from the silo areas. Our Platoon Sergeant, Chris Phelan, decided he'd had enough and addressed the protestors. He told them too many men were being taken from official duties to baby sit the protestors at the fence and that he was relieving the men of their duties and sending them back to the silos, with one exception – Ron Duffy. He introduced Ron and gave them a summary of his résumé. The girls, unsure of whether Chris was bluffing, jeered on. Unfazed, Chris ordered the lads to return to their original duties and stood back. Ron moved to a more central position and stood staring at the protestors, confidently nodding his head. The girls tentatively started to climb the fence and so Ron moved closer. I'm convinced it was the intensity of his eyes but for whatever reasons the girls soon understood Ron was not to be messed with and gave up, moving off to other areas. Chris was pleased with his decision – but Ron felt cheated.

I was promoted at Greenham Common. Major Easton called another soldier and myself over and enquired why we were incorrectly dressed. Dress was quite relaxed at the camp, so we wondered what he was on about and said nothing. 'ET' held his hand out and presented each of us with a Lance Corporal stripe and told us to get them sewn on to our uniform as quickly as possible. Being just a few weeks past my nineteenth birthday, I felt quite awkward with my promotion, as there were many individuals who were older and had served for much longer. I knew my promotion would bring comments and grief from them. I decided to sew the small, inconspicuous green and black L/Cpl patch on to my parachute smock and leave the larger white stripes, for my jumper and shirts, until told to do so. This unfortunately only delayed the process for twenty-four hours when I was required to march the lads down to an area in jumper order, and was once more incorrectly dressed. The promotion did bring its comments and some grief but that is the nature of the Parachute Regiment.

At Greenham Common I first experienced the awesome might of the American war machine. Throughout our stay, the Americans would fly aircraft into the camp daily, offloading new machinery, weapons and supplies. We were ordered to provide perimeter protection for one arrival, which was obviously carrying a sensitive cargo. Seeing the aircraft coming in I was flabbergasted: even from a distance its silhouette commanded the horizon – it was gigantic. The inbound aircraft was a C5 Galaxy. With a wingspan in excess of 220ft and a body the size of a football pitch, it stood sixty-five feet from the tarmac. When it eventually landed our platoon went to encircle it, to provide protection but the thirty-odd men we had were insufficient and the remainder of the Company, ninety men in all, was sent for. Once station-ary, the aircraft's cockpit hinged skywards and its 'landing gear' knelt to assist with the discharge of its cargo. Lorry after lorry, their trailers fully laden with supplies and weaponry, drove out of the aircraft's cargo bay. The traffic flow seemed never ending.

The Galaxy was the largest operational aircraft in the world at the time and was capable of carrying 125,000lbs of cargo over a range of 8,000 miles. The Yanks were obviously proud of their plane and the engineering that went with it but to me it was a grotesque monster.

The next time I encountered the US war machine came during an exercise on camp. The Americans had decided to undertake drills involving the deployment of their mobile missile units, similar to the 'scud' units that caused such mayhem during the Gulf War. We were tasked with the outer perimeter protection of these units, while the Yanks deployed their infantry throughout the closer confines. Patrolling our section's area on foot during the early hours of the morning, I noticed that a group of Americans had gathered and were looking at something. Curiosity getting the better of me, I moved closer to the fence. Struggling to get a clear sight of what they were looking at through the trees and the early morning mist, I pinned myself against the fence. I could make out what seemed to be a ramp or launch pad attached to a vehicle of lorry-size proportions. As I watched, a siren sounded and the pad's hydraulics screeched into life. As it reached the various stages of its ascendancy different coloured lights on the side of the pad came on, just like the floor indicators in a lift. From the groaning hydraulics, the missile was obviously of considerable weight and its deliberate rate of elevation implied there was no room for error. The final incline had to be perfect. It was all so foreign to the warfare I had known; of men staring into the eyes of their enemy with their rifles and bayonets at the ready, each with the same opportunity of life or death, dependent upon their skills and luck on the day. This was of another league, of smartly-suited men sitting comfortably behind well-polished desks ordering red buttons to be pressed. I thought how useless one man and his rifle would be against such weapons of destruction and I concluded how useless the best-trained regiments would be. Warfare had moved on and maybe it was time I did the same. Noticing my presence and over-interest at the fence, a couple of Americans came over to remind me my duty was to protect the outer perimeter and that my observations would be better suited looking outward instead of in. The Yanks dictating to their British ally once more, I thought, and moved off grudgingly. Greenham Common, like the C5 Galaxy aircraft, came and went.

It wasn't until April, 1984, that 3 Para went on tour again and this time for six months in Belize, Central America. Belize or British Honduras, as it was formally known, has Mexico and Guatemala on its western border and the Caribbean Sea to the east. El Salvador, Honduras and Nicaragua lie to its south. Its history is marked by territorial disputes between the UK and Guatemala, which delayed its independence until 1981, although Guatemala refused to recognise this for another decade. The country suffers high unemployment and has an increasing involvement with the South American drug trade. Our brief was to maintain its borders, pushing back any illegal Guatemalan squatters and destroy any drug crops we came into contact with. B Company was stationed in Salamanca Camp, down south, in the middle of the jungle. Roads were dirt tracks and the majority of transport was undertaken by foot or by helicopter.

Being in the jungle was fantastic. It was a completely new experience of breath taking magnitude. The jungle was incredible to patrol, with its monstrous trees untouched for hundreds of years and creeping vines that rose out of eyesight high into the jungle canopy. The animals, birds, insects, the snakes and the noises, all completely unique to the jungle environment. It was an exciting place, where something interesting or something new was always happening. Jungle warfare required patience, stamina, alertness, and fitness. Not only was there an enemy to consider, in this instance the Guatemalans, but the soldier also had to be conscious of his surroundings, the dangerous animals and the weather. Monkeys commanded the trees, providing an early warning system to others of any foreign or unwanted presence, while jaguars cautiously patrolled beneath, searching for prey. At certain times of the day, due to the position of the sun, a soldier's shadow would be projected in front of him, betraying his position. On other occasions when the sun was at its highest point, patrolling even for a short time became exhausting and dehydration was a constant concern. Minor injuries could bring quite serious secondary infections. To combat this, the majority of us purchased small pocket size, battery-operated electric shavers, to reduce the risk of facial cuts. Personal hygiene became important to the point of obsession. Fungal infections were commonplace, attacking the moist parts of the body under the arms and between the legs. The jungle floor was a complete universe of its own creation. From floor level to about eighteen inches high lived a complete food chain of ants, insects, bugs, snakes and the like. Anything stationary for a considerable period of time had to be above this height for fear of being consumed. To this end makeshift A-frame beds would be constructed to ensure the soldier was clear of these dangers while sleeping. Foreign smells and aromas would travel great distances. It was said a

Mars bar or soldier's soap could be smelt up to a mile from his position. Cooking, in any tactical area, was a complete no-no.

The main observation post at the Guatemalan border was called 'Tree-Tops', which was a short helicopter ride from Salamanca Camp.

I can recall as a boy listening to my radio late one night in my room, when a woman had called in and asked the DJ to play a record for her husband. He was serving with the British Forces in Belize and was at 'Tree-Tops'. I can remember having mental visions of what the observation post might look like with its jungle surroundings, and I wished I was a soldier stationed there. Now, at the age of nineteen I was – and enjoying every single minute of it.

The initial months were spent vigorously patrolling the border areas, submitting reports on each patrol undertaken and the terrain encountered. This intensive programme proved to be successful and within three months we had achieved the boundaries as defined, and as long as these were maintained, could now undertake a 'hearts and minds' programme with the locals.

This usually meant patrolling into one of the villages, after approval had been given by the village elder, and spending time with the locals, assisting with whatever tasks they were undertaking. First aid and medication would be given to anyone in need, mainly the cleaning and dressing of cuts from their over-active machetes. Where first aid was given, the sharing of food and drink, as a 'Well done for being so brave' would follow it. These patrols were beneficial to everyone: the kids in the villages loved to see the soldiers and their weapons, and would mimic us as we entered their location.

The young adolescent girls with their 'mocha' coloured skin and dark brown eyes, loved the attention the soldiers paid to them and would gather in a group giggling, their naked breasts exposed to the delight of the lads. The men of the village always kept their distance although I believe they appreciated the deterrent we provided against the Guatemalan guerrillas. On one occasion, undertaking a patrol of a village on the Guatemalan border, I was told to keep my radio operator with me and spend the night with the elder and his family. A member of his family had been extremely ill and it was considered good practice to keep a presence on the ground to show our respect. Sending the rest of the patrol back to base, Mick James, the radio operator, and I prepared for a night at the village. As we made our way to the elder's atap we were confronted by a small group of men, all of his family, who refused us entry to his house, unless we left our weapons outside. Of course this was impracticable and with us being so near to the border we decided to keep our weapons to hand and basher up just outside his house. Just before last light the elder came out and invited us in. We informed him, through broken English and hand signs that we could not leave our weapons outside. With a toothless smile he waved his hands in the air, beckoning us, and our weapons, inside. The atap was a wooden beamed construction with branches and leaves for a roof and a mixture of mud, twigs and tree stumps for walls. Chickens ran around the hard earth floor and in the centre was a large open fire used mainly for cooking but also providing heat throughout the night as the temperature dropped. As we settled by the fire the women of the family, with the exception of the elder's wife, left and climbed into their hammocks, which were hanging from the roof beams. At first the conversation was difficult to say the least, but as time progressed we got the hang of the hand signs and their broken English. Lads being lads around the campfire, the conversation turned to women and us asking how each couple managed their conjugal duties, with so many couples sharing the same atap and there being no partitions? The elder seemed perplexed by the enquiry and so a younger member of the family told us how each night the men would gather round the camp fire and discuss which couple's turn it was to make love that evening. Once agreed all the other men would go off to join their wives in their hammocks and get a good night's sleep. The remaining chap would wait a few moments for the others to settle, before climbing into his hammock to merrily swing the night away. Lovemaking is a definite skill at the best of times but performed in the confines of a hammock, with your family looking on beggars belief. Mick and I congratulated the men on their sexual prowess and enquired as to whom the lucky chap was this evening and at what time the 'show' was due to start? With the exception of Mick and me, everyone roared with laughter. The 'show' had been cancelled for the night. As the laughter died down the elder's wife began to make coffee. The water and coffee beans were placed in a pot together and brought to the boil on the fire. Once done, she looked around for a bowl to put the hot coffee in. At first she couldn't find one and a small row broke out. Eventually one of the younger members found a bowl on the floor being used by one of their pets as a makeshift bed. After disturbing the animal from its sleep, he wiped the bowl free of dust with his hand and gave

it to his mother, who poured some of the coffee and the majority of the beans into it. The bowl was passed to the elder who
took a large mouthful, including the beans that apparently
substituted as a sweetener. The elder then spat the beans back
into the bowl for use by the next person. He passed the coffee
to the man to his left, who repeated the process. As I was but
a few members of family away from the bowl I urged Mick to
get his webbing mug out. Understanding the dilemma I was
about to face, Mick purposely procrastinated and by the time
he had pulled his mug out of his webbing my lips were
already attached to the bowl. With eyes firmly closed and
thinking of merry England, I took a large mouthful, beans and
all, and swallowed the hot beverage. It was not a pleasant
experience. Spitting the beans back into the bowl I turned to
hand the drink to Mick, who by now had removed his
webbing mug and had poured some of the remaining coffee
from the pot on the stove into his mug. The elder beckoned
me to finish what was left, before the bowl was refilled. My
stomach heaved in anticipation as Mick nodded his head in
gratitude to the elder's wife. All eyes returned to me in expectation of the same gesture. Mick gave me a huge grin. With no
option available and all chances of escape removed, I emptied
the contents of the bowl into my mouth, and hoped Mick
caught malaria, or some other incapacitating illness.

In the morning the lads from our patrol revisited the
village. Mick and I made our way to the police station, which
was positioned on the highest point overlooking the
Guatemalan border, where our new Platoon Sergeant, Sgt
Dennis 'Woody' Woodhart, was talking to two Belize policemen. Apparentley there had been a number of Guatemalan

border raids throughout the night and we should keep our eye out for any insurgents. As we were talking we became aware of activity in the maize crop a hundred yards to our front. Immediately everyone's attention was drawn to the maize field and the discussion stopped. A man carrying a large machete came running out of the maize. He was extremely animated and waving his machete in the air in an aggressive manner that would indicate a threat to anyone he encountered, and headed straight for Woody. Cocking my M16 rifle I took aim and was about to shoot the man when Woody stepped towards him and straight into my line of fire. The man still heading in Woody's direction started to shout and scream. I shouted at Woody that I had the man firmly fixed in my sights, and to step to one side to enable me to release my shot. Sgt Woodhart didn't move and motioned to the man to calm down by slowly gesturing with his hands, up and down. This brought about no change in the man's manner and as he was only twenty yards away I moved to one side to again get a clear line of fire. Taking up a kneeling firing position I informed the man that I had in him my sights and was about to fire, believing Woody's life was in danger. Although only Woody, as the senior serviceman present, could give the order to fire, I felt it was my duty to issue the warning in the hope it would bring about a change in the man's actions and the threat as I saw it.

Woody ordered me to lower my weapon and once more stood in front of my line of fire. The man was soon upon Woody, with his machete held over his head in a stance not dissimilar to a Knight on his first crusade, bawling and screaming at him in his native tongue. The policemen, who had retired to a safer distance, came back and started to interpret what the man was screaming. He was a Guatemalan farmer whose wife was pregnant and was experiencing severe problems with her labour. Needing help and being unable to transport his wife to a hospital, he had walked through the jungle and over the Belize border to seek assistance from the Army medics. After a few minutes dialogue with the police Woody asked me if I would go and give the man the medical assistance he sought. This meant crossing over the border into Guatemala, which was out of bounds to British troops, into the unknown and without any military backup.

"I may have a kid," I told him. "But I've never delivered one!"

Woody smiled and waited. The man feeling that he had wasted his journey despondently started to walk back towards the maize field.

"Okay," I said. "But not alone."

Taking Mick the radio operator with me we hurried after the man, who had by now disappeared into the field. We followed him for what seemed an eternity as he sped off through the jungle but it was most likely a couple of hours before we finally reached our destination. There, in a small clearing, was his modest single-room atap. A mongrel dog stood barking at us.

Giving him a moment to inform his wife of our presence, Mick and I stood sweating and panting heavily outside. Mick removed one of his water bottles and we started to wash our hands, necks and faces, in basic preparation for what was to follow. The man called us inside. His wife lay on a wooden platform off the mud floor on a makeshift bed, covered in sweat, with a facial expression that told us that she had been experiencing pain. A blanket maintained a degree of modesty. It was obvious that she felt relieved by our presence. Her face lit up as we entered the room and she tried to offer us both a smile.

Never having delivered a baby before I thought back to when I was present during my wife's delivery and tried to remember the conversations between the midwife and the doctor. I felt the woman's stomach to check the baby's position. A normal delivery is defined by the baby's head being in a downward direction. I knew the conversation always turned to how frequent the contractions were and how much the pregnant woman was 'dilated'. I also knew that this was not referring to her pupils. Looking at the husband for approval, I gestured to advise him that I needed to raise the blanket. Holding his wife's hand firmly he nodded in approval. As I raised the blanket, I could see the woman's knees were raised, in anticipation of the arrival. I could also see the baby's head was engaged. The vagina was so dilated a small piece of the dark scalp hair on the baby's head was visible. Her contractions were almost constant. Remembering the breathing sequence we had been taught as an expectant couple going to pre-natal classes, I mimicked the teacher.

"HA, HA – HEE, HEE," I said, trying to assist her breathing. She copied my example, and together we continued. As the baby started to make its arrival I coaxed her to relax as best she could between pushes, remembering how the doctor had advised us that this was the point where internal injuries can be caused unnecessarily. Within moments the child, a boy, was out and lying on his mum's chest. Mick and I left the room and washed. The man cut the child's umbilical cord and stuffed it with cotton wool, which had been soaked in a solution. He took the placenta outside and buried it. Mick and I stood for a moment, pleased with our achievements. The man reappeared and with warm thanks gestured that the boy would be named after us. We smiled. Tom-Mick, I thought. The kid's going to love us!

He then offered us coffee, which we both politely, but very quickly, declined. Saying goodbye to his wife and his newborn son, the man escorted us back to the border, where he once again thanked us and bade us farewell. It seemed unbelievable that ten hours previously I had been willing to take this man's life. The consequences did not bear thinking about. Fortunately that had not happened. He was now a proud father, an ally of the British Forces and I had successfully delivered a healthy baby boy.

The patrols in Belize consisted of four to six men plus a scout, usually one of the locals, whose knowledge of the area and general fitness was legendary. Most of the patrols were transported from Salamanca Camp to a pre-arranged drop off point by Puma helicopter. The patrol would conduct whatever the patrol brief was, normally over a two or three-day period, before making their way to the pick up point and being transported back to base, again by helicopter. On one occasion, when receiving my orders from Major Easton up in the Intelligence Cell of the Operations Room, I was informed that the Brigadier in overall charge of British Forces in Belize would be joining my patrol. I was to meet him at an agreed rendezvous point, brief him on the patrol's mission, carry out whatever tasks were needed in the village and then take him into the jungle to spend the night. In the morning I was to take him to his pick up point, where his helicopter would collect him and whisk him off. Feeling quite nervous that the Brigadier would be with us for the majority of the patrol, I went back to brief the lads. No one was impressed.

"Why us?" they asked.

"I don't know – that's the brief so lets get on with it," I replied.

The helicopter dropped our patrol off and we made our way to the designated village. There we met with the elder and informed him that we would have a distinguished guest with us and that we would be very happy if the elder could take time out of his busy day to meet with him. The elder liked the thought of meeting with our distinguished guest and called for the schoolteacher. The school had broken up for the holiday but the elder instructed the teacher to gather as many children as she could, so that when the guest arrived he could be shown the children sitting at their desks, happily working away. The children, happy that they were to be the centre of attention, all ran to the school and sat behind their desks awaiting the arrival of the important white man. Our patrol made our way to the pick up point, just outside of the village, where we met up with Major Easton, the Brigadier, and his radio operator. Introducing myself to the Brigadier, I noted how tall he was. He was wearing a sand-coloured SAS beret, with his chief-of-staff badge, and his grey hair gave him a distinguished look. He had piercing brown eyes and a radiant smile that oozed confidence. All in all, he had incredible presence and I immediately knew I was going to like him. I then introduced him to the other lads in the patrol.

ET pulled me to one side and told me not to 'cock up'.
Leaving the Brigadier's radio operator with Major Easton,
our patrol started back towards the village. The Brigadier,
who was without a weapon, was positioned in the centre of
the patrol. As the village came into view I informed the
Brigadier that the tribal elder was expecting his arrival and
had put on a welcoming party. The Brigadier smiled. Soon the
two men were shaking hands and nodding their heads in
appreciation of the other's standing. The elder, with his chest
pushed forward, proudly escorted us into the school hut,
where the children immediately burst into song. The
Brigadier enjoying the moment, his smile beaming, clapped
his hands in rhythm to the children's song. The elder beamed
with pride. Observing their smiling faces, I felt pleased with
myself that the initial introductions had gone so well. Making
our way through the village I pointed out the areas of interest
to the Brigadier. The elder's house, the small Christian church
constructed of branches and leaves, the fields of crops, and
the pens for their livestock.

The village was well organised, self sufficient, disciplined
and happy – and so was my distinguished guest. As we
settled under an atap for shade, I informed the Brigadier that
it was my intention to eat scoff, clean the weapons and patrol
out into the jungle, back-tracking to a suitable resting up
place, to spend the night. The lads prepared the food, as the
kids from the village looked on, and alternately cleaned their
weapons. The Brigadier told us stories of SAS operations and
of Belize in general. We all clung to his every word. With food
eaten and weapons cleaned, I briefed the lads on the route we
would be taking, the approximate duration of the patrol, and

the method of backtracking that we would be employing. Backtracking was for our own safety, and in order for us to hide our tracks so that the enemy, or any other undesirables, couldn't find our eventual resting up place. Everyone packed their kit and prepared for a couple of hours patrolling through the dense jungle. After an hour or so our patrol looped round to rejoin its initial path, some three-quarters of the way up the patrol route, before venturing off to the resting up place. There we lay in all-round defence for about an hour as last light came and went, after which I informed the lads of the sentry roster and went over to the Brigadier, who again was positioned centrally, to ensure that he had everything he needed for a good night's sleep. With that completed I went back to my position and zipped myself up, into my bivvie bag. A bivvie bag is best described as a 'Gortex' body bag. Made of breathable material, it covers the body completely ensuring mosquitoes, ants and all other bugs that live in the jungle foliage, don't eat the soldier alive. The lads regard it as a pukka piece of kit.

Just before stand-to at first light the last sentry woke all of us, with the exception of the Brigadier, and we again positioned ourselves in all round- defence. As I lay there peering through the half light and trees, with Martin Clarkson-Kearsley, known as CK, to my left, I could hear rustling out in front. At first I thought it may be an animal, but the noise became more regular and drew nearer. Getting CK's attention I pointed to the area of concern. Both of us nervously took up firing positions, unsure of what was to our front. As we looked on, the noise grew louder. My heart pounded in my chest. All I was thinking was please don't let this be a

Guatemalan attack. Please don't kill the Brigadier, my career will be finished. Imagining the stick I would get back in camp, if I didn't act quickly, I motioned to CK for him and I to move towards the noise for a closer inspection. As we started to move forward a head popped up over a fallen tree trunk in front of us and a small boy from the village we had visited, stood up held out his hand and said "Bisskit?" I nearly jumped out of my skin. Not wanting the Brigadier to know a seven-year-old had tracked us, I placed my finger to my lips and urged him to be quiet. The kid nodded at me and was soon joined by one of his friends who, not knowing the form, also enquired, "Bisskit?" Telling him also to be quiet I reached for my webbing pouch, removed a packet of Army biscuits and threw them in their direction. I then motioned for them to go away, which fortunately they did.

Later, I woke the Brigadier, who thankfully was none the wiser. After he packed his kit away, we made our way back to the village for breakfast. The Brigadier debriefed me on my patrolling and leadership skills, telling me that he had enjoyed his visit and would put in a favourable word to my OC. I didn't tell him about the kids, but the two of them came and sat with us, during the debriefing, merrily chomping away on their prizes. The Brigadier didn't notice their rations and CK and I said nothing.

Eventually the time came to escort the Brigadier to his pick up point. Wishing us all the best for the future, and giving me an approving nod, the Brigadier was handed over to our OC and our patrol went back to the village. Although it had been stressful having him with us, I had learned from his mannerisms and words. I felt confident the patrol had gone well and that I had benefited from the overall experience.

Rest and recuperation (R&R) was fantastic in Belize. Our Platoon Commander, Lieutenant James Chiswell, was an avid sailor and had arranged for some of us to hire two very new eight-berth yachts. Most of our platoon enjoyed two weeks' sailing around the Mexican Islands. Our days were spent out on the reef swimming, diving and sunbathing, while our nights were spent on whichever island took our fancy. One that springs to mind had beautiful sandy beaches, trees that were covered with a bark that looked and felt like hair, air-conditioned restaurants, and bars with sand covered floors and portholes, so that when you looked down you could see the fish and turtles swimming under your feet. We spent some of our evenings in a bar, listening to tapes of the chart rundown with DJ Tommy Vance that someone's girlfriend had taped and sent out, while chatting and eating fresh lobster curry. It was paradise. Another island we visited was owned by some God-zillionaire. It included a golf course and an airport and had been bought with the intention of turning it into a gambling den to rival Las Vegas. The owner had spent millions importing white sand for the beaches, modernising the airport and hotels, and upgrading the golf course, only to be refused the gambling licence. As our yacht sailed up to one of its jetties, a few of us dived into the beautiful blue sea and swam up to the shore. It was idyllic.

Making our way to the wooden slatted jetty at the far end of the Island and to the rear of the hotel, we lined up and dived once more into the crystal clear water, where several stingrays took flight and gracefully swam off. Returning to the jetty I lay for some time soaking up the sun and staring into the cloudless blue sky, enjoying every moment. I acknowledged a couple walking by with a toddler and they returned the compliment. The chap was a captain in the SAS, enjoying his R&R with his wife and child. What a life, I thought, that'll do me – SAS, attractive wife, lovely kid, beautiful scenery, what more could anyone want?

Another time CK and I spent a couple of days R&R on a small island where water-sports activities were run by a young water-borne 'hat' who, with his blond hair and tanned body, was a little too fresh for his own good. With his small dog as a companion, he would show off on his windsurfing board, reminding us daily how incompetent we were. Before long we all grew very tired of his accomplishments and looked to sailing to restore our pride. Unfortunately for us he'd obviously sailed the Atlantic single-handed in a previous life and excelled again, which pissed us off even more. During one voyage around the island he told us all to sail over to his boat and connect all the craft together as a storm was brewing. Looking up at the cloudless blue sky CK and I ignored his advice and continued to mess about with our boat. Within minutes we were battling tropical winds and lashing rain. When the storm had passed he restored his sails, sailed over to us and told us to make our way back to the jetty, as it was scoff time. Looking like drowned rats, and feeling sorry for ourselves CK and I started to make our way back but the wind had dropped and the boat stood stationary. Once again 'Chay Blyth' sailed over to us and told us to tic-tack back to base.

"Easier said than done!" we shouted as he sailed out of view, homeward bound. After about twenty minutes of going nowhere, we'd had enough, jumped ship and swam back to shore. When we arrived the 'hat' came over and in his cocky arrogant manner enquired, "You eventually made it back then? Where's your boat?" Reminding him that it was not our boat but his, we pointed to the middle of the blue yonder and said, "Your boat is out there!" and walked past him and joined the queue for scoff. He was not impressed but as there was very little he could do, he had no other option but to swim out and retrieve his boat. The 'hat' had been taken down a peg!

Back in camp, the Platoon Commander announced that he had found a location while out patrolling, and decided it would be perfect for a bit of platoon recreational fun. So the next weekend we loaded up the wagons with beer from the NAAFI and the camp's inflatable dinghy, and set off. The location was incredible, a clearing in the jungle complete with log cabin, waterfalls, rock pools and a huge cave. We all immediately jumped into the clear water and like kids, splashed about. After a while we decided to take the dinghy into the top pools and explore the cave, which was extremely dark and the water appeared very deep. Occasionally we could see the white blind catfish coming up for air and then disappearing quickly from view, back to the safety of the darker depths. There were four of us in the dinghy at the time and as we turned the craft around to head back out of the cave, into shallower waters, the front of the dinghy got sucked in by a whirlpool created as the water escaped into a lower cavern. The boat's rear end rose out of the water and we were all immediately thrown from it. Someone started to mimic the Jaws theme tune and everyone scrambled to get out of the water, as quickly as they could. Taff Illiac, the expedition corporal tried desperately to save the boat from slipping into the abyss, by placing one of the paddles through the canvas loops situated on either side of the inflatable. The rest of us looked on as Taff battled with the whirlpool but the pressure was too intense causing the paddle to give way and snap in two. The dinghy slowly disappeared from view as one of the lads hummed the Last Post while the rest of us stood to attention and saluted the boat's final moments. Making our way out of the cave, in hysterics, we informed the Platoon Commander of the dinghy's fate. He was not impressed and asked who had signed for it. Taff admitted that it was his signature against the withdrawal of the boat from the stores and was ultimately responsible for it. Arriving back at camp our laughter soon stopped. We were informed that the dinghy played a vital role in the evacuation plan of the camp and had been given the status of a 'star' item. A 'star' in Army stores is an item of importance or of some value. Losing a 'star' item instigates a board of enquiry, which if found guilty of negligence can lead to the soldier involved being jailed or ultimately to his dismissal from the Army. Taff became very concerned for his future. Believing that he had done nothing wrong, we all told Taff not to worry and that we would all support his case if the situation arose. Within days everyone present at the cave was ordered to attend a board of enquiry into the dinghy's disappearance. Venue: Holdfast Camp, Dress: No.2s. We were informed to pack sufficient supplies of wash kit and normal working dress in the event that we didn't return to Salamanca Camp. The next few days were spent bulling boots and pressing our No.2s, a uniform usually only taken from a soldier's locker for special parades or functions.

On arrival at Holdfast Camp we were separated and individually interviewed by the Board of Enquiry. Two Regimental policemen guarded the entrance to the enquiry room, reminding us that should the board find us negligent in anyway, then we would be immediately placed in their charge. The atmosphere was tense. Taff looked ill. By the time I was called for Taff and the Platoon Commander had already given their evidence. I was shocked by some of their questions, which implied we might have sold the boat to locals, or worse still, the Guatemalans. After giving evidence, I saluted the officers who sat on the board, marched out and took my seat with the others outside the entrance to await their findings. Taff sat with his head in his hands, convinced his career was over. I felt it was all a complete waste of resources and a typical Army overkill to something that had quite simply been an accident. Eventually we were all marched back in, this time with the Regimental policemen as escorts, to hear the board's conclusions. After much rambling, it turned out the board's findings were inconclusive and required further investigation. They were now going to summon an Army diver, who would enter the cave and report his findings when an ultimate decision would be taken. Taff was to remain at Holdfast Camp while the diving expedition took place. The rest of us would report back to Salamanca Camp. If the board required us further we would be called for. None of us could believe the lengths the board was going to. After a couple of days Taff rejoined the platoon at Salamanca. All charges had been dropped. The diver had entered the cave but could not investigate the whirlpool, as there was no longer one in existence. Although he had found a hole in the floor of the cave that could have led to the cavern below he was unable to prove this as something was obstructing the passage. He had also entered the cavern beneath the cave but had found nothing. A passageway to the upper cave was also blocked. The water level in the top cave had certainly risen recently and his conclusion was an item was blocking the passageway between the two caves. This obstruction had dramatically slowed the natural leakage of water from the top cave into the cavern below. In his mind it was certainly feasible that the dinghy was located somewhere in the passageway between the two caves.

My conclusion was that the inflatable dinghy must have cost the Army a few hundred quid. With the five of us summoned on full pay to the enquiry, our transport, the three Army officers who investigated the matter, the Regimental police, the Army diver, and all his expenses incurred, the board of enquiry must have cost the British taxpayer thousands of pounds. Incredible logic!

The biggest event at Salamanca Camp happened one night after a tactical discussion between two NCOs regarding the camp's ability to protect itself went wrong. I was duty NCO, which meant making sure the NAAFI was locked and secure, and that the keys were placed in the guardroom under the direct supervision of the guard commander. The guard commander on this particular night was L/Cpl Dominic Gray. Dom was a legend in 3 Para, highly respected by all as an individual who had excelled during the battle for Mount Longdon. Dom along with another Private, Ben Gough, had personally secured several enemy bunkers after dispatching their 66mm anti-tank rockets into one and taking the others by rifle and bayonet. Eventually Dom had been shot in the head, the bullet traversing his skull and exiting his helmet on the other side. He had continued fighting for several hours only to collapse through loss of blood. It is well known that Dom had received a letter from a Colonel who was sitting on the Army's medal awards board, congratulating him on receiving the Military Medal. Unfortunately politics dictates the Army can only distribute a certain number of awards and Dom's MM was eventually downgraded to a Mention in Dispatches. Dom never really forgave the Army for this.

Anyway, as I entered the NAAFI just before closing time, I could see the two corporals deep in discussion at the bar. With the exception of the two corporals, everyone got up to leave. The bartender pulled the bar shutter down, removed the money from the till and left. Telling the two corporals it was time to go, I went over to the back door and locked and bolted it. I will not name the two corporals, although their names are known by all who served in B Company at Salamanca Camp. I will refer to them as Cpl A and Cpl B.

Cpl A was a highly respected and highly qualified section commander. He had served with 3 Para's pathfinders, D Company, and was HALO – High Altitude Low Opening – and HAHO – High Altitude High Opening – trained. HALO involves parachuting from around 35,000ft, complete with oxygen and all equipment and free falling to a few thousand feet below radar, before opening the parachute. HAHO is also parachuting from around 35,000ft, complete with oxygen and all equipment but opening the parachute at high altitude. The parachutist then navigates his descent by map and compass to a designated landing point. Cpl A was a career soldier who was going places. He was considered by most to be one of the Battalion's finest soldiers.

Cpl B had requested to join the Parachute Regiment after serving six years with the SAS. His original unit had been a Guards regiment, I believe. Nevertheless he was also considered a highly qualified section commander, if a bit of an unknown quantity as he had not been with the Battalion long.

Cpl A believed the officers were complacent in their approach to the defence of the camp and should the camp be attacked, the Company would be at risk. He believed retrieving ammunition from each soldier at the end of every patrol placed the men at huge risk. If the camp were to come under a surprise attack each soldier had to race to the store to be issued with ammunition before he could put up a fight. If the officers believed the men could not be trusted with the ammunition throughout the night, then suitable defensive positions with sufficient ammunition should have been strategically located around the camp perimeter. These positions could ward off any would-be attacker, allowing sufficient time for the remaining soldiers in the camp to retrieve their ammunition from the store and stand-to.

Cpl B believed the camp was under no such threat and that Cpl A was being melodramatic. Cpl A became irate and asked what I thought. "I think it's time for bed," I replied and both corporals left the NAAFI.

I made sure the windows were fastened and secured the front door, took the keys to the guardroom and retired to bed. Next thing I knew I was being woken and told to get my section into their defensive positions. Not entirely sure what was going on, I immediately roused the section and told them to stand-to. Once in position, Sgt Woodhart come round and distributed the ammunition. He also confirmed that everyone had been issued their arcs of fire.

"What's going on?" I asked believing the stand-to was simply a drill.

"There'll be a briefing in a couple of minutes," he replied. "I will inform you from there."

Waiting in position, combat helmet and webbing on, rifle aimed in the direction of my field of fire, I became concerned that this was not a drill. Word on the grapevine was that Cpl A had gathered the officers together at gunpoint during the early hours of the morning. He had informed them they were taking the camp's security lightly and he would show them just how insecure the camp was. He had then wandered off into the jungle with his weapon and ammunition. The general consensus was that Cpl A had no intention of attacking the camp or his comrades but the Company would remain in their defensive positions until told otherwise.

It was rumoured that someone had asked at the briefing, "What happens if he does attack, sir?" and the reply had been, "You have all been issued with your orders for opening fire in Belize cards, yes? These cards cover all types of eventualities of opening fire, this type of incident included. If you are fired upon you may return fire."

As the hours passed by the briefings and rumours continued and the tension increased. It became a real possibility that Cpl A could be shot if he entered someone's arc of fire. The lads were not impressed with their predicament, Cpl A was not only a switched-on soldier but he was hugely respected and liked by them. No one wanted the situation to prevail or worse still deteriorate to a higher status but there seemed very little anyone could do but wait and hope.

At first light Cpl A walked up to the main entrance to the camp where he was met and escorted to the OC. The Company stood down. I believe the official conclusion thereafter was that Cpl A had no intention of attacking the camp and had gone off into the jungle, to calm down, spend the night under the stars, and to think. He had taken his weapon and ammunition with him for personal protection only, and for no other reason. Everyone was thankful that the matter had reached a suitable conclusion, although Cpl A did not complete his tour of duty in Belize, and was soon on a plane back to England. However, he was not disciplined by the Army for this incident.

The last weeks of serving in Belize brought about a return to the intensive patrolling regimes which the Company had employed during its first few months. This was in preparation of handing the area over to the in-coming 'hat' regiment. The lads' mood changed as everyone had the homeward journey fixed firmly in their minds. They all undertook these patrols with the same professionalism but without the same enthusiasm. One time, I was ordered to patrol and clear a specific route. The Royal Anglians had been unable to complete the patrol after encountering several problems en route. We were taken by helicopter to the village where the Anglians had ended their patrol. Initially the route was reasonably easy going but the terrain soon changed and it became difficult to continue. Making regular contact with the ops room by radio, I informed them of our progress and advised them that we would continue, as best we could. We soon encountered a huge incline where the rocks and moss underfoot proved difficult to combat. It was around here the Anglians had turned back.

Everyone was of the opinion that the ground could be tackled and that the patrol should continue. Battling against the terrain we persevered, manhandling our equipment up the steep incline, rock by rock. After a couple of hours we managed to get to the top, where we crossed a flat area of ground only to be confronted by a sheer drop. As we stood at the cliff edge looking on top of the jungle canopy some two hundred feet below I knew our journey had come to an end.

Feeling dejected, I immediately radioed the ops room to inform them of our position.

The message that came back wasn't what I had expected. The ops room believed the patrol could continue and that I was exaggerating my situation. Packing the radio antenna pole away, I informed the lads that we would be tackling the cliff face and to prepare the limited number of ropes that we had for a descent. Each soldier would descend to a pre-determined spot without his equipment as he would need both hands for climbing. Initiating the climb down the cliff face, I stopped at a ridge and waited for my equipment to be lowered to me. Baz Barrett, the next man, then started his descent. To the amazement of everyone, Baz had returned to the Battalion after being shot in the Falklands. He had initially been written off by the medics as someone who would never walk again. Parachuting, he had been told, was out of the question. Baz being Baz, had proved them all wrong, by learning to walk again and completing the Regiment's physical tests. He had also parachuted. As Baz made his way down he slipped and tumbled down the face, crashing against several rocks. Eventually we managed to secure him. He had a large gash across one wrist. Fortunately for him, his artery had not been severed. Telling everyone to stop, I requested my webbing be lowered down. Baz couldn't climb back up the cliff face and so I had no alternative but to administer first aid where he was. Taking a solution from my medical kit, which I diluted with water, I placed it into one of my mess tins, cleaned his wound and prepared him for suturing. Baz needed five or six stitches, which I did as best I could. I cleaned and closed his other cuts with butterfly sutures. Taking a decision to carry on, I shouted for the next man to start his descent. Col Carter started but also slipped and yelled out in agony as his ankle caught awkwardly between two rocks. I immediately aborted the descent. Back at the top of the cliff I radioed the ops room and told them that I had two injured parties and would make my way back to the village for transportation. Transport was declined until the morning.

My patrol now faced a dilemma. Should we stay out on the ground overnight in unfamiliar territory or should we go back to the village and spend the night there? We only had a couple of hours before nightfall and the village was still some six or so miles away. If we opted for the village the tab back would need to be at a fair pace for us to get there before last light and Col's ankle was playing up. The alternative was to stay out on the ground in an uncertain environment without back up. The patrol opted for the village. Going back down the incline proved much easier than getting up it and we were soon at the bottom raring to get on with the tab. Contrary to normal routine, I plotted a route back to the village that took in several established tracks. This enabled us to set a fast pace that would not be affected by the jungle foliage we would otherwise have encountered. Things were going great until one of the patrol struggled with the pace being set. If it had been Baz or Col I could have lived with it, considering their injuries, but it wasn't. It was one of the new recruits, who had recently joined from depot. Stopping the patrol I asked him what was wrong? He offered no other reason but that he was tired and struggling with the heat. The rest of the patrol came round and understanding the situation took his kit from him and evenly distributed it. It was agreed that he would forfeit his turn in carrying the GPMG. With that done we sped off once more.

We made the village with little more than ten minutes to spare before darkness fell. The villagers had all gone to bed and the place appeared deserted. I decided to make camp in the church, which in this instance also acted as the school-house. If we were attacked and outnumbered, the villagers might at least give support to us if their church was at threat. It also appeared to be a solid construction. We made our way inside the church and closed the big wooden door. The few candles we found were lit while we took stock of our surroundings and our injured. A sentry roster was agreed and we rested on the mud floor. The tables and pews were too awkward and too uncomfortable to sleep on. Throughout the night, rats ran around the floor and across our bodies. Just before first light we made contact with the ops room, requested transport and within a couple of hours we were whisked off back to camp. When I was debriefed by the Company 2 I/C he apologised and explained that another patrol report, previously unfound, had been filed by a member of A Company, stating exactly what I had reported. He said the OC, who had been overseeing all patrol activity, had been suffering from malaria and that the ops room hadn't been operating in its usual fashion.

I acknowledged his apology and requested permission for Baz and Col to be excused duty for the immediate future and until they had reported to the Company medic. This was granted and nobody said anymore about the incident.

Our stay in Belize ended in October, 1984. 3 Para flew back to Aldershot and settled back into barrack room duties. This was soon disrupted when on 12th October the IRA detonated a bomb inside the Grand Hotel during the Conservative Party Conference in Brighton. Prime Minister Margaret Thatcher and her Cabinet survived the blast but the explosion left five people dead and thirty-four injured. I was in the Company office when the order came through to dispatch a group of soldiers to secure an Army barracks near Brighton and was detailed by the CSM to be one of the NCOs in charge.

Our brief was to provide access/egress control to the main entrance of the Army barracks and maintain a high level of presence on the ground by continually patrolling the barrack confines. We were briefed about various suspect cars, their make/model, description and registration plates. We were also each given a 'pink' card – "Orders for Opening Fire, United Kingdom". None of us even knew of its existence. My previous experience of these things had been limited to the famous yellow card – Orders for Opening Fire, Northern Ireland – and the white card – Orders for Opening Fire, Belize. Now at twenty years old I had in my possession what some referred to as a 'get out of jail free card'. My problem was that it was for use on my own doorstep. A very sobering thought.

Brighton in the main was uneventful. The camp was full of Pay Corps 'hats'. They rarely wore uniform and provided as much a threat to the IRA as a primary school kid with a water pistol. The 'hats' were supported by a large number of civilian staff, all women, who had been briefed that the Paras had been sent for to ensure the safety and security of everyone who worked at the camp. The ladies were ecstatic to see us and when our patrolling duties began they would lean out of their windows whistling at us and inviting us into their offices for coffee and a chat.

Unfortunately, not everyone was as pleased to see us. Sitting in the guardroom one morning, I could overhear an argument. Grabbing my weapon I went outside to see one of our blokes standing toe-to-toe at the vehicle checkpoint (VCP) with a delivery driver. The driver had refused to open his truck for inspection and as a consequence was being refused entry to the camp or exit from the VCP. In a calm rational manner I explained that all vehicles entering the camp had to be searched due to the current security level status. I was taken aback when he replied that the whole situation was stupid and that due to us holding him up he would be late for his other deliveries. He continued to rant that we were all little boys, playing at soldiers and should all grow up and get proper jobs.

Playing at soldiers – proper jobs, I thought and swaying more towards the American attitude of when you have them by the b*ll*cks their hearts and minds will follow, I informed the driver to stop talking and empty the entire contents of his truck onto the grass verge by the side of his vehicle.

"But my truck is full of bread deliveries and other stuff not due for here," he protested. "Can't you just look inside?"

The time for pleasantries had now passed. I once more instructed him to open the back of his truck and empty its contents on to the grass. Knowing that there was nowhere for him to go, the driver reluctantly opened the back of his truck and slowly started to off load his deliveries, dramatically emphasising the weight of each crate. Not giving a damn for his discomfort I stood and watched as the last crate was lifted from the vehicle and placed on the grass. Staring the driver in his eyes, and without looking into the rear of the vehicle, I nodded and nonchalantly said, "You can put it all back now, sir. Thank you for your co-operation."

The driver was livid and claimed that I was without a father, but my point had been made and from that moment on that particular driver gave us no more hassle.

We were eventually stood down and called back to Aldershot but this was not before the civilian ladies in the camp had put on a farewell party to thank us for what we had done. The party was arranged for the night before we were due to return to camp and was held in the 'hats' mess. Being on duty for the first part of the do I couldn't attend until later and, deciding that I wouldn't change, I went straight from the guardroom to the party. As I entered the room I could see our lads all having fun chatting to the girls, who outnumbered the lads some ten to one, and a large cheer went up. Acknowledging everyone's appreciation, I was swept to the bar and a pint of lager was thrust into my hand. As I stood chatting, being complimented on my dress and how nice it was to see men in uniform and proper men at that, I was tapped on the shoulder by one of the 'hats'.

Preferring the company I was in, I ignored it and continued to soak up the compliments being offered. Within seconds I felt a second tap on my shoulder, this time with more conviction. Placing my pint on the bar, I turned around to see a skinny, older man who was dressed in civvies and standing with another nonentity. "Can I help you?" I asked, expecting some kind of comment about jumping out of perfectly serviceable planes or bird shit and the like, but instead this guy pointed at my head and said in a most disrespectful manner, "Take off your hat!" and turned away from me. My initial thought was what a prat – and so I turned back to my company and ignored him. He once again tapped me on the shoulder and said, "I told you to take off your hat!"

Feeling slightly chastised by his constant attention I stared at him and replied, "It is not a hat and no I won't take it off." The bloke squared up to me and said, "Do you know who I am?" Not giving a damn and knowing that he wasn't one of us. I replied in my most arrogant way, "No, and I don't give a shit – so f-off!"

The 'hat' replied by enquiring as to whether I thought I was a hard man and that if I was he would meet me in the corridor outside the mess. Not giving it a second thought, I apologised to my company and made my way outside of the mess and awaited his arrival. The 'hat' soon appeared, with the other bloke who had been standing at the bar with him and promptly introduced himself as the RSM of the camp. He informed me that no one wore headdress in the mess and that rule included me. I acknowledged his status and told him that I had no way of knowing who he was and that he had provoked my actions.

He laughed and said, "You Paras are so touchy – it is, after all, only a 'hat'."

I corrected him. Ours was a beret that had to be earned and that I would not stand by while he mocked it. With that said I started to walk back to the mess. He stopped me and apologised and it was agreed that I would enter the mess first wearing my beret. After a few moments he would re-enter the mess and ask me to remove my "beret". I would then, of course, oblige.

I went back to the bar and the obvious enquiries as to what had happened outside. I informed everyone that nothing had happened and that the bloke at the bar had simply followed me to the loo and was still in there. They told me that he was the RSM and, appearing shocked, I replied, "In that case I'd better take my beret off!"

Shortly afterwards, the RSM reappeared came over to me and said, "Take your beret off – mess rules".

I looked at him for a moment and was busting to say, "I've told you no – now piss off!" but I didn't. I simply nodded, removed my beret and placed it into the inside pocket of my smock. The following morning I left Brighton and returned to Aldershot.

In February 1985, I asked for an OC's interview. 3 Para had become stagnant and with no immediate tours up and coming I had decided to ask Major Easton, B Company's OC, whether he would approve me for SAS selection. If approved I would re-engage with the Army signing for at least a further three years, if not I would leave the Army when my three-year term was due to finish – 30th June, 1985.

My future in the Army was now firmly in the hands of my OC.

CHAPTER ELEVEN

I Kings

The Davidic Succession

My decision to ask for an interview with the OC B Company, Major Easton, had not been taken lightly. In my mind the Battalion appeared to be standing still and I was far too head-strong and impatient to let the weeks drift into months without anything new or exciting happening. The SAS seemed the obvious career route for me to take. The SAS were held in the highest regard by the Regiment and any individual taking their name in vain, or misplacing his 'present standing', could be chastised beyond repair. In other words if the interview went badly my time with the Battalion could be over. To my benefit I had completed every course that had been placed before me with more than satisfactory passes and had been promoted well within the desired time. My annual reports were more than favourable and my fitness was at an all time high. Surely, I thought, it would not been seen as conceited to ask for the opportunity to go on SAS selection.

On my way from the B Company block I reminded myself not to be too demanding or cocksure. Everyone hates a cocky twat, I thought. It doesn't matter what profession you are in. And as the decision to release me lay firmly with the OC, he needed to like me. Be confident and respectful, maintain eye contact at all times and let him know that this is your wish, your career, your everything!

The Company clerk met me on the stairs to the B Company offices. "He's clear and expecting you," he said. "Wait directly outside his door. I will tell him you're here," and with that he disappeared into his office. This adjoined the CSM's office, which in turn adjoined the OC's office, three offices in a convenient 'L' shape. Usually you would have to pass through all three doors before standing in front of the OC, ensuring the CSM's beady eye didn't miss anything that was going on.

Today, because I had stated that my interview was of a personal nature, I had been excused this palaver, although I was certain that the CSM would be conveniently at his desk, eavesdropping on everything that was said.

As I waited, I watched through the upstairs window the Provo staff beasting some 'hats' on the parade square. This was a regular occurrence. 'Hat' regiments would often send their prisoners or offenders over to the Battalion for a beasting session. With the Para Regiment's hatred for any other soldier in the British Army other than its own, combined with the sadistic mannerisms and characteristics of a Provo staff member, the offender would be guaranteed to be treated as cruelly and inhumanly as physically possible. Reports from the prisoners and their treatment by the Americans at Guantanamo Bay, are like postcards from kids having fun at a Butlin's camp in comparison. The half a dozen 'hats' had all been brought to their knees by the continual carrying, at the double, of a Wombat Shell weighing 45lbs, made all the harder by the loose cobblestones that bordered the parade square and the Company offices. Two of them were crying, again not an unusual sight, but an indication to the Provo member that his motivational methods were taking hold and that if he stepped up the heat the others were sure to follow. The two Provosts were screaming expletives at their prisoners, advising them to get to their feet and not to let the shell touch the hallowed surface of the parade ground, the worst possible offence imaginable. As I watched I was joined by the Company clerk. We stood for a while just looking, not saying anything. It was after all part of the Battalion daily routine. Then he spoke. "Poor bastards," he said sympathetically. It was the first time I had heard anyone speak compassionately about a 'hat'.

Lifting my gaze from the victims on the parade square I turned my head towards him, "He's ready for you now," the Company clerk said not taking his eyes from the 'hats'. Checking my dress in the reflection of the window, I knocked on the OC's door and waited. In the background I could still hear the Provosts screaming at the 'hats'.

"Enter."

Major Easton sat behind his desk perusing a file, pencil at the ready. Standing to attention, in the usual over-emphasised way when addressing a senior officer, I saluted and waited for his command to stand at ease.

"Relax, Corporal Thomas", he said without raising his head from the file, "I'll be with you shortly."

Knowing the Commanding Officer's policy of, 'Make them wait, it gains their respect', I relaxed from my attention position to a more comfortable I-bet-you-can't-tell-me-the-name-of-the-person's-file-you're-pretending-to-read stance.

After a moment or two Major Easton closed the file and moved it to one side. Sitting upright in his chair, then leaning slightly back he placed his hands apart on the desk and looked up at me. "What can I do for you today, Corporal Thomas?" he inquired. Trying not to be too intimidated by his huge frame, deep voice or shovel-like hands I spoke out. "Sir, I wish to be considered for selection."

The room fell silent. A thousand thoughts raced through my head. Should I follow up the statement immediately or wait for his reply? Was it my turn to speak again or his? Jesus, I'm going to be joining the 'hats' on the parade square in a minute, I thought. Major Easton pursed his lips and turned his gaze from mine to the CSM's door. Shit he's going to get the CSM in here, I thought. Returning his gaze to me and nodding his head several times, he started to speak. Missing the opening lines through my anxiety I scrambled to catch up with his conversation. Making some headway, I could make out that he was talking about my time with 3 Para, my experiences in the Falklands and how I had put them to good use, my courses, my achievements, my early promotion, my battle fitness test times, my combat fitness test times, my infantry combat fitness test time, my leadership qualities, experience, personal presentation and all manner of other things. In all he was being very complimentary, A positive step in the right direction, I thought, he's going to approve my request. Then, like every party I had ever attended, it ended.

"The Battalion's strength at the moment is at an all-time low," he said. "We are especially short of Junior NCOs. In fact we're bloody short of everything. Christ, you know that Thomas, your own platoon has experienced a Lance Corporal as its Platoon Sergeant before now. The Battalion already has too many men on secondment, and although to the everyday eye these men have left the Battalion, they remain on the Battalion's register." He paused for a moment. "You see, the powers-that-be inform the Government that the Battalion is at full strength and battle-ready but the facts are we have never fully recovered from the losses sustained from the Falklands, whether through fatalities, casualties or leavers come to that. Thomas, we are seriously undermanned and for me to release you at this moment in time would not be in the best interests of our Company or Battalion."

He stopped for a moment to assess my facial expression, which by now gave my disappointment away. "Look, son, you are very young. What are you, twenty? You have a bright future in front of you if you carry on doing what you are doing. You're now married with a daughter, why sod off around the world with the SAS? You'll never see your family!" My facial expression didn't change and, as it was obviously still not my time to speak, I continued to look straight at the man who seemed to be missing the plot and my huge disappointment.

"What I suggest, Thomas, is that you undertake the Junior Brecon course at the next available opportunity, successful completion of which should ensure your next promotion". He smiled, "And we all know promotion brings money and with your new toddler I'm sure that won't go amiss. Just give it a couple of years then we can revisit your request."

He started nodding again in that arrogant, I've-just-given-the-best-speech-of-my-life- but-have-missed-the-plot-totally-self-conceited way and I knew my time had come to speak.

"Is that your decision, sir?" I asked.

"Yes, Corporal Thomas it is," he responded quickly as if to bring the interview to an immediate end.

So in my best hard-done-by, f-u sir voice I replied, "In that case, sir, I will be leaving the Battalion." After a small speech on the Battalion needing its experienced soldiers and a recap on manning levels I was excused, dismissed to be frank.

B*ll*cks, I thought, as I trudged back to the block. That didn't go quite to plan.

No doubt by the time I had reached the B Company block, Major Easton would have already handed back to the Company clerk the file he had been perusing. On instruction the company clerk would have probably already filed the personal file marked '24583175 L/CPL Thomas' and, to them, the matter would be closed. To me it wasn't. What I needed was a change of heart from the OC, but how I was going to achieve that God only knew.

Climbing the stairs to the top floor of the B Company block, I plonked myself in a huge comfortable armchair in the television room and sulked.

BFT – *Battle Fitness Test*
   1.5 miles in 15 minutes followed by a one minute break then 1.5 miles in ten and a half minutes.
CFT – *Combat Fitness Test*
   2 miles in full kit, webbing weighing 35lbs, plus platoon weapon, in less than 18 and a half minutes.
ICFT – *Infantry Combat Fitness Test*
   8 miles in full kit, webbing weighing 35lbs, plus platoon weapon, in less than 1 hour 30 minutes.

CHAPTER TWELVE

II Kings

The Second Book of Kings

Turning on the television I sat back and flicked through the channels. Sgt Woodhart, the Platoon Sergeant poked his head around the television room door. "What's going on?" he asked.

"I've just had my OC's interview," I replied. "I'm waiting for the lads to return." He nodded then predictably asked, "How did you get on?"

"Shite," I said, emphasising the point. "I requested selection and was rejected." Woody paused for a moment, "I can't see you being rejected, Corporal Thomas", he said. "What did he say to you?"

"Oh, some bullshit about the battalion being under strength and needing every Tom, Dick and Harry at the moment," I replied. "He wants me to do Junior Brecon, get promoted and reapply after that."

"Well that's hardly a rejection."

"In your book it might not be, Woody, but in mine it is!" I snapped back, feeling my disappointment once more. Woody fully entered the room and took his beret off. "Look, Tom," he said in his best fatherly voice. "You're disappointed now but think about it. Junior Brecon, promotion, it's not such a bad thing you know, and how old will you be then? Twenty-two and a full-screw, it's not bad going if you ask me."

He waited for me to reply to his suggestion that I'd be a full Corporal in two years. "Woody, I don't just want to sit around for two years waiting," I said. "I want more!"

Woody looked sternly. He obviously didn't understand what I was on about. "Tom, you're a good lad but sometimes you've got to wait for the others to catch up," he said. "This isn't a one horse race you know."

In fairness to him, Woody meant every word he was saying. He had been promoted early and had reached Sergeant within five years of first being promoted, quite an achievement with the Paras. Woody was fit, comparatively intelligent and extremely loyal to the regiment that had been good to him, but he, like Major Easton, appeared to be missing the plot. I want more! I screamed in my head.

"With respect…" I started and then thinking better of it, paused and said, "No, you're probably right."

"That's the spirit," he said. "Time flies when you're having fun." With that he put his beret back on and walked out. F-ing idiot, I thought as the door closed and continued to feel sorry for myself.

Within a week I was no longer a section commander in B Company but had been transferred to HQ Company, as an additional member of the Provost Team. It had obviously been concluded that I could be a risk to the other members of the platoon, should I continue my ultimatum of selection or Civvy Street. As most lepers know the best solution is to remove the contaminated person from the environment. So I was ousted from the platoon I had been with ever since join-

ing 3 Para and told to report to the Provo Sergeant.
Unfortunately, no one bothered to revisit my request or re-
educate my thinking, just a simple notification to report to the
Provo Sergeant on Monday morning.

Life as a Provo was extremely dull in comparison to the
excitement of a section commander within a rifle platoon. The
majority of the day was spent escorting prisoners from their
cells to various tasks throughout the camp. All tasks undertaken by the prisoners were mundane to the extreme and
purposely uneventful. The prisoners always seemed to make
light of their duties and would turn the slightest incident into
a comedy show, much to the amusement of the Provo staff. In
return regimental prisoners were given preference with tasks
and the odd back was turned while they enjoyed privileges
normally restricted to them. 'Hats' on the other hand were not
shown any compassion at all and Pete, the ex-professional
heavyweight boxer and long-standing member of the Provo
team, took much enjoyment in exercising his 'Provost
prowess' on the parade square, at every available opportunity. Ralph, an ex 'D' (Patrol) Company full-screw and I,
however, were both biding our time and always took a more
leisurely approach to the day's activities, preferring those that
took us away from the camp or the watchful eyes of the
Battalion's company offices.

In April I was informed that the CO, Lieutenant Colonel
Rupert Smith, wanted to see me. Being marched into his office
by the RSM, after several others had undergone their interviews, I wondered what was going on. The CO informed me
that he had received a letter from my father. My stepmother
was ill and that my father was requesting my early release

from the Army to assist him with running his pub. With life at that particular moment being extremely dull and not wishing to prolong my agony with the Battalion any longer than was necessary, I jumped at the chance. "When can I be released, sir?" I asked.

"About as quickly as you can hand your kit into the quartermaster and return your married quarters over to the Families Officer," came the reply. With that I was marched out. My kit was soon returned to the quartermaster and the necessary arrangements made for the 'hand-over' of the married quarters.

Life would be better in Civvy Street, I promised myself.

Epilogue

I can clearly see the green woodpecker, through the study windows, as it forages amongst the grass for ants and their pupae to feed on. The sun appears warm and bright, an unexpected and pleasant surprise for early March. The unfortunate side to this is that the study windows need a clean. I am now forty-two years old, remarried with a daughter and son – and a lot has happened in the twenty-five years since I served in the Falklands.

My marriage to Laura at 18 ended before my 21st birthday. Separation brought the inevitable arguments and blame – concluding in me losing all contact with my daughters.

My first year of Civvy Street saw me returning to the Army careers office contemplating signing back on. What a complete let down Civvy Street appeared to be. If the 'hat' recruiting sergeant hadn't been such an arsehole I probably would have rejoined. Instead I walked away from the office and applied for every single job vacancy I saw in the paper. Everything from double-glazing salesman, insurance representative, factory worker, security officer... you name it. If it didn't need A levels I applied. I even applied for a Scene of Crimes Officer vacancy thinking my paramedic training/qualification would be recognised, but of course it wasn't and when I was told that part of the curriculum included attending several post-mortems I decided that I'd seen enough dead bodies to last me a lifetime.

Through a family contact I even got a job interview at Whitehall. I bought a brand new suit, shiny shoes and a copy of The Times, believing I was going to be the next James Bond. I thought I had done exceptionally well but the advice the interviewer gave me was to start my own business or something, "As you have sooo much EN-ER-GY". I can remember thinking, what a prat. How the hell am I supposed to start a business with no money and living in rented accommodation?

In the end, I took a security job with a newly established local firm. I worked seven nights a week, up to sixteen hour shifts, for the princely sum of £1.35 per hour. When I had finished my shifts, I would harass the owner by telephoning and telling him that he needed me in the office and he should immediately promote me to sales manager on a salary. Of course, he didn't.

Eventually, the owner gave in and allowed me to work in the office for commission only, although initially I still had to work my night shifts to maintain an income. That was the break I needed. The energetic telesales person with a will to work, a determination to succeed and an ability not to take no for an answer – became a salaried Sales Manager, who then became Area Manager, Regional Manager, Senior Consultant and finally Director, all within three years.

In 1988, after a short spell trying to establish a souvenir/gift item business in Barbados, I formed my own manned guarding security company, which eventually became a NACOSS approved Central Alarm Monitoring Station. In subsequent years my wife joined me and the company evolved from being primarily a manned guarding company to a CCTV installer/monitoring station and vehicle/equipment tracking station. Our monitoring station has now a National Security Inspectorate (NSI) Gold accreditation to be proud of.

Together our business has allowed us directly to employ at times in excess of 300 people, to travel the world, to buy the cars of our dreams, to purchase a beautiful farm with 30 acres as our family home and to send our son to a private school.

These achievements are impossible without the obvious hard work and endless sleepless nights that preceded them, but they would have been inconceivable for me without the constant love, affection, understanding and solidarity of my wife Trish.

Trish has witnessed the nightmares, the flashbacks, the depressions, the guilt, and unfortunately, the inevitable drinking sessions. She understands more about the Falklands, Post Traumatic Stress Disorder, Regimental pride, British stiff upper lip syndrome etc. than most lecturers. As the Falklands will live with me for ever so it is for her. We have been together since 12th June 1985, the third anniversary of the battle, and we married on the 12th June 1990. In my reckoning I am probably one of the few husbands who will never forget his wedding anniversary.

In an ironic twist of fate our 17-year-old son has announced his intention, on passing his A levels, to enter military service as an officer. However qualified I feel to be able to tell him the woes of war, he is as we were, young, proud and undiscovered. It is, and must remain his future, and therefore his choice. He is well educated, fit and well aware of his parents' love for him. In conclusion, if everyone sat and listened to our veterans, wars would be a thing of the past. Unfortunately this is not so.

Our daughter is another military buff and although the allure of wearing a military uniform never quite took her fancy, she is enjoying her job at the Imperial War Museum.

My relationship with my mother, father and sister has gone from strength to strength, and I can honestly say that I love them all dearly, and enjoy their company on the rare occasions that we manage to get time together. I did get talked into playing cricket, on leaving the Army, and my first game after nearly six years absence from holding a bat saw me score 108 not out for Horton Kirby Cricket Club. Dad was obviously ecstatic and asked me to consider the game professionally once more, which I decided against. I did however get elected as a playing member of the MCC, which is an honour indeed. I have toured South Africa and Barbados and I have played in a televised game against the French National Team, with a Kent County Cricket Club seniors side. I have even played cricket for Holland against the MCC, although that is a story in itself. My greatest cricketing memory however was when my father, my son and I took the field at my old club in a 20-20 exhibition game.

In all honesty, I wish the Falklands had never happened – as I would now be enjoying telephone calls, emails and texts from three dearly-missed friends. All of whom I am sure would now be parents complaining bitterly that their kids do nothing to help them and that the kids of today have it easy: because when they were their age, they were off fighting wars. In contrast, I also acknowledge that the events of the Falklands in general and of Mount Longdon in particular have shaped my life, for both good and bad. The one overriding factor for me has always been the motivation to achieve for myself the things that my friends were unable to.

There is not a day that goes by when I do not think of them.

God bless you all – 'til we meet again…